THE ENTREPRENEURIAL
SPIRIT OF AGGIELAND

Tales of Success from Former Texas A&M Students

Rusty Burson

© 2017 Rusty Burson

All Rights Reserved.

No part of this publication may be reproduced, stored in a retrieval system, or transmitted, in any form or by any means, electronic, mechanical, photocopying, recording, or otherwise, without the written permission of the author.

First published by Dog Ear Publishing
4011 Vincennes Rd
Indianapolis, IN 46268
www.dogearpublishing.net

ISBN: 978-1-4575-5462-9

This book is printed on acid-free paper.

Printed in the United States of America

TABLE OF CONTENTS

Chapter 1: Fadi Kalaouze 3

Chapter 2: Alan Roberts 17

Chapter 3: Lou Paletta 29

Chapter 4: Dan Allen Hughes, Jr. 41

Chapter 5: Terrence Murphy 55

Chapter 6: Artie McFerrin 68

Chapter 7: Lyle Eastham 80

Chapter 8: Neal Adams 93

Chapter 9: Michelle Lilie 105

Chapter 10: Larry Hodges 117

Chapter 11: Jay Graham 130

Chapter 12: Casey Oldham 142

INTRODUCTION

Timing is everything in life, and God's timing is always perfect…and sometimes quite astonishing. This book is proof of that.

For many years while working at the 12th Man Foundation on the Texas A&M campus, I pondered how I could possibly connect the fabulously successful entrepreneurs I had the privilege of meeting because of my role with the organization and the bright, goal-oriented and ambitious students who strolled the sprawling campus in College Station. In fact, I pondered that possibility so many times that I knew God had placed it on my heart. He was calling me to do something, but I wasn't sure how I was going to answer that call.

In the meantime, I was blessed with the opportunity to write quite a few books: biographies on A&M legends like linebacker Dat Nguyen, NFL referee Red Cashion, World War II hero Roy Bucek and women's basketball coach Gary Blair; compilations on Texas A&M's football history, the history of hockey in the Lone Star State (it's deeper than you think) and the Texas Rangers' baseball history; business books with my good friend and insurance agent extraordinaire Warren Barhorst; and tradition-detailing books on Reveille and the yell leaders. Still, I had this calling to go deeper and to tackle a project that would fulfill my own entrepreneurial desires and inspire others to follow their dreams.

My wife has joked that I have written more books than I've read. That's not true, but it is true that I had not been reading as much as I should. So, in the summer of 2013, I vowed to read more meaningful pieces of literature than what I found in *Sports Illustrated*. A friend recommended an easy-to-read, thought-provoking book called, "The Traveler's Gift," and I figured, "Why not?" I went to the bookstore, picked up a copy and carried it with me for a month or so while I crisscrossed the state with my son and his travel baseball team. I should emphasize the word "*carried*." I brought it everywhere, but I didn't open it until I attended one of my son's games, and he was not in the lineup. Quite frankly, I was disappointed he wasn't playing, which gave me the perfect opportunity—or excuse—to finally open the book while sitting in the stands of a ballpark.

Once I started reading, I couldn't put the book down. It was such a great read that I bought another book by the author, Andy Andrews. While reading "*The Noticer: Sometimes, All a Person Needs is a Little Perspective*," one of the quotes I read practically leapt off the pages: **"Remember, young man, experience is not the best teacher. Other people's experience is the best teacher. By reading about the lives of great people, you can unlock the secrets to what made them great."**

I read it again and again and again. Then I highlighted it. It was my eureka moment, as I knew I needed to write a book that spotlighted some the great entrepreneurs and business people I had befriended while with the 12th Man Foundation.

Still, there was something missing. There needed to be another element. My vision for the book was clear, but the purpose was cloudy. That's when I picked up a copy of *The Battalion*, the student newspaper on the Texas A&M campus. Honestly, that's not something I normally did. But for whatever reason, on that particular day in the fall of 2013, I picked up the paper and clearly found my purpose and heard God's calling. On the front page of that particular edition was a story about a new business incubator and accelerator on campus called Startup Aggieland. I had never heard of it before, but as I read about its mission—helping students nurture their entrepreneurial dreams—I knew I had been called to write the book and to donate all proceeds to Startup Aggieland.

Writing the book was a long journey—longer than I had envisioned. But interviewing and working with the 12 remarkable subjects in this book has blessed me beyond belief. All their stories are different, but they are also essentially the same. There is no secret recipe for success, and the term "overnight success" is typically made for fairytales. Entrepreneurial success is about courage, self-discipline, vision, belief, capitalizing on opportunities, overcoming obstacles and, most of all, hard work.

These stories inspire me. They will inspire you, too. These 11 men and one woman have walked in your shoes across the Texas A&M campus. They were at one time where you are. And if you want to go where they have gone, it is possible. They are living proof. As you begin reading their stories, keep one thing in mind, young man or young woman:

"Experience is not the best teacher. Other people's experience is the best teacher. By reading about the lives of great people, you can unlock the secrets to what made them great."

Here's to unlocking your greatness. Gig 'em, God bless and go for it!

1.

Fadi Kalaouze

Founder & CEO, Kalcorp Enterprises, Inc.
Owner of Aggieland Outfitters
Texas A&M Class of 1990

KALAOUZE'S PATH TO TEXAS A&M

The Kalaouze family

Undeniably, I was afraid of dying. Exploding bombs, rocket launchers, sirens, rifle-firing soldiers and bloodshed in the streets were routine parts of my childhood in Beirut, Lebanon. I vividly recall one time, in particular, being with my father when a rocket hit the bottom of the building where my family lived. As I write this today, that was more than three decades ago, but sometimes when I close my eyes and think back in time, I can still hear the explosion, shattering glass and screams of scared women and children. According to various sources, Lebanon possesses the most religiously diverse society in the Middle East, and at that time—the early 1980s—a civil war was essentially being waged between Christians and Muslims. Fighting was sometimes intense, and the combatants on both sides were often barbaric. Danger, destruction and death lurked at every street corner. As a teen-ager, it was quite easy to envision that one day a bomb would land on my floor or a stray bullet would find my chest. The odds of living a long and prosperous life were not favorable…even if you never participated in the violence or chose a side.

On the other hand, the fear of dying was not the driving force that led me out of Lebanon and to Texas A&M. The most dreadful thought that haunted me was that if I stayed in Beirut, I would ultimately be required to kill other people. I was already receiving military training, and I had already seen enough bloodshed and brutality to know I wanted no part of it.

I am a Christian, who'd been raised by my parents as a Catholic. During church services, we learned about the sacrificial love of Jesus Christ, who instructed his followers to "turn the other cheek" and to "love your enemies." But on Saturdays and Sundays, high school kids like me would be taken to military camps where we were trained to maim and mutilate Muslims. Please don't misunderstand. I'm not saying that the terrorist Muslims in Lebanon were any less barbaric, and I certainly understand the principle of defending your faith. But I wanted no part of fighting this "civil war," which I believed was more about power and money than religion. Besides, I couldn't read about modeling Christ-like behavior one moment and then torture others with differing perspectives.

At that point in my life, I'd already been exposed to a couple of appalling incidents that had been emblazoned in my mind. During one of the battles, our leaders kidnapped some Muslim children and extinguished lit cigarettes in their faces. Our leaders also brutally battered women, punching them in the face and then instructed the women to smile when they turned on video cameras. One trainer grabbed a piece of scrap metal, carving up a woman's face with the jagged edge as she screamed and blood gushed.

Ghastly images shook me. And I knew that when I graduated from high school, I would be expected to join the warfare, killing others before I was killed and justifying my actions in the name of my faith. Deep-down, I couldn't believe that was the plan Jesus had for my life, and I couldn't stop thinking about my older brother, Fayek, who at that time was a graduate student at a place called Texas A&M.

I had never previously visited the United States, and I'm not sure I could have located College Station on a Texas map. But my brother's descriptions, along with the educational opportunities, peaceful campus and overall camaraderie of the student body at A&M, made Aggieland sound like as much of a dream destination as Disneyland. My brother, who is three years older than me, left Beirut for the United States in 1978, when the intensity of the war in Lebanon had not yet reached a boiling point, and there was no need for mandatory military training for high school students. The more tranquil times also made it easier to acquire a visa for international travel.

My father was not a rich man, as he and my mother raised three children in a modest home. My sister was born in 1959, my brother came along two years later and I was born in '64. We all shared the same bedroom growing up, which gives some indication of our humble financial status. But we never lacked for any necessities. My father made enough money so that my mother stayed home to raise the kids, and my father worked hard to provide the most important things. When my brother, Fayek, expressed a desire to attend college in the United States, my father found a way. Fayek had done well in high school and attended the equivalent of a junior college in Lebanon. He made good grades, and administrators at the school helped him with the application process to American universities. He was accepted into what was then called Memphis State and began his collegiate career in 1978 (he ultimately transferred to Texas A&M for his postgraduate degree).

Fadi Kalaouze as a child attending Catholic school in Lebanon

My brother and I wrote letters to each other, and as I read about his life experiences, I dreamed of attending college in the United States, as well. Three years later, however, when it would have been time for me to apply to American universities, leaving Lebanon was not an option. The escalating tensions of a war-torn country took a negative toll on the economy. Money became increasingly harder to earn, and my father's financial resources grew smaller. Visas also became more difficult to attain, as more Lebanese residents sought to escape the hazards of war. And for me personally, the biggest obstacle hindering my "study abroad" dreams was the threat that had been made to me and my other Christian friends during our military training sessions. In no uncertain terms, we'd been warned by trainers that if we attempted to escape from our "duty" of annihilating Muslims, our family members would suffer serious—perhaps deadly—consequences. In other words, not serving was not an option.

As much as I would have loved to follow in my brother's footsteps, I wasn't willing to jeopardize the safety of my father, mother and sister. I grudgingly and fearfully accepted the fact that I would be required to participate in a war I did not believe in and would—in all likelihood—die because of my reluctance to kill others.

It wasn't until an acquaintance chose to escape from his military service duty that I began to ponder other possibilities. This particular acquaintance possessed a true rebellious spirit, and he simply disappeared one day, escaping military training with no physical or financial pain being inflicted on family members he left behind. The realization that it had been an idle threat opened my eyes. I vowed to leave my war-torn country if I ever received an opportunity, and I believe God presented me with the chance.

I was visiting an Armenian friend one day at his home in Beirut and I told him how I strongly opposed joining the war effort. His father overheard our discussion and suggested that I apply for a visa at the American Embassy as soon as possible. He knew someone at the embassy and knew that five-year visas were being issued for a limited time. This was not publicized information. My friend's father overheard our conversation. He happened to know somebody at the embassy, and he knew my brother would soon be graduating from A&M, which would make me a prime candidate for the visa.

In the midst of the war, the American Embassy had been extremely selective about issuing visas. To obtain one, you essentially needed to be rich because the Americans didn't want broke and/or desperate Lebanese refugees seeking jobs, financial aid and asylum in the United States. As such, the visa application process was typically stringent and decisions were made primarily based on a family's financial resources. If you had plenty of money, it was assumed you would be likely to return to Lebanon after visiting or studying abroad. But anyone who wasn't wealthy was considered a flight risk because he/she would be likely to seek employment and long-term residency in the U.S. The interview/application process was typically loaded with numerous financial questions and proof-of-income requirements. But the timing of my brother's graduation, along with the invaluable nugget of information regarding five-year visas from my friend's father, opened a door for me that would have been previously bolted shut. My father wasn't required to provide bank statements and we were not asked financial questions. We simply told them about my brother, and by the grace of God, I was granted the visa. One huge hurdle had been cleared. One more was left.

My father, who already had a visa, scraped together enough money to purchase two airline tickets to the United States. Even though I had a visa, I needed to avoid being detected by the Christian militia. They routinely set up barricades near the airport to prevent teen-agers like me from escaping their duty. My father devised a plan to take three vehicles to the airport, with one of my uncles driving the lead car and another driving the trail vehicle. My father and I were in the middle vehicle, which would allow me at least a few moments to hide or possibly slip out the back door if we encountered a barricade where militia members were checking IDs. Fortunately, we were not detained on our trip, and the airport was not closed, which was often the case when fighting from the war escalated. I don't remember much about the flight, but I thanked God all the way from Beirut to New York City, where we landed first, and then traveled on to Houston.

I didn't speak English, and I could not have possibly anticipated what God would have planned for me in the United States, but I remember being so grateful when we landed in Houston, where my brother picked up my father and me. I was happy to see Fayek, but I was ecstatic about the fact that I would not be required to kill anyone or risk my life in a war I didn't support. Upon arriving in Texas, I vowed to make the most of my opportunity. Fayek had been an excellent student in the U.S., and he had enjoyed A&M. That was a good enough reason for me to apply to A&M, but first I needed to learn English well enough to at least pass the Test of English as a Foreign Language (TOEFL). After my brother graduated and before my father returned to Lebanon, I enrolled in the English Language Institute. I learned enough in the ensuing year and a half to pass the TOEFL and then was accepted into A&M. Meanwhile, Fayek didn't find a career opportunity that appealed to him in the U.S. after his graduation, so he returned to Lebanon to join the rest of my family, leaving me truly on my own in College Station.

I was nervous and excited about starting classes at A&M in 1985, and since my father no longer needed to pay for Fayek's expenses, he could send me a monthly check. That was the plan for the duration of my college experience. If that had actually transpired, I might have ultimately been successful in this country or I possibly would have returned to Lebanon like my brother. But I certainly would not have become the entrepreneur I am today if my father had continued to pay my way. My short-term plans and long-term future changed almost overnight when the value of the Lebanese lira crashed. During the 1980s, Lebanon became second to Columbia in the international drug trade, and drug money kept the economy afloat temporarily. But ultimately, a number of factors involving the war contributed to the dramatic decline of the lira, which went from an exchange rate of 5 LL to $1 to 2,000 LL to $1. In other words, my collegiate fund completely disappeared overnight. A savings account of 50,000 Lebanese lira was once the equivalent of $10,000 in America. After the crash, however, the 50,000 in savings amounted to only $25.

My father had no money to send, and I had no way of paying tuition expenses, the rent for my apartment, food or anything else. I had been thoroughly enjoying college life at A&M, relishing the freedoms and opportunities in this country. But after the Lebanese financial crisis, I received a phone call from my brother telling me it was time to come home. I had always followed the instructions of my parents and older siblings, never rocking the boat. I was a "pleaser." But there comes a time in life when everyone must take a stand for himself. This was my time.

My brother told me I had to come back. There was no other financial option. He said I could attend college classes in Lebanon, as my sister had done years earlier. I listened to everything he said, but I took a stand, telling Fayek I wouldn't return to Lebanon without a degree from A&M. "You won't survive on your own because you are too weak," he said angrily. "Without our father's money, you have no chance." Those words were hurtful, and we fought over the phone. He hung up on me, and as I sat in my apartment thinking about my next move, I realized I was truly on my own.

At that moment, I made an important realization—one I believe everyone must make in order to be successful. Sitting alone in my apartment, I comprehended for the first time that my destiny was entirely up to me. I was completely responsible for my future and my actions would determine my success or failure. That was an extremely frightening and powerfully liberating discovery. There was no longer a financial safety net. My father would not be sending money, and I could no longer afford to attend A&M or stay in my apartment. But deep-down, I believed God had opened a door and granted me the chance to be in the United States. This was the land of opportunity, and I was determined to chase the American Dream.

The first really good decision I made on my own was to say "no" to a golden—but suspicious—opportunity presented to me by one of the friends my brother made at A&M. I was in desperate need of money, and out of the blue, I was contacted about a great opportunity in Houston. My brother's friend and I drove to Houston and met a man who explained to me that he was going to help me buy a new Nissan 300 ZX without me putting in a dime of my own money. He would take me to the dealership, place the vehicle in my name and I'd drive it for a couple months. Then he would contact me one Saturday and I would drive the Nissan 300 ZX to a Houston hotel, where I'd check in for the night. The car would then be stolen from the parking lot, and all I had to do was to tell the police that it was, indeed, my car. To sweeten the deal, he promised me that a beautiful woman would be at the hotel to have sex with me. He further explained that the vehicle would be stripped of its valuable equipment and abandoned on the side of the road. Once the insurance was filed, I would be given $4,000 for my part of this scheme. He tried to convince me there was no risk on my part and that I wouldn't actually be doing anything wrong. At that time, $4,000 would have covered my tuition fees, apartment and expenses as I searched for a job and stayed in school. It was a tempting offer, especially since I didn't understand the illegality of the scheme and I'd never been with a woman in that way.

Thank God I didn't agree to do it. Even though I didn't understand the scheme, I sensed something shady. Maybe it was my conscious or the Holy Spirit, but after giving it some serious consideration that night, I decided to pass. A couple of months later, the *Houston Chronicle* reported that the man who'd tried to recruit me had been busted, along with several accomplices, for insurance fraud. A couple of his recruits were foreigners like me, and they were deported. That could have easily been me, but I believe God led me in a different direction.

Instead of driving a new 300 ZX, I took the money I had left in the bank—money that had been converted to U.S. currency before the lira's demise—and spent it on a much different mode of transportation. I bought a van for $800, which may have been the best investment I have ever made because it also became my home and entrepreneurial office. Besides, if you are about to begin the ride of your life, it helps to have wheels.

KALAOUZE'S WILD ENTREPRENEURIAL RIDE

For a moment, I desperately hoped it was only a bad dream. But then I cautiously opened my eyes and discovered that the swaying back and forth sensation was real. So were the angry voices outside my van. I closed my eyes and prayed, asking God to protect me from the drunken men who were screaming slurred obscenities and shaking my van violently in the parking lot of Culpepper Plaza at the corner of Texas Avenue and Harvey Road in College Station. It was about 3 a.m., and I quickly concluded that the men—probably three or four of them—had wandered out of the bar in the shopping strip center and stumbled in the direction of my van, which was parked in the vicinity of what is now a Chick-fil-A restaurant. I had no idea if their intent was malicious or mischievous, but lying there alone, scared and wearing only my underwear in the sultry summertime humidity, I was in no position to confront or question them. I tried not to make a sound, practically holding my breath as the inebriated men rocked my world back and forth.

Fortunately, they had rather short attention spans after an apparent lengthy night of pounding longnecks. After shaking the van and cursing prolifically, they called it a night without doing any damage to the one possession I could simply not do without at that time. That van, held together miraculously by prayers, took me on numerous adventures and misadventures in my unlikely route from financial desperation back to full-time student status at A&M. The maroon-colored, full-sized Dodge van featured a small bed in the back, thick curtains covering the windows and a tiny sink that drained directly onto the pavement. It didn't feature any running water, so I was constantly in search of the next available location to use the bathroom and shower (thank goodness for the old G. Rollie White Coliseum on the A&M campus and truck stops), but I could at least brush my teeth in the van's sink as long as I had some sort of drink. I slept in the van for three unmercifully hot months during the summer, parking it wherever I thought I would be least likely to be towed.

Primarily, though, the van was my rolling sales office. After the collapse of the lira, I could no longer pay my tuition to A&M, I was kicked out of my apartment, and I had to begin searching for ways to make money. A friend told me about a man in Dallas who made a living selling flags. Hoping he might allow me to become a distributor, I headed north to "Big D" with just enough money to pay for gas. By the grace of God—that's been my life's theme phrase—the man in Dallas stocked my van with flags and didn't charge me up-front fees. Depending on the design of the flag, I sold each for $10 to $15 apiece and paid the supplier in Dallas half of the retail price. I initially parked my van on the roadside in high-traffic locations in Bryan/College Station and then moved to other cities across the state. I sold all types of flags, representing countries like the U.S. and Mexico, rock bands like AC/DC and Pink Floyd and even Confederate flags, although I did not have any idea at that time in my life what those flags symbolized.

I made decent money, but I continually had to relocate, moving from one city to the next. For whatever reason, I seemed to sell the most flags when parked in high-traffic locations in Plano. I could easily sell 10 to

15 flags a day, grossing $175 to $200 on a good Saturday afternoon. After a few days, I would have a considerable amount of cash in the van, which is why I purchased a BB gun. I displayed it carefully by adjusting the curtains so that it might appear to be a 12-guage shotgun. My only intent was to scare away potential thieves, but my carefully displayed gun backfired on me one night in Dallas.

Again, I was sleeping in my underwear along the roadside when I was startled by a police siren at 2:30 in the morning. Seconds later, I heard a voice ringing in my van coming from a police megaphone/bullhorn. They obviously saw the BB gun and demanded that I step out of the van immediately. I did just that, holding my hands above my head and stepping onto the street in nothing but my underwear as cars passed by and passengers gawked at the Middle Eastern man in his boxers. That was a particularly embarrassing moment, but after verifying it was indeed a BB gun and doing a background check on me, the police apologized and let me go back to sleep. Humiliating moments like that stick with you and tend to motivate you.

Acts of random kindness stick with you, as well. Whenever possible, I've looked for ways to help others, especially in times of need, because it's the right thing to do. I also believe it's a way of showing my appreciation for the people who helped me along the way…like the stranger who came to my aid in Plano. On another flag-selling expedition in north Dallas, I parked one night on a hill, and to my dismay, the van would not start in the morning. I didn't know what to do, especially since I had not sold any flags the previous day and I only had a couple of dollars in my pocket. As I was worrying about the dire situation, a man and his wife pulled beside me. They were a normal-looking, middle-aged couple, but they were heaven-sent angels to me. The man asked if I needed more fuel, and I told him my gas gauge indicated there was at least a quarter of a tank left. Of course, as anyone could plainly see, the van was practically as old as Methuselah—or at least almost as old as me—and it was quite possible that the needle wasn't reading accurately. The man encouraged me to hop in his vehicle so he could take me to the nearest gas station and buy me a little gas. I had no other options, so I did just that. He bought me $5 worth of gas and returned me to my van. After I added the gas, my van cranked up relatively quickly.

Later that day, I found an ideal location and sold numerous flags, giving me enough money to fill my tank, return to College Station and pay for several expenses. But I would have never found that location without that couple. I'm not sure what I would have done without their help. I only wish I would have asked for contact information so I could let them know how much they helped me. I've certainly thanked God for sending them my way, because my financial situation began to improve steadily after that event. I sold enough flags throughout the summer to pay for rent for an apartment I shared with three other people. I learned how to eat inexpensively, buying beef liver from the grocery store meat department for $1.25 per half pound and a box of rice for even less. I'd put butter on the liver, fry it and eat for a week on just a little over $2. I saved as much money as I could because I needed to return to school as quickly as possible. After all, my visa featured an expiration date.

Finding an affordable apartment and cheap sustenance were steps in the right direction, but the leap forward came when I met someone who introduced me to a new product called the "auto sunscreen," which could be placed on the front dash of a parked car to reflect the sun and reduce the inside temperature of the vehicle. The auto sunscreens featured various patterns that could also reflect the personality of the vehicle's owner. My new acquaintance told me he was driving to California during spring break to meet with the manufacturer and to become a distributor. I was intrigued by the concept, and I eagerly accompanied him when he asked if I would like to tag along on his drive to California.

My friend purchased the auto sunscreens and we began selling them inside the Memorial Student Center on the A&M campus after spring break. But our initial sales were so agonizingly slow that my friend completely lost his patience and bailed out of the auto sunscreen business, offering me the chance to sell his remaining inventory and repay him only his initial investment. The wholesale cost of each sunscreen was .68 cents, and we were selling them for $5 apiece. The profit potential was much better than selling flags, where I was pocketing 50 percent of the retail price, and I agreed to take the remaining inventory and repay my friend as I made sales.

Once again, this turned out to be a monumental blessing. As the weather heated up, the auto sunscreen sales picked up, especially when I made the decision to utilize my flag-selling strategies instead of staying in the air-conditioned MSC. I first parked in front of an automotive parts store in Bryan, placed a sunscreen on the front dash of my van and began selling them steadily. As April turned to May and then May became June, sales skyrocketed. I ordered more from the manufacturer and routinely sold 30 to 35 per day, which allowed me to net $130 to $150 a day. By the end of the summer, I had enough money to buy my way back into A&M. A wonderful woman in the immigration office at A&M assisted me in my reinstatement efforts, and I paid all my previous debts to A&M, as well as my tuition fees for the next semester.

The downside of the auto sunscreen business was that as the weather cooled, so did sales. I needed steady income, as I was taking classes at A&M and Blinn Junior College. Since I had done so well with sunscreens, I figured I needed to stick with sales. I used some savings to pay for a trip to New York to explore business ideas. In the Big Apple, I was intrigued by imitation perfumes that smelled like the designer originals. For example, while Chanel No. 5 perfume cost hundreds of dollars in retail stores, the knockoff that smelled just like it—at least to me—could be purchased for $2 for a small bottle in New York. I believed I could strike it rich by designing a special label for the small perfume bottles and selling them at the MSC. My creation was called "Lady Aggie Perfume."

Unfortunately, I generated far more jokes than sales because of the fliers I placed on cars, which stated: "Do you want to smell like an Aggie?" I experimented with different scents and names, but I didn't know the first thing about selling perfume. Nevertheless, I continued to regularly set up my perfume table at the MSC, selling three or four bottles each football game weekend, until another salesman at the MSC named "John" took me aside and bluntly asked me why I was continuing to sell perfume. John's favorite adjective was the "F word," and he was crude, but he gave me the best business advice I ever received. John was selling tons of T-shirts every weekend, and he strongly suggested I do the same. At that point I began drawing T-shirt designs.

While I had some success selling T-shirts, I decided to take a full-time job, working the graveyard shift and making minimum wage as a gas station/convenience store cashier on the corner of Highway 6 and Booneville Road in Bryan. I worked 40 hours a week, but it still wasn't enough to cover all my expenses, so I took another job as a busboy at the Texas Tumbleweed restaurant in College Station. I'd go to school in the morning, come home and grab a couple hours sleep, go to the Texas Tumbleweed at 3 and work until 11 and then go to the gas station to start my eight-hour shift at midnight. Every day was not like that, because I was not permitted to work more than 40 hours a week at either job. But I didn't sleep much.

I also sold my gas-guzzling van and bought a moped, which was great for gas mileage, but not so great when the weather—or other drivers—made conditions hazardous. Dodging raindrops could be difficult, but flying beer cans were especially perilous. I was running late one evening after working at the restaurant, and I decided to save some time by hopping on the feeder road of Highway 6 for the drive from College Station to Bryan. Top speed on my moped was considerably less than the speed limit, and apparently, I agitated other late-night drivers with my slow-moving pace. Most drivers merely honked or waved their middle fingers, but a bunch of boys in the bed of a pickup truck began tossing beer cans in my direction as they passed and cursed me. I was minding my business, meandering along as fast as the moped would allow when—BOOM!—a beer can pelts me. It was another one of those moments I'll never forget that served as motivation for me to make something of myself.

I had moments like that at the restaurant, as well. Cleaning up vomit and backed-up toilets were bad enough, but I specifically remember times when several Lebanese students from A&M came into Texas Tumbleweed, flaunting their money. Their parents had obviously been made aware of the pending economic collapse before the lira took a tumble and had exchanged their savings to U.S. dollars. Whenever I would see them with plenty of cash, I often asked myself, "Why me? Why couldn't my family have known in advance, too?" In hindsight, I'm grateful I had to make my own way because I learned so many lessons, but there were definitely some hard and humbling times as I worked my way back into school.

Fadi Kalaouze on his graduation day at Texas A&M

One particularly terrifying moment ended my gas station cashier career. In the wee hours one morning, a man pulled his car up to the pumps and walked inside to give me his credit card. He instructed me to charge his card for $30 worth of gas. When I did, I received a message on the vintage terminal of that era, instructing me to hold his card. I politely told him I could not process his request and that I needed to keep his card. He unloaded a barrage of "F bombs" and threatened to come back and rearrange my face. As he left, I scribbled down his license plate and reported it to the police, who informed me that he was wanted for a third-degree felony. That scared me, and I called my manager at home at 3 a.m. to report what had happened. His response shocked me. He was furious because he was worried the man would come back and damage the station, throwing a brick through the glass or something like that.

Meanwhile, the police continued to maintain a presence at the gas station, so I felt somewhat better about my immediate safety, and I temporarily breathed a sigh of relief when the police informed me at about 5:30 a.m. that they had arrested the man. Unfortunately, my sense of peace disappeared when another man showed up two hours later, informing me that he was the cousin of the man who'd been arrested. "The minute my cousin is released from prison, he's coming after your (blankety-blank)," he warned me. "He'll never forget your face."

That's all I needed to hear. Working the graveyard shift was fine, but ending up in the graveyard was not. I said goodbye to the gas station and went to work for McDonald's, where I was fired after only one week (apparently I spent too much time cooking McNuggets and not enough time flipping burgers). I also had stints delivering newspapers and making door-to-door sales with a book company. Those jobs and others helped me pay my expenses and save a little money as I progressed toward earning my degree in industrial engineering and graduating from A&M in 1991.

In the meantime, I continued to sell T-shirts, and my first two designs sold well. But it was the third one that really opened my eyes to a world of possibilities. In 1991, *Time Magazine* voted Diet Pepsi's catchphrase "you've got the right one, baby"—belted out by Ray Charles—as the best advertising jingle of the year. The jingle took direct aim at Diet Coke, and my modified T-shirt took aim at A&M's biggest rival, Texas. My T-shirt featured a sketched drawing of three babies, a boy in the middle kissing a happy baby girl in an A&M outfit and a crying baby girl on the other side with a Longhorns logo on her outfit. It also featured the, "You've got the right one, baby" catchphrase.

That T-shirt took off in 1992, and I soon became the top-selling salesperson in the MSC. I continued to sell that T-shirt, along with others, and also sold posters and flags in the MSC. And perhaps my greatest sales job was in convincing a beautiful woman I first noticed while selling T-shirts in the MSC to eventually become my wife. I first noticed Hege when she passed through the MSC with a fellow Lebanese student I knew named "Rita." I called Rita and asked if she could introduce me to her friend. She suggested that I meet them at one of the clubs on Texas Avenue on Friday night at 9. I dressed to impress and showed up at the club by myself. But shortly after 11, I figured out they weren't coming. I called Rita the next day and she said Hege had been sick. Rita and I then arranged for a meeting the following weekend at a house party. Once again, I showed up, and once again I was stood up. Fortunately, I did see Hege a few weeks later on campus as she was walking toward her bus stop. Realizing this might be my only chance, I hopped on the bus even though I had no idea where it was going and proceeded to sit next to her. We talked briefly, and I asked her out to dinner before the bus stopped at her apartment complex. I was deflated by her response, as she informed me she had a boyfriend.

I figured that I might never see Hege again. But one year later, I was selling T-shirts again when I noticed her walk into the MSC Bookstore. I asked a friend to watch my things momentarily as I again "stalked" Hege, tracking her down at the checkout line and trying to make it appear that I had not followed her. I casually sauntered up to her and we began a conversation that led us to the Flag Room across the hall from the bookstore. She seemed engaging and even joked about T-shirt design ideas. I decided to risk another blow to my ego and muscled up the courage to again ask her to dinner. This time, she accepted as one full year of persistence finally paid off. I had won the date I coveted, but then I began to panic as I pondered what I would drive.

By that time, I had purchased a car for about $500. It may have been overpriced. It didn't have air conditioning and didn't have many more miles left before its junkyard destination. I wanted to make a positive impression on the elegant Hege, and I knew that wouldn't be possible in that vehicle. I rented a Chrysler New Yorker, picked her up in style and took her to dinner at Café Excel. It was probably the first serious date of my life, and I had a wonderful time. I assumed that she also had fun because she accepted my invitation for a second date. But this time I knew I couldn't continue to mislead her by renting a car that was far more expensive than I could afford. This time, I picked her up in my $500 jalopy. It was a typically hot and humid late May night, and by the time we reached the restaurant, Hege was sweating bullets and her makeup was running sprints. She never complained, though, and she again accepted my invitation for another date. I knew then that she was genuinely interested in me. We were engaged in 1993, married on May 15, 1994 in Houston and the first of our three children was born in 1995. To this day, we've never had what I would call a "serious fight."

Hege slipping a wedding ring on Fadi's hand

Marrying Hege gave me confidence in other areas of my life, as well, and we both decided it might be time to move my T-shirt/poster/flag sales business out of the MSC hallways and into the mall, giving us a real storefront (Barnes & Noble taking over the MSC Bookstore and forcing any competitors out of the MSC also played a role in that decision). We came up with the name "Inspirations," and we started with a small store at Post Oak Mall and $5,000 in inventory. We couldn't initially afford to do much decorating, so we opened the store by hanging the posters that were for sale on the walls and "displaying" our T-shirts on metal racks. We designed as many A&M-related T-shirts as possible, and we offered shoppers a 25 percent discount on their first purchase. Patrons merely had to tell us they were new customers, and we'd offer the 25 percent discount. Many repeat customers thought they were pulling a fast one on us when they lied about coming into the store for the first time, but we were fine with giving everyone a discount…as long as they were buying something. My wife managed the store and I began thinking of ways to grow the business.

I researched trends and traveled frequently to purchase the "hottest" clothing lines and posters. For example, in the early 1990s, California-based designers Shawn Stussy and Mossimo Giannulli hit it big with the Stussy and Mossimo sportswear lines. They were big in California, and we believed they'd sell in College

Station, as well. We were right, and we were also ahead of the curve in bringing in other products such as Far Side T-shirts and the Magic Eye 3D, hidden-image posters that were all the rage in the mid-1990s. We bought posters from as far away as England, and Inspirations became a mix of new and exciting brands. Anytime a new product was introduced, we strived to have it first. We also customized popular products geared toward the A&M audience. We were the only retailer in the community selling a 3D hidden-image poster that featured the "A&M" logo. We made good money by staying aggressive, keeping up with national trends and being creative with A&M merchandise.

The College Station Inspirations was doing so well we opened a second location in San Marcos that carried the same national products and specialized in Southwest Texas State merchandise. The San Marcos store never did as well as the one in College Station, but it was a solid business, and we were duplicating the same strategies and product lines in both stores. We learned the retail T-shirt/casual clothing business inside and out, and we generally made wise decisions about what to carry and how to promote products.

Unfortunately, our next decision was not our wisest. Instead of building upon our foundation, we decided to open a fast-food franchise…in Lebanon, of all places. As we built Inspirations into a profitable company, I heard from family and friends back in my native country that the economy had rebounded and restaurants were doing particularly well. For various reasons, a friend and I decided to give the fast-food business a shot in Lebanon, taking American restaurants to the Middle East. I arranged for my brother-in-law to oversee the Inspirations operations, while I took my wife and 1-year-old daughter to Lebanon. My friend opened a Subway franchise, while I opened a Schlotzsky's. Neither venture was a wise investment. The biggest issue was that we had to import all of our food items from the United States or other countries, and suppliers were not equipped at that point to deliver what we needed in a timely manner. We had to charge a higher prices, we had very little support from local officials, and it was just a bad overall investment. I could write about the many reasons we lost money on the Schlotzsky's experiment, but it was a relief when I sold it and returned to Aggieland in 1999. I knew Aggies; I knew clothing; and I knew I needed to stick to my area of expertise.

When we returned, we seriously evaluated our store in San Marcos. It was making money, but we were not generating the revenues we were in College Station. We decided to close the San Marcos store and focus our efforts on College Station. That was one of several positive decisions we made shortly after the not-so-good attempt to open a Schlotzsky's. Another extremely beneficial move was expanding our A&M-logoed clothing line to appeal to former students of all ages, as well as current students. Why limit ourselves to T-shirts? My wife and I noticed former students visiting campus on game days often wore collared and button-down maroon and white shirts. We figured a high-end A&M clothing line would do well with men and exceptionally well with women.

We weren't abandoning T-shirts, and I didn't want to mess with the success or feel of Inspirations at Post Oak Mall by overloading it with more expensive merchandise. Instead, we opened another store in the mall that carried A&M apparel called "Aggieland Outfitters." I was confident it would work because, while the merchandise was somewhat different than what we sold in Inspirations, it was still clothing. I wasn't venturing completely into unfamiliar territory…as I had by opening a Schlotzsky's. For the most part, we made good decisions and began turning a good profit almost immediately.

One other relatively risky, but wise decision we made after returning to Aggieland was to purchase the copyright of the "saw 'em off Longhorns logo" from a couple of students who'd designed it. My brother-in-law told me about how popular the design was on campus. I contacted the two students, who were nearing graduation and had plans to begin their professional careers in Austin, and said I was interested in buying the copyright from them. They politely declined, but I continually followed up with them. I just had a good feeling about that logo, and I finally offered to pay them such a significant amount that my wife and accountant thought I'd lost my mind. But I believed it was one of those risks that needed to be taken. To be a successful entrepreneur, you can't always play it safe. You need to be wise with your money, but at the right times, you also need to be proactive. I thought this was an investment worth making, and the two students happily handed me the copyright, which was legally transferred to me in 2001.

KALAOUZE'S MOST DIFFICULT CHALLENGE

Because of the success of the Aggieland Outfitters store in the mall and the astounding popularity of the "saw 'em off" merchandise, we began looking for opportunities to open additional locations, especially if we could give Aggieland Outfitters a presence near campus. Thanks to the advice of one of our store managers in 2002, we looked at a small grocery store in the Southgate area on George Bush Drive near Wellborn Road that was for sale. Previously, it had been a gas station, and it had never done particularly well as a grocery store because, quite frankly, it was rather small—at least by grocery store standards—and somewhat of an eyesore. A liquor store on the east side of the building gave it an increasingly seedy feel. Nevertheless, we loved the location, and the owner of the grocery store told me he wanted $40,000 for it.

We certainly didn't have that kind of capital. But after negotiations, he agreed to let us pay him $20,000 up front and to finance the remaining $20,000 over four years. Once again, many people thought we were crazy, especially since we didn't even have the $20,000 up-front money. Besides, buying a grocery store had nothing to do with our T-shirt and A&M-logoed business. But we were convinced the location would provide the perfect presence near campus we were seeking, so we basically bought the location and remodeled it by putting all the expenses on credit cards. I'd never do such a thing now, but we believed then it was a risk worth taking.

Thankfully, we were right. Two years after opening the Aggieland Outfitters in Southgate, the landlord approached us about renting the liquor store space on the east end of the building, which we gladly did because we were outgrowing our existing dimensions. Eventually, the Southgate location did so well that we purchased the building from the landlord so that we no longer had to pay any lease. The success of the Southgate store led us to open another storefront on University Drive, and in the fall of 2013, we expanded that location to become our 8,000-square-foot flagship store. It took years of negotiations to expand the University Drive store, as we bought two houses on one side of it and another house on the other side to build a parking lot to accommodate all of the customers who shop the store, particularly on football game-day weekends. As we have grown the business, we've also been able to add key personnel members through the years.

The Kalaouze family in front of the store on George Bush Drive

Business is, indeed, booming and we continually thank God for blessing our efforts beyond our wildest initial expectations. We are especially thankful today because we realize how closely we came to going out of business when a lawsuit filed on December 4, 2006 by the University of Texas System Board of Regents against us threatened to destroy everything we had worked to achieve. The UT System lawyers accused us of trademark infringement for selling merchandise that featured the "saw 'em off" logo. Our lawyers believed we were protected by First Amendment freedoms to sell the parody of the Longhorns' logo, but it was quite intimidating to be confronted by the entire UT System, with all of its powerful and mega-rich lawyers. In my mind, it was not coincidental that the lawsuit was filed 10 days after the Texas A&M football team went into Austin and shocked the No. 10-ranked Longhorns, 12-7, to knock Texas out of Big 12 title contention. Hundreds of A&M fans—maybe thousands—attended that game with 12th Man towels that featured the saw 'em off logo printed on them. We also sold thousands of T-shirts right after that game featuring the logo and the final score. I believe we ruffled feathers in Austin.

The UT powers-that-be responded with a lawsuit seeking a permanent injunction preventing us from selling the logo. That wouldn't have ruined us, but the lawsuit also sought attorneys' fees, damages and profits our company made through the sale of University of Texas trademarks. We'd have gone belly-up bankrupt if we had been required to pay UT for all the profits—roughly $2 million at that time—that they sought in the lawsuit. Unlike the war in Lebanon during my teen-age years, this was a battle I knew we had to wage. We had no other choice, as this could have spelled the end of business as we knew it.

Of course, we first needed to arm ourselves with a lawyer willing to defend us. I searched the Internet for the top 10 lawyers in Texas, and I sent them all emails explaining the case and our position. Only one of them, Allan Van Fleet of the Greenberg Traurig law firm, responded. He called and said, "Fadi, I graduated from Baylor Law School, but my father was in the A&M Corps of Cadets. I'll help." We were grateful to have one lawyer, but as Allan began explaining to me how the court system worked, I realized that even though we had done nothing wrong, the UT System was quite capable of draining all of our financial resources by simply extending and delaying court appearances and decisions in an elaborate legal delay of game. They had plenty of time and plenty of money, and I had plenty of sleepless nights. But Allan came up with a brilliant strategy that leveled the playing field. He explained that we had to take our fight to the media to win the court of public opinion.

That's exactly what we did, and the publicity was amazing. First, the *Bryan/College Station Eagle*, the local television and radio stations and TexAgs.com shared our story. Then it was the *Dallas Morning News*, the *Houston Chronicle* and the *Austin-American Statesman*. Eventually, even *USA Today* told our story, and with each article and telecast, our company seemed to gain support as the little underdog fighting for its First Amendment rights against the greenback-packing, burnt-orange bullies. In the meantime, we began producing "Save the Saw 'em Off" T-shirts that were selling so rapidly we could barely print them fast enough. We quickly sold 5,000 shirts at $20 apiece, as Aggies rallied to help our cause and defeat the Longhorns' lawyers. Thankfully, the case never went to court, as it would have cost us at least a half million in fees.

Enough public pressure and negative media scrutiny led UT officials to agree to a meeting with my wife and me, along with our artist and law team, in Austin. We met with UT lawyers, along with then-athletics director DeLoss Dodds and other UT officials. I'll never forget how Dodds refused to shake my wife's hand. There was plenty of back-and-forth legal dialogue, but I eventually had a chance to state my case and provide them with six alternate designs that an artist had produced. The artist had produced 60 designs featuring variations of the sawed-off logo that were slightly different than the one we'd been producing. My hope was that we could settle the suit out of court by agreeing on an alternate logo.

The UT officials examined the six alternate designs I provided. Those six designs were the logos that many Aggies viewed as their favorites that would keep the tradition alive. I later explained to the UT officials that our artist had actually produced 60 designs. Without much hesitation, they said, "We want to see the other 54." Dodds, who retired as Texas' AD in August 2014, is a wise man who has won many negotiations, and he has probably out-smarted many adversaries like me. But not this time.

After the meeting in Austin, we emailed the other 54 designs to UT officials, who then emailed us the six logos they'd accept. We picked our favorite of the six they had chosen and then our artist made 10 variations of that logo, making the blaze and the nostrils on the steer's head 10 different sizes. Anticipating that UT officials would do everything they could to spite us, I presented the logo that we actually liked the least as the first on the top of the page, and I labeled it as our favorite. Instead of numbering them 1 through 10, I positioned them from our favorite to our least favorite. But in reality, I completely reversed the order, so that the one we liked the most was presented last, and we labeled it as our least favorite. It was really just a game, as I anticipated their next move. We then returned to Austin for another meeting. After two and a half hours of discussing options for the logo, the Texas officials picked the logo we had listed as our least favorite one…just as we'd suspected. In reality, it was the logo we wanted. Texas officials then agreed to settle out of court, primarily because they were taking a public relations beating, and they were livid about the fact that so many media members sided with us.

We settled out of court in late June 2007, and we agreed to accept the logo we labeled as our "least favorite" under the condition that they would not block our trademark efforts. We intentionally made a big deal out of begrudgingly taking their offer, even though the logo that they chose was really the one that we wanted. We also agreed to pay a $20,000 court fee to settle the whole thing, but they allowed us to pay it over four months. The great thing is that we couldn't have possibly bought all the positive publicity we received throughout the entire ordeal, and even though we paid $5,000 a month for four months to cover the court fees, sales of our saw 'em off-logoed apparel increased 30 percent the rest of the year. So, what started off as potentially the worst thing that could ever happen to me and my wife as entrepreneurs became something that expanded our brand and overall business operations beyond what we could have imagined. God truly blessed us through the storms, and we are proud of the way we stuck to our principles and fought for our rights under the letter of the law.

KALAOUZE'S ADVICE TO YOUNG ENTREPRENEURS

Whether you are contemplating a future career path or virtually anything else, I encourage you to always look at the overall picture. Try to always envision in advance how important decisions will affect you over the long term. It may also be of great assistance to look at the big picture in examining why you are being led in one direction or another.

Imagine all of us are in race from the beginning, and each person becomes wired in a certain way and receives certain connections in their brain pushing them in various directions in life. Some of us want to become lawyers because we saw injustice in our childhood. My friend became a doctor because, when he was young, he watched his father die after he failed to receive proper medical treatment. Some people are driven to be great business leaders because they had so little money growing up. For many people, these careers are viewed as a "life mission" because of how they have been wired.

It's great to satisfy any desire you have in mind, to follow where you believe that God has led you and to use your natural talents to pursue your dreams and goals. But I encourage you not to make the mistake that many people do by focusing so intensely on one goal that you miss out on the simple pleasures of enjoying the people around you and the journey it takes to reach your goal. Some people focus so much on making money that they fail to make friends, to make time for themselves and others and to make a positive difference in the world. Focusing too much on personal goals can cause you to miss out on many important things in life.

From the beginning of our lives, we're programmed by everyone around us—parents, friends, teachers, etc.—to believe certain definitions and to think in certain ways. Typically, we are a product of our childhood environment. Some of us are raised in an ideal setting and we are programmed in positive ways. But sometimes, people receive corrupted information or data, and they experience negative situations that generate counter-reactions in their mind when something is said or done. So many things that happen to us growing up can affect the way we think or react to certain situations. And at a certain age—usually in our late teens or early 20s—we become a hard-wired package, as we are trained to think in certain ways. At that point, it's hard to change who you are, how you think and the way you look at the world. That's why I encourage you now to look at the big picture, whether it involves business, pleasure or anything of the sort.

I encourage you now to form your own opinions, examine the way you think, analyze why you think certain ways and then make your own definitions. That way, you'll be prepared to help your own kids look at the big picture. If you're not next to your kids when they are growing up, you may miss an opportunity to help them define the important things in life: Love, commitment, religion, trust, fun, etc. If you miss that opportunity, your kids may end up with another definition in their heads that is completely different from the one that's in your mind. For example, if you're not there to help them define "fun" in a positive way, their definition of "fun" may be using alcohol or drugs with friends. Some definitions might end up hurting them or misleading them the rest of their lives.

To stay next to your kids, you may be required to sacrifice some of your personal goals in terms of how they relate to your career. Likewise, to develop and maintain close relationships with your spouse, relatives and friends, you may need to sacrifice some of the time you spend chasing your personal and professional goals. I know many rich people who are miserable because they have focused so much on making money and making a living that they have not really made a difference in the lives of others. Before you die, is it enough to merely say, "I was one of the best lawyers, doctors, CEOs, etc. in the world?" Or is it more important at the end of your life to say, "I was a good businessman and a great spouse, parent, friend, etc.?" Consider the big picture.

The other thing I'd like to emphasize is that to me, it's obvious that our world is created and driven by two powerful sources: Positive and negative. You can call them God vs. the devil or any other names you want. But even when you examine the simplest atom, it contains positive and negative charges. All life forms are dictated by positive and negative, and you must decide early what guides your value system: good or evil? Do you want to add more positives or more negatives to our world?

Most entrepreneurs would love to make lot of money. But is it enough to die with plenty of money in your bank account…and then to be forgotten a few years later? Or would you like to be remembered for adding more positives to this world before you die? Perhaps the legacy you really want is to establish a company or organization that continues to generate more positive contributions to this world even after you die…like Jesus or many other religious leaders. It doesn't have to be a religious organization, as your company could help young parents or kids by educating them about real life and real consequences. Or perhaps your organization could help change negative circumstances into positive results for people in their physical, mental or spiritual development.

There is so much that can be done to make our world a more positive place. Always consider the big picture and how you can use your talents to contribute in meaningful and lasting ways. Making money and being successful in your business is important, but it is not as important as making positive differences in the lives of others.

2.
Alan Roberts
Founder and Owner of Pumpco, Inc. Pipeline Construction
Texas A&M Class of 1978

ROBERTS' PATH TO TEXAS A&M

The Roberts family and friends

According to the Texas State Historical Association, oil may have first been accidentally discovered in Refugio County near the Texas coastline and the Mission River around 1870 while workers were digging a water well. But it wasn't until half a century later in the mid-1920s when the Refugio economy was stimulated significantly by the oil and gas industry as serious explorations began. The spark that first ignited the fiscal boom in Refugio was the completion of a pipeline owned by the Houston Gulf Company.

Ever since then, pipelines have played a major role in fueling the Texas economy, and the industry has most certainly been a driving force in the life of this particular Refugio native. I was born and raised in Refugio, which is located about 40 miles directly north of Corpus Christi. Like so many other men in the region, my father, W.D. Roberts, worked on the pipelines as a welder. During his childhood, he never had much of an opportunity to earn an education, as his mother—my paternal grandmother—died shortly after giving birth to my dad. My father was the youngest child in the family, and he had to start working at a very early age just to help my grandfather and the rest of the Roberts clan make ends meet.

Because of that background, my father was an extremely hard worker, and he placed a major emphasis on earning a higher education. He absolutely did not want any of his three sons following in his blue-collar footsteps. We knew from an early age that education was extremely important to him, and it was always a foregone conclusion that we would attend college and use our minds—not just our hands—to make a living. I was the youngest of three boys by a significant amount of years. I have always assumed that I was probably not a planned pregnancy, as my oldest brother, David, is almost 11 years older than me and my other brother, Jimmy, is eight years older. By the time I was mastering the ability to read and write in elementary school, David was already out of the house and enrolled at Texas A&M, where he eventually became the Commander of Company B-2 in the Corps of Cadets. I was probably 6 or 7 when David first went off to Texas A&M, and I looked up to him with tremendous admiration. I recall listening to many Aggie football games on the radio and being quite envious that my brother was probably at all of those games.

I remember visiting him with the rest of my family from time to time when he was in college, and I have a vague recollection of being inside Kyle Field on Thanksgiving Day 1965 for one of the most famous plays in Texas A&M history, "The Texas Special." Early in the second quarter of a scoreless tie, Texas A&M quarterback Harry Ledbetter bounced a lateral toward halfback Jim Kauffman, who picked up the ball, stomped his feet in anger as the fans at Kyle Field thought it was a busted play and momentarily took a step backward toward his own end zone. All of the Aggie players acted in disgust, as if Ledbetter had grossly underthrown an incomplete pass…rather than a lateral. But Kaufman then looked up and connected with a wide-open Ken "Dude" McLean, who had drifted 15 yards past the Texas defensive backs. The field judge had been tipped off before the game by head coach Gene Stallings so that an inadvertent whistle would not be blown when the lateral hit the ground. McLean caught the pass some 40 yards from the line of scrimmage and raced 91 yards for a TD and a 7-0 lead for the Aggies. The play, which was the longest in Texas A&M and Southwest Conference history at the time, staked the Aggies to a 17-0 halftime lead. I remember Kyle Field being so energized at that point. Unfortunately, it wasn't enough, as Texas rallied for a 21-17 win.

Nevertheless, the majesty of Kyle Field, the atmosphere of the campus and the fact I was such a big admirer of my oldest brother sold me on one day attending Texas A&M. Long before that happened, though, I gained a full appreciation for my father's work, along with why he was so adamant about us earning degrees. By the time my middle brother was nearing his graduation from Southwest Texas State University in San Marcos (now Texas State), I had begun working in the oilfields as a welder's helper. My dad would never allow me to do the actual welding, because he thought it offered great short-term pay that might deter me from going to college. In hindsight, he was probably right because that kind of pay may have kept me as a young man from pursuing higher education.

Although I didn't do any actual welding as a teen-ager, I worked extremely hard in the oilfields beginning at the age of 15. While he was based in Refugio, my dad actually worked all over the state, traveling wherever there was oilfield and pipeline-related welding work. When I wasn't in school, I'd follow right along with him. I worked on the pipelines throughout the summers, and when school was in session, I worked as many weekends and holidays as possible. My mother, Bertie Lea, was a devoted homemaker, who thoroughly enjoyed her domestic responsibilities and taking care of my father and her kids when we were at home. As a young man, I developed a great reputation for possessing my father's work ethic among the other pipeline workers, and many of those guys often requested that I served as their assistants. I earned quite a few raises and was given the opportunity to earn extra hours because of my dedication and attention to details.

That's how I first learned the pipeline business, and those experiences of working with different people and implementing various strategies would benefit me tremendously in the future. Being on my own for long stretches at a time as a teen also taught me how to be quite independent. I learned to cook, clean, do my own laundry, shop for my own groceries, balance my own checkbook and fend for myself long before many of my peers in high school. When I did finally enroll at Texas A&M, my roommates and buddies always used to joke with me, saying that I was such an organizer and enjoyed grocery-shopping, cooking, house-cleaning and so forth that they were looking for a woman to marry just like me…with some much different physical features, of course.

My parents, especially my father, were ecstatic when I enrolled at A&M. My older two brothers had already earned their undergraduate degrees, and I was now on track to do the same. In my dad's way of thinking, he'd gone three-for-three in one of his top parental objectives. To further motivate me to finish my degree plan once I arrived at A&M, my father vowed to buy me a car when I graduated.

Alan and Robyn Roberts on the sideline of Kyle Field with former A&M standout Ryan Swope

I went to A&M without any definitive plans for my future, other than obtaining a degree where I could better myself. Once I started at A&M in the fall of 1974, my initial thought was to pursue a degree plan that would lead me to medical school. I took plenty of chemistry and biology courses—extremely difficult classes—that seriously cut into my enjoyment of Aggie football at the time. A&M had a strong run under Emory Bellard in the mid-1970s, winning at least eight games every season from 1974 through 1978. I attended as many home games as possible, but the medical school track kept me extremely busy. I was doing well in school until my grades fell during my junior year. Once my GPA dropped to around 2.8, I realized medical school was probably no longer an option and made the switch to the business school, which is now the Mays Business School.

My chemistry and biology courses weren't necessary for the accounting degree I began pursuing, but my switch in majors is what pushed my graduation back from 1978 to '79. Once I graduated, I went to work for a CPA firm in Victoria. It didn't take long to realize that I hated the desk work I was doing. I worked on my fair share of tax returns during part of the year, and when it wasn't tax season, I was doing audits. I would go through boxes of bank statements, manually inputting balances. Then I'd take the statements to the partner, who would approve or alter the audits. It wasn't difficult work, and it wasn't necessarily awful. But it was B-o-r-i-n-g, with a capital "B." After almost two full years with the CPA firm, I went in one day and turned in my resignation. I had been contemplating doing something on my own in the pipeline/oil and gas industry, and the Austin Chalk boom was in full force.

After turning in my resignation, I went to my parents' home and told them the news. As you might imagine, my dad was furious. He couldn't understand why I would leave a good, white-collar job with no assurances, and he was really livid when I told him I initially planned to start a construction business in the oilfield.

ROBERTS' PATH TO ENTREPRENEURIAL SUCCESS

I am sometimes amazed by people who simply assume that I have always enjoyed the lifestyle, comforts and luxuries that my family can now afford. Nothing could actually be further from the truth. When I left the CPA firm to pursue my own entrepreneurial efforts, I lived with three other roommates in a modest, rather small place in Victoria that was anything but the "lap of luxury." And the only "marketing/advertising tool" I could initially afford was a daily box of donuts.

My business vision was to provide an oilfield construction and repair service to take advantage of all the activity surrounding the Austin Chalk play. The Austin Chalk formation covers some 300 miles in length and 40 miles in width along the U.S. Gulf Coast from Texas to Florida, but the center of the original play was located in Giddings, which sits on U.S. Route 77, almost exactly 100 miles north of where I was living in Victoria. Conventional drilling with vertical wells had not initially been particularly successful in developing the tight, fractured Austin Chalk reservoir. The development of horizontal drilling techniques, however, greatly enhanced the productivity of the wells. In the midst of the early-1980s boom, some 300 oil-related businesses were located in Giddings, and many rigs were operating in the outlying areas just beyond the city limits. I just figured that with so much activity, a construction service and repair company could do extremely well.

In August 1981, with no large capital, I officially opened Pumpco, Inc. I would leave Victoria at 5 in the morning each day and drive the 90 to 100 miles into Giddings. Depending on the amount of fog and/or traffic I encountered on the drive, which was mostly a two-lane highway, I'd arrive in Giddings at 6:30 and stop by the donut store. In an attempt to make as many connections as possible with company owners and office managers, I quickly discovered that I was far more likely to move beyond the receptionist and receive some face-to-face time with a decision-maker if I had a box of donuts with me. As I began to meet more and more production people, I started earning a job here and there. I was literally willing to do just about anything to make a few bucks and build a strong reputation. I had a used pickup truck and a bed full of tools, and I'd tackle virtually any challenge, from pump repairs to building fences and painting.

Within about four months, I had enough business to give up the daily, 200-mile, round-trip drive from Victoria and back, and I moved in with a friend in Giddings who had a 24-foot trailer. He already had a roommate living with him, so I slept on the floor of the trailer. At that point, I realized—quite literally—that nothing was "below me." On the positive side, though, at least I could sleep a little longer on the floor since I was no longer making the long drive.

I was obviously just trying to make ends meet, and at times my meal money came from the loose change jar. But after about a year or so of living in Giddings, I was generating enough business to hire two full-time employees. Then I added another and another. Business picked up so much and I was doing so well that I began buying more tools and equipment and moved out of the trailer and into an apartment with a couple of friends. One of the friends, Mike Morgan, was also starting a company that is still thriving today—Morgan Petroleum Testers—and we literally had two phone lines hanging on the wall next to each other of our rental property, one that was devoted to Pumpco and the other to Morgan Testers. Neither one of us could afford to hire a full-time person to answer the phone lines, so we took turns answering each other's calls. I was a morning person, so Mike would answer my calls early in the day when I was making sales calls, and I would answer his calls in the afternoon when he was pursuing business leads.

Fortunately for me, my business just kept growing in the early 1980s. It was great to see things expanding before my eyes, but it also made for some awfully long days. I typically put my accounting background to use late at night following all the sales and service calls, doing payroll, balancing the books, overlooking the bills and so forth. I never really devoted much salary to me personally; I just kept putting whatever we made back into the business by buying equipment, tools and supplies and adding new employees. Things were progressing steadily into the mid-1980s when a couple of events occurred that forever changed my life on both a professional and personal level. First, I made the decision to transform Pumpco from an oilfield service company into a pipeline construction company. As my business grew, I visualized a seemingly unlimited amount of opportunities for pipeline development and expansion across Texas, the United States and beyond. Whether most people realize it or not, pipelines play a huge role in our everyday lives, and they are essential to the nation's industries. According to various reports, the United States in 2014 featured a liquid petroleum pipeline network of 185,000 miles, while the natural gas pipeline network covered 2.4 million miles. In the late 1980s and early '90s, however, much of that pipeline network had yet to be developed, providing great opportunities for someone ready to enter the pipeline construction industry.

The second life-changing event of the mid-1980s was going on a double date to a Texas A&M-Baylor football game. On that double date, I met my ultimate partner in business and life, then-A&M freshman Robyn Meyer, who would eventually become my wife. The first time I met Robyn was before the football game at what was then considered a fairly upscale restaurant in College Station on the corner of Texas Avenue and Southwest Parkway called Pelican's Wharf. To clarify, she was not even my date; I had been set up to go out with the other woman. But Robyn definitely left the biggest impression on me at the restaurant.

She was also originally from Giddings, where I'd established my business operations, and she eventually earned an accounting degree, which was my collegiate academic background. Beyond that, at dinner she reached across the table and grabbed something off my plate to taste it…without asking. I was stunned at her audacity, but I was also intrigued by her initiative and personality. Neither one of us remembers when our second date occurred, but we kept running into each other. After all, while Giddings (population 5,665 at the 2010 census) had once been at the center of the Austin Chalk play, it was not exactly a major metropolis.

The more I talked to Robyn, the better I liked her, and she eventually began working for me (without pay) when I actually moved Pumpco out of my apartment and into a used office trailer. She was still a student at Texas A&M, but she arranged her schedule so that she didn't have classes on Fridays. She would drive home to Giddings on Thursdays, stop by the office late in the day and begin assisting Becky, who I had hired to oversee office operations. Robyn would then spend all day Friday and Saturday helping in the office, whether she was organizing bills, handling payroll or running errands. We began dating in the late-1980s, and I knew I liked her right from the start…at least after I overcame the initial shock of her grabbing something to eat off my plate. But I guess I didn't realize how much I loved her until she received two job offers following her graduation from A&M in '89: one from Houston Power and Light Company and the other from Browning-Ferris Industries.

I suggested that she go to work in Houston, which would make it much easier for us to continue dating. Instead, she told me that she had decided that it was best for her career to go to work for BFI in San Antonio. I respected her independence and business insight, and I didn't necessarily disagree that it was the better move to go to San Antonio. Shortly after she took that position and moved to the Alamo City, however, I realized she was not just another girlfriend; she was *the* one. I asked her to marry me, she said "yes," and as if I needed any further proof that she was the ideal, resourceful, thorough and thrifty mate for me, she won her wedding dress on the weekend closest to Valentine's Day. She literally filled out every raffle drawing imaginable, and she was rewarded with $1,000 toward a new wedding dress, which was a ton of money at that time. We were married in July of '89, and Robyn wore what amounted to a free wedding dress.

We could not, however, afford for Robyn to work for Pumpco. We really needed a guaranteed salary so Robyn went to work for a local insurance agency as its controller. She worked there until the birth of our second daughter. But even though she worked at the agency, her heart was always at Pumpco. We poured everything we had—time, money, resources, effort, etc.—into building and growing Pumpco. We made mistakes along the way; we made errors in judgment; and we made some decisions that were ill-advised. We really complemented each other, though, and when we made the decision for Robyn to stop working at the agency and to start working at Pumpco, she understood the support role she had to fulfill. I had an innate, big-picture understanding of business, and I possessed an ability to pinpoint existing problems and to foresee future issues that might negatively affect business operations. Meanwhile, Robyn was far more detail-oriented and meticulous in terms of the day-to-day office routines and operations. Together, we have made a great team, and I have always appreciated her frugal nature and willingness to continually invest in the company.

People have asked us many times if there was a specific moment early on when we knew that the business had turned the corner and that we were destined to succeed. Honestly, we never looked at it in that fashion. We viewed each day like participants in a baseball game of sorts. We tried not to focus on the scoreboard, but instead placed all of our attention on executing and winning the next inning. We both have a great appreciation for sports, and I believe our competitive, team-oriented approach has been critical to our successes. Robyn was a basketball player at Giddings High, who had no ties to Texas A&M other than the fact that she wore No. 12 in high school basketball. Obviously, the No. 12 is revered in Aggieland, which is part of the reason she chose to be an Aggie…and eventually met me.

We certainly treated the business like a team from the start, especially in terms of how we treated our employees. No matter the role he/she played, we viewed every employee not just as a hired hand, but rather, as a valuable part of our team. And we didn't just preach that; we proved it with our actions, and we still do today.

I knew from a fairly early age that I was not often going to be the smartest guy in the room, so I wasn't going to necessarily inspire others with my ingenuity or strategic brilliance. But I felt like God had blessed me as a leader with the ability to communicate, motivate and rally everyone in the boardroom or the locker room—even the guys much smarter or more talented than me—in order to work together. I'm a really big believer in allowing everyone to provide input/ideas and then making sure everyone is on the same page and moving forward together. I tell my daughters and the young people who work for me all the time that working together is the key to success with any team or practically any business endeavor. As the great entrepreneur Henry Ford once said, "Coming together is a beginning. Keeping together is progress. Working together is success." And as Ken Blanchard, author of *The One Minute Manager*, stated even more succinctly, "None of us is as smart as all of us."

An Aggie family: From left, Allyson, Alan, Jennifer and Robyn

It's been my experience that one of the best ways to inspire others to share their constructive ideas and thoughts is to make sure they all really feel like part of the team. Many years ago, I'd cook for all of my employees who would work on Saturdays. I can remember many times in the early 1990s when I would fire up the barbecue pit in cosmopolitan locations like Snook, Texas (population approximately 500) and grill a seemingly endless array of hamburger patties and pork chops for lunch or dinner at a job site. Also, for many years, I'd drive down to the Gulf Coast to buy hundreds of pounds of fresh shrimp and oysters to cook the week before Christmas on a Saturday night. I encouraged all the employees to bring their spouses and kids, and I rented the Fireman's Hall just outside of Giddings for a truly festive holiday feast.

For me, it was always very important to cook, as opposed to merely having lunch or dinner catered, because I wanted to be a servant, as well as a leader. I have always wanted my staff members to know that I view them as part of my business family, and if they are family, they are entitled to a home-cooked meal by Robyn and me. It's all about creating a team atmosphere, and you cannot do that without investing time in the team.

Likewise, you can't transform a small start-up business into a multidimensional and thriving organization without investing money back into the company. To do that, Robyn and I were committed to live within our means. As the business grew, we didn't reward ourselves with expensive luxuries, sports cars or even a dream home. We stayed in our modest, three-bedroom, 1,200-square foot home through the birth of our first daughter, Jennifer, and just continued to invest back into the business by adding staff, upgrading the benefits we provided for the employees and purchasing the heavy-duty equipment that is essential for the growth of a pipeline construction company. To build a pipeline across the county or the country, it's imperative to own fast and effective trenching machines. A hydraulic trackhoe excavator can range in price from $125,000 to $300,000 or more, so each one is obviously a major investment. Today, Pumpco owns a fleet of dirt-moving heavy equipment (roughly 180 backhoes and trackhoes), but in the early days of the company, each new purchase was a major financial stretch that was essentially the equivalent of buying a new home.

Disposable income was non-existent, and our entertainment options were sometimes limited to riding together on site survey expeditions. I remember one time, in particular, when Robyn and I were riding with an operator and another gentleman surveying the landscape of a job that Pumpco had just been awarded. Without being too technical, there are two general types of energy pipelines: liquid petroleum pipelines and natural gas pipelines. Within the liquid petroleum pipeline network there are crude oil lines, refined product lines, highly volatile liquids (HVL) lines and carbon dioxide lines (CO_2). The entire oil and gas industry, which includes pipeline construction, features its own vocabulary of terminology. For example, a "Christmas tree" refers to an assembly of valves, pipes and fittings used to control the flow of oil and gas from the casing head. And the term "it is a little coyote" is utilized in describing the conditions and terrain of a project that is very tough. As we were riding along a dirt road in a pickup truck, we were surveying the creeks and conditions of the property and I mentioned that "it was a little coyote." Robyn nearly broke her neck looking for a literal baby coyote. My fellow co-worker and I shared a good laugh when we noticed how hard she was looking for the coyote.

But she eventually picked up the lingo, as well as practically everything else regarding the business. She handled a variety of roles, from managing the office to delivering parts to me when I was on a construction site. Robyn has always been extremely attentive, quick to adapt and highly proficient in keeping me up to date on everything I've needed to know. Unfortunately, I haven't always been quite as reliable in keeping her completely in the loop.

Shortly before the birth of our second daughter, Allyson, in 1993 a worker from one of the oil and gas companies asked me if I would be interested in selling the 1,200-square-foot home we had in Giddings since we were adding a second child. I told him that if the money was right, I would certainly be interested in selling the home to him and upgrading. He asked if he could take a look at the house later that evening, and I told him to stop by at 8. In hindsight, it probably would have been a good idea if I had mentioned that fact to Robyn, who was eight months pregnant and cooking dinner when the doorbell rang. Much to the surprise of my wife, it was the gentleman I had been talking to earlier, and he ended up buying the house a week later. My wife was not exactly delighted with my lack of communication or moving when she was eight months pregnant.

Nevertheless, she once again managed to multi-task, juggling everything without missing a beat. And in addition to moving homes and adding another child, we also grew the business significantly during that timeframe. In fact, on the day Allyson was born—October 25, 1993—I was in an important meeting that would take the company from roughly 100 employees to 350. My mind was racing and my stomach was churning with excitement as I prepared for an 11 a.m. meeting that would lead to the biggest job in our organization's history. Unbeknownst to me, Robyn was back at the insurance agency in Giddings when she began enduring labor contractions that were two hours apart. The business manager side of her was tempted not to call me until after the meeting. Finally, one of the women in the office practically insisted that she call me. I picked up the phone right before the meeting and she said, "I wish I could wait, but I think it's the day." It was, indeed. As it turned out, we managed to expand the family and our business on the same day. It was one of the most memorable days in our lives for numerous reasons.

ROBERTS' MOST DIFFICULT CHALLENGE

In all sincerity, it's rather difficult for me to single out one or two specific challenges that have really defined or stretched us as entrepreneurs. In reality, there have been hundreds upon hundreds of challenges—some major, some fairly minor—that have tested, molded and strengthened me as a business owner ever since I left my first job in an accounting firm and told my parents I was going to start something on my own. In fact, breaking that news to my father may have been one of the toughest challenges of all. I was genuinely nervous about telling him I was not going to pursue a career in my accounting degree field.

In many ways, the challenges we have encountered have continued to grow as our business has expanded. But for the most part, they are so much easier to tackle now than they were 20 to 25 years ago because Robyn and I have evolved as business owners, and we have constantly been motivated to surround ourselves with the most talented people we can find. Our business would not have prospered like it has if we had not remained adamant about investing in high-quality people.

There were many times in the past when I absolutely felt like I had to be in the middle of every negotiation and present at every construction site in order to ensure that a contract or a job was done correctly. That's certainly not the case any longer because I am so confident in the people we have hired and placed in positions of responsibility. My role now is to be less of a hands-on, Jack of all trades and to be more of a visionary and tone-setter. After so many years of being intimately involved in practically every moving part and transaction, adopting a new leadership style and looking at the overall business from a big-picture perspective were initially quite challenging. But I firmly believe one of the signs of maturation as an entrepreneur is the ability to delegate as you come to the realization that no individual—not even the most talented and astute businessman on the planet—can do it all or manage it all as a business grows.

That sounds like a pretty easy concept to grasp, right? In theory, it's a no-brainer, but the reality is that most entrepreneurs go into business for themselves because they are independent, self-reliant, autonomous and confident that they can tackle any obstacle. Those qualities and beliefs are tremendously valuable during the start-up phase of a business, but they can also hinder long-term growth if you are reluctant to hand over some of the roles and responsibilities you once handled yourself. Again, that sounds simple, but some of the mistakes I made as a business owner, especially in my early years, were the result of trying to do too much and juggle too many responsibilities.

No matter where they travel, the Roberts always enjoy an adventure

Fortunately, Robyn was often able to remind me that it was time to pass the torch to someone else or to add a new position to our payroll. Case in point: My decision to buy a helicopter to make the best use of my time. Beginning in 2012, my "Bell 429" helicopter began receiving quite a bit of media attention when I offered the Texas A&M football coaching staff the opportunity to use it in recruiting. I first mentioned the availability of the helicopter to A&M assistant coach Clarence McKinney, and head coach Kevin Sumlin took me up on the offer prior to the first game of the 2012 season against Florida.

Houston St. Pius X was playing Sealy on a Thursday night, nationally televised game on ESPN, and Sumlin was particularly interested in making a strong, positive impression on Sealy wide receiver Ricky Seals-Jones and St. Pius quarterback Kohl Stewart. There was no way, however, for Sumlin to attend Texas A&M's practice in the late afternoon and still make it to Houston in time for the game. At least there was no way to do it by driving. Instead, the head coach hopped in the chopper after A&M's afternoon practice, and the pilot flew past the rush-hour traffic on Highway 290, circled the crowded football stadium and landed the helicopter at the nearby high school baseball field. Sumlin later appeared on the sideline of the football game, where he was videoed by the TV crew. The entire flyover created quite a stir inside the stadium and an even bigger commotion on the Internet. I knew the prospective recruits would be impressed by the helicopter, which retails for about $6 million. After all, practically everyone who has seen it up close—from the CEOs of oil and gas companies to our new entry-level staffers—has raved about it. I was not at all surprised to learn that both Jones and Stewart eventually signed with the Aggies, although Stewart later chose to play professional baseball. Nor was I surprised when Sumlin used the helicopter in ensuing years to land other top prospects.

What did catch me somewhat off guard, though, was the fact that the helicopter took on a life of its own on social media and Internet websites. Shortly after Sumlin first used it to scout Jones and Stewart, I was told that the unofficial new name for the Bell 429 had become the "#SwagCopter." That name stuck in A&M circles and took off even more on National Signing Day in February 2014. When asked about Sumlin and the A&M recruiting presence that has included the head-turning helicopter, former Texas coach Charlie Strong dismissed the idea of an aerial arms race. "The University (of Texas) speaks for itself," Strong said. "We don't need gadgets. We're not going to be a gadget program." Quite frankly, I was amused that anyone would refer to a $6 million helicopter as a "gadget." But I am delighted that Texas A&M's coaches have utilized an extremely valuable tool to make the best use of their time and effort.

That's certainly why I first invested in a helicopter many years ago (the original was much less attention-grabbing than the Bell 429). As Pumpco began to expand rapidly in the mid-1990s, I would often leave the house at 4 in the morning to drive to remote locations across the state. With two young daughters, I wanted to make sure I was home at night as often as possible. But I was also committed to doing whatever it took to build the business. Robyn would be so nervous about me driving across the state in a sleep-deprived condition that she would wake up with me and stay on the phone with me as I drove from our home to a construction site. Not only was this extremely expensive—this was back in the days when all cell phone usage was billed by the minute—but it also left Robyn, who was typically awakened at all hours of the night by our infant daughter, doubly exhausted. My solution to this ongoing situation was to explore the use of a helicopter, which turned out to be a great benefit.

Thanks to my do-it-all mentality at that time, I initially began taking helicopter pilot lessons in 1994. Robyn immediately grounded those flight plans, making the case that if we could afford a helicopter for the company, we also needed to be able to afford a full-time pilot. As she pointed out—rather sternly—her primary incentive in supporting the addition of a helicopter to the business was to give her greater peace of mind while I traveled, not to increase her worries. I realized once again that she was making a great point, and the lesson I learned from that experience has become a metaphor of sorts for me through the years as I attempt to delegate more and micromanage less: *You don't have to pilot the helicopter—or anything else—to steer the business.*

The Roberts family at Miramont Country Club

In other words, you don't need to be in control of all things to lead. That may not have been a huge challenge to overcome, but it was a necessary hurdle for me to cross. Perhaps the biggest challenge for Robyn and I personally, however, was building a business while also raising a family. It can be so difficult to grow a business while also finding enough quality time to devote to your kids, especially since Robyn and I were often building Pumpco together. I'm not sure if the parenting experts or child development psychologists would agree with our solution to finding quality time together, but it definitely worked for us. Instead of separating business time from family time, we actually brought our daughters into the business as early as possible. We viewed it as part of their overall education, supplementing the theoretical and abstract lessons they were learning in school with real-life business applications. Both Jennifer and Allyson are now grateful for the practical experiences we provided them, which gave them a head start on their own business endeavors.

Some of our customers would often joke that we were breaking the child labor laws when the girls were answering office phone lines when they were as young as 13 or 14, but we always pointed out that we weren't actually paying them; they were merely earning their keep. That's a joke, but we really did gradually involve the girls in our business at a very early age. Because of the time demands on us as parents, we taught them to be independent at early ages. They were probably the first kids in their schools to have cell phones because we absolutely needed to know when and where to pick them up on a daily basis. We couldn't afford to waste precious minutes in the day guessing when a coach might decide to end a practice.

Their basketball coach from the time they were in fifth grade through eighth grade was none other than Robyn, who was quite the technician, strategist and disciplinarian. Robyn and I always encouraged our daughters to play team sports not because we believed they would become Division I college athletes, but because of the life lessons that could be learned and applied. There are so many things you can learn as part of a team, particularly gaining an understanding that you can accomplish so much more as a group than you can as an individual. The girls both attended private schools until they reached Giddings High, and the fans who watched the Immanuel Lutheran Knights girls' basketball team quickly learned that I was not the only family member with a tremendously strong competitive drive.

Robyn became known as "the stomper" as she coached the girls. In one game, she stomped so hard that the heel on her shoe fell off. It was practically impossible not to laugh at the sight of her hobbling/balancing on one shoe, but just to make sure the girls knew she was dead serious, she dropped her clipboard on the floor. She was the definition of intensity.

Because we were a private school without an abundance of players, the dads would participate in practices as the scout team, and even the fathers learned quickly about Robyn's relentless will to win. Those were fun times, and in juggling work/school, coaching, homework, practice, etc., we often ate dinner at 9:30 or later. Our hectic schedules and time demands also made it necessary for our daughters to handle many things on their own. From a relatively early age—and especially once they reached an age where they could drive—we taught them that if they needed a haircut to make an appointment. If they weren't feeling well, we encouraged them to make their own doctor's appointment. If we needed groceries, it was up to them to go shopping. Most teens are not placed in that position of responsibility. But it was a necessity for our lifestyle, and it certainly made Robyn and I feel more confident about sending them both to Texas A&M. We had absolutely no worries about them being able to take care of themselves once they arrived in Aggieland.

They also knew their way around the campus long before they were ever students. Since we didn't have much time to spare on a day-to-day basis, we didn't have much vacation time, either. Robyn made the decision early on that we could also make our shared passion for Texas A&M and Aggie athletics a family affair. Our early vacations as a couple and as a young family often revolved around Aggie football. And I did finally convince Robyn that it would be the wisest use of time and money to purchase a nice recreational vehicle. We'd drive from Giddings to College Station—or some road destination where the Aggies were playing—on a Friday, pick up a babysitter on the way, park the RV near the stadium, and Robyn and I would go to the game while the girls would stay with a babysitter when they were young. As they grew older, we didn't need the babysitter, and we would explore the surroundings in new destinations. Like the helicopter, the RV purchase was not necessarily a luxury item. To me, it was a tool to follow the Aggies, expose the girls to Texas A&M, make the best use of our family time together and create a lifetime of memories. We have upgraded the RV over the years, but we still drive it to most Texas A&M games in College Station.

We rarely ever went on what might be described as "dream vacations" and we didn't indulge in some of life's more extravagant pleasures until a Coral Gables, Florida-based telecommunications contractor

reached out to me about buying Pumpco. For years and years and years, we had invested practi
thing we made back into the company. We were growing, and we were doing well, but I didn't
have a line of credit large enough to take the business to another level and have complete peace of
some ways, I had stepped onto the treadmill, running fast but going nowhere. But in 2007, MasTe
Jose Mas contacted me about his desire to diversify his company. We began talking rather seriously
once I learned that MasTec did not own another pipeline construction business, I was quite interested, e
cially when I learned that they wanted me to continue overseeing the operations of Pumpco. Basically, Mas-
Tec offered us enough to give us the flexibility and financial stability to take things to an entirely new level.
MasTec is now a $3 billion company, and its financial support allowed Pumpco to go from a successful, family-owned business to a thriving, financially secure major pipeline construction company.

Since the buyout became official in 2008, we have expanded our horizons in numerous ways. We have started other companies; we've delegated more; we've stressed less; and our family vacations have evolved from road trips to Austin and Waco to fishing trips in Alaska and vacations in world-renowned destinations. Pumpco now has more than 1,500 employees, and in 2012, our payroll exceeded $80 million. After more than 30 years in business, it is no longer necessary to invest every bit of profit back into the business. We now have complete financial security and freedom, which has allowed us to invest back into the things that mean the most to us: our church, our charities, our family passions, Texas A&M, Aggie athletics, dream vacations, fishing boats and so much more. But please allow me to reiterate a point: We didn't travel to Italy, France or Australia when we first made a profit; we didn't buy dream homes when we were investing in backhoes; and we didn't overextend our finances when we were extending the hours we worked and the demands we accepted.

ROBERTS' ADVICE TO YOUNG ENTREPRENEURS

In all sincerity, I am somewhat uncomfortable in giving advice. But I am more at ease highlighting a couple of the key points that have been essential to my success as an entrepreneur. First and foremost, I believe it's critical to follow your heart. It's probably not impossible to be successful in an industry that you don't enjoy, but life is too short to be miserable in your profession. Besides, if you enjoy what you do, you are at least twice as likely to be successful at it financially and to be satisfied and/or fulfilled. As the Chinese philosopher Confucius once said, "Choose a job you love, and you will never have to work a day in your life."

I'm thoroughly convinced that I did the right thing by leaving the accounting field less than two years after I started in it. It didn't fit me, even though I tried desperately to convince myself that it was a good career and that I could be happy as a CPA. But I finally realized I could not be happy by living out my father's dreams. Even though I knew he would not be pleased with my decision to initially leave my white-collar career to start my own oilfield repair service—to use my hands to make a living—it was something I felt like I had to do. Telling him was tough, but it was easier than staying in a career field that bored me. Eventually, even my father realized that I had done the right thing. I've always believed that if you follow your dreams and work hard, success will eventually follow you. That has certainly been applicable in my life and my career.

Another critical component to what has made me successful is my commitment to treat people the right way. Not just my friends. Not just my customers or prospective customers. I have always strived to treat everyone around me the way I would like to be treated. That's the biblical "Golden Rule," and it should also be a top priority for any entrepreneur or business owner. Quite frankly, I believe treating people with respect, dignity, kindness and compassion should be a top priority for every person on the planet, regardless of whether you are building a business or not. But it is especially important to treat every employee as a key employee, which will create loyalty, unity and solidarity.

Today, we do so much to reward and encourage our employees. We host tailgates at sporting events—particularly Texas A&M football games—where we have numerous televisions set up around our RV, and have hosted as many as 175 people, who were all employees, family and friends. At the 2013 Texas A&M-Alabama game in College Station, we literally had so many people at our tailgate that we passed out wristbands to make sure we could manage the crowd. Throughout the years, I cooked and prepared food for everyone before and after games. I could have had it catered, and I certainly could have hired people to serve everyone. But that would have defeated the purpose of hosting the tailgate. I wanted to show my appreciation toward my employees, customers, colleagues and friends by serving them.

We have created a tremendous team-oriented atmosphere, and I truly believe most of our employees are quite pleased to be working for an organization that values them and their efforts. We work hard, and I expect great things from our employees, but I try to be a leader who coaches, inspires and motivates instead of merely acting as a dictator. When you encourage someone to perform at a peak level it is far more effective than demanding someone to do more. It's a subtle distinction that makes a world of difference. And through the years I've been able to retain great people because they enjoy working for us. I've even been able to hire longtime friends and some family members, making our atmosphere even more enjoyable. My brother Jimmy, for example, came to work for me after a career in teaching and banking, and he now oversees all of our safety policies and procedures, and I am proud of our safety record.

In addition to investing in people, Robyn and I have always invested back into the company by purchasing equipment, upgrading technology and providing our staff with all the resources to be successful. For roughly three decades, I didn't really take a salary. We paid our people, paid the bills and paid for more "yellow iron" before we took any income for ourselves. Even the most expensive purchases—like an airplane and helicopters—have been made to propel our business ventures. We're doing work in Wyoming, North Dakota, New Mexico and various other locations across the country, which makes a private plane far more of a necessity than a luxury. But as an added benefit, we have been able to use the plane and the helicopters to help people in a variety of other ways.

Our plane contributed indirectly to one of Texas A&M's national championships, as I occasionally accompanied former A&M women's basketball assistant coach Vic Schaefer to Kansas City to recruit Danielle Adams, the star of the Aggies' run to the 2011 women's basketball national championship. Vic really didn't like to fly. So, we would go together, and he would talk to the player and the family, while my pilot and I would hang out at the airport. We would then fly back, stopping in Dallas for dinner at a place like Pappas Bros. Steakhouse and then we'd drop him off back in College Station.

Of greater importance, we've also been able to use the plane and helicopters to help friends and family in times of need. In the summer of 2010, Vic Schaefer's son, Logan, had a severe wakeboarding accident at a camp that required emergency surgery in Tyler. At the time of the accident, Vic was with his daughter, Blair, at a basketball tournament in Cincinnati, while his wife, Holly, was at home in College Station. We were able to immediately fly Holly from College Station to Tyler, and after Vic caught a commercial flight from Cincinnati to Dallas, we had the helicopter waiting for him at the airport to fly him to Tyler. Fortunately, everything worked out for the best. Logan recovered from the subdural hematoma he had suffered, and we felt blessed to make sure that his family was together as quickly as possible. We couldn't have done that without our longtime commitment to investing in tools for the company. It would be my strong recommendation to any prospective entrepreneur to do the same thing, practicing delayed gratification for any personal luxuries and unnecessary expenses, while investing everything you can back into your business.

Finally, I believe it is imperative to establish yourself within any industry as a businessperson of integrity, honesty and morality. I see businessmen and women who cut corners and fail to deliver on their promises all the time. Some people really believe that the key to making a profit is to over-charge and under-deliver. But if you focus on doing things the right way, treating people the way you would want to be treated and exceeding expectations, you will eventually distinguish yourself and your business within any industry. Focus on building a strong reputation and everything else will take care of itself. As Albert Einstein once said, "Try not to become a man of success, but rather, try to become a man of value." Success will follow men and women of integrity, honesty and value.

3.

Lou Paletta
Partner and Chief Operating Officer of Kildare Partners
Texas A&M Class of 1978

PALETTA'S PATH TO TEXAS A&M

Lou and Wanda Paletta

Throughout much of my life, I have often been intrigued by the various factors that motivate and propel entrepreneurs or businesspeople to achieve high levels of success. Obviously, no two people are exactly the same, so it stands to reason that no two people are inspired by identical circumstances or backgrounds to pursue excellence in their field. On the other hand, it's been my observation through the years that money—whether someone grows up with it or without much of it—usually plays a significant role in someone's internal drive to succeed. I have read numerous stories—including several in this book—and heard about plenty of people who have come from difficult financial childhood situations and have been inspired by the lack of money to build a much different lifestyle as adults. I have also read and heard about plenty of people who grew up around money and learned valuable lessons from their parents about building businesses, turning profits and acquiring wealth.

I suppose I am a bit of an oddball—or perhaps just an extremely fortunate soul—in that I actually experienced both economic extremes in my childhood. We never did without any necessities, but some of my earliest memories are of living in a loft that was above the family-owned grocery store that my parents operated. My maternal grandparents eventually came to live with us, meaning that at one point, there were six of us—my grandparents, parents, sister and me—living in a loft in downtown San Antonio that had no more than about 1,100 square feet to it. The loft had three small bedrooms, one bathroom and virtually no privacy whatsoever. But that's what families, especially Italian families, did back then. Besides, we didn't have much of a choice at that time.

My maternal grandparents both arrived in America from Southern Italy, where their families had been involved in farming and agriculture (food is a family theme). My mom's dad came to the United States on a boat when he was just 13, serving as an apprentice barber. He didn't initially have a trade, but his parents believed he could build a better life for himself in the United States, so they found a barber who was also moving to the U.S. and sent their son along with him. I can't imagine essentially being on my own in a foreign country when I was just 13, but times were different back then and my grandfather did fine.

Meanwhile, my paternal grandparents also can trace their roots to Italy. My dad's father started a business in San Antonio back in 1915 that eventually became known—and known quite favorably in the local marketplace—as Paletta's Imported Foods. He first started the business by selling produce off a horse-drawn wagon before upgrading to a truck. There was a significant Italian presence in San Antonio, so he would drive around the streets and downtown neighborhoods to sell produce. Eventually, he grew the business into more of a grocery store and began importing specialty goods—foods, wines and non-consumables—from Italy. My grandfather did well and built a strong reputation in San Antonio. There's no telling how well he could have done or how big he might have grown the business if his health had permitted it. But unfortunately, he died from an aneurism in his 50s, and my parents eventually took over the business.

Obviously, my father had grown up around the grocery/food business. But he had visions of doing something else. My father—like many of my great uncles and other relatives who also settled in San Antonio (my paternal grandmother had eight brothers and sisters)—attended Texas A&M, although he never graduated. My dad would have been in the Class of 1948 at A&M if he had actually stayed in school. But after enrolling at Texas A&M and becoming part of the famous Texas Aggie Band as a freshman (even though he couldn't technically read music), he left College Station early to enlist in the Armed Forces. Dad joined the Navy and ended up becoming a part of the Construction Battalion (CB), which became known as the "Seabees." The earliest Seabees were recruited from the civilian construction trades and were placed under the leadership of the Navy's Civil Engineer Corps during World War II. As the name suggests, the Seabees were "busy bees" in the area of construction support for the war effort. More than 325,000 men served with the Seabees in World War II, building major airstrips, bridges, roads, gasoline storage tanks and Quonset huts for warehouses, hospitals and housing. The Seabees were officially organized in the Naval Reserve on December 31, 1947, and my father enjoyed his experiences in the Seabees—at least for the most part—because he had been studying engineering at Texas A&M. The Seabees allowed him to put some of his engineering/construction "know-how" into practice.

When my father left the Navy, he returned to San Antonio, and who knows where his career might have taken him if my grandfather had not had health issues. My father and mother met in their early teens when my mom would visit Texas with family relatives. My mom, who was a professional musician at age 16 playing the accordion and piano among other instruments, moved to San Antonio from Albany, New York to marry my dad. My mother was an ambitious woman, and my father was a hard-working young man with natural people skills. Together, they made a great team, especially in terms of running a business together. When my grandfather died, my parents took over the grocery store. My mom was a visionary/strategist with a great mind for business, while my dad was more of a marketing-oriented people person. They worked hard right from the start and built a growing business. My mother's vision was to keep on growing and expanding, building a deli sandwich operation that could become some sort of franchise. Keep in mind that this was in the 1960s, and my mother's vision in the South was similar to Fred DeLuca's in Bridgeport, Connecticut. With a $1,000 loan from a friend, DeLuca opened his first submarine sandwich store, Pete's Subway, in August 1965. According to the website, SUBWAY® now has more than 42,000 stores in 107 countries.

Perhaps my parents could have done the same, except that my dad was comfortable keeping the grocery business as it was originally. I remember talking to my father at one point about growing the business significantly, and he said he didn't want the headaches associated with starting a franchise. He worked hard, and he was comfortable in his element, but he was just not as ambitious as my mother…or her side of the family. My maternal grandmother was also a hard-working woman who, beyond just being willing to work, was also wise with her money. She made plenty of shrewd investments and did extremely well in the stock market. She lived well below her means, didn't feel the need to flaunt her income or spend money frivolously on herself and instead invested a major portion of her wealth in her children, which was not uncommon in those days. My maternal grandmother helped my mom and dad build a luxurious residence in one of the nicest areas in San Antonio that was my mother's dream home. Thanks to her help, we went from what was becoming an increasingly questionable downtown neighborhood to living a completely different lifestyle.

In fact, I could have been considered the Italian "Fresh Prince of Bellaire," and our family could have been the 1960s, San Antonio version of "The Jeffersons," a popular sitcom in the mid-1970s and early '80s. We weren't living in a high-rise luxury apartment complex, but like the theme song from The Jeffersons we were most certainly "moving on up." I was probably in the fifth grade—about 10 years old—when we moved from the tiny loft above the grocery store to our luxurious, six-bedroom home that had about 5,000 square feet and a swimming pool in the backyard. I definitely thought we had made the big-time when we made the move, and things did seem to be going well as we left our humble roots behind. But in what amounted to one of my first real-life lessons in going from one socioeconomic extreme to another, I soon discovered that money cannot buy happiness—certainly not marital bliss.

For the most part, my mom and dad had seemed to have many things in common as they were growing the business and living paycheck to paycheck. They both loved to be the life of the party and they certainly loved to entertain. That was a good thing for a while, but over time, I think my father became envious of my mother's ability to play practically any instrument—piano, violin, accordion, etc.—and to immediately become the center of attention in social settings. My mom, on the other hand, wasn't the jealous type, but she probably had some pent-up frustration toward my father that dated back to their earliest days of marriage. When they first were married, they lived next door to my grandmother (my dad's mother), which is not an ideal way to start a marriage. Living next door to her mother-in-law created some stressful situations for my mother and probably prevented my parents from really bonding with each other and relying on one another early in their married days. They had business-related stresses, and then along came my sister and me.

From my viewpoint as a kid in a crowded loft, my parents seemed to get along most of the time. Mom was always thinking of new strategies for the business and new ways to make money, while my father was a workhorse putting in the hours to provide for his family. He worked six days a week, every week of the year, except for one long weekend he would annually take off for the family vacation that was always in Corpus Christi. My parents were working class, but they were making ends meet and making things work. When we moved into the big house, however, there no longer seemed to be a question of whether we'd make it or not. The financial struggles, long work hours and meager living conditions may have masked some of their bigger marital issues. They were so busy making a buck and making the most of their opportunities that they often didn't notice—or at least didn't point out—the things each one did that drove the other person crazy.

That changed when we moved out of the loft. To quote the Righteous Brothers—a popular band in my childhood—my parents seemed to "lose that loving feeling" after the move. In the tiny loft, they pulled together. But in the expansive house it was never quite the same. Ultimately, it ended in an ugly, bitter divorce, which really started about the same time my sister went to Texas A&M for her freshman year and I was going into my freshman year in high school. When things finally went completely wrong, my mother locked my father out of the house. And just to make sure he didn't enter the house, she also taped up the doors and roped it off. My sis and I ended up having to testify at the messy divorce hearings, and I didn't spend nearly as much time with my father after the divorce.

My father remarried, my mother did not. But she was bound and determined to do everything she could to keep me, my sis and grandfather (my grandmother had died by then) in the dream house. She was only 20 when she married my dad and started running the grocery business, and she no longer believed she could return to being a professional musician. So, after the divorce, she took a job as a hostess at a restaurant along the River Walk. She typically wouldn't make it home until 1 a.m., which required me to grow up in a hurry. Not only did I need to fend for myself each night, I also had to make sure that my grandfather had something to eat every evening. My mom was working hard to keep us in the dream house and keep the bills paid, and she met a man at the restaurant—a purely platonic relationship—who had a vision to open his own business.

I suppose my entrepreneurial/ambitious genes come mostly from my mom, because she always had some sort of plan in the works and some kind of business vision in mind. While working on the River Walk, she and a visionary man from India decided to join forces and put together an extremely unique business

"Sweet Lou" speaking at the Texas A&M campus

model for a restaurant that would be an Italian deli during the day and an upscale Indian restaurant at night. It was just bizarre enough to be a big hit. My mom poured her heart into the restaurant and it attracted the Who's Who among San Antonio's most well-known personalities, including many of the Spurs players from that era. I met some of the great San Antonio players in the late 1970s and early '80s—guys like George "The Iceman" Gervin, Mark Olberding, Billy Paultz and James Silas—because they frequented my mother's restaurant. She and her partner ran that restaurant for years before it took a turn for the worse and she eventually shut it down. Afterward, she also sold the big, six-bedroom house. Even after her father died and I moved out of the house to go to Texas A&M, she was still reluctant to let go of that house. It was her pride and joy. Nevertheless, she finally parted with it and lived the next 30 years on her own in a small apartment. Even though she remained single until her death and battled a severe case of macular degeneration that took her eyesight in her late 60s, she was happy and always there to provide spiritual guidance to my sis and me.

My father, on the other hand, struggled financially for many years after the divorce but always found a way to stay content and happy. He initially moved into a one-bedroom apartment and barely had any furniture except for the coffee and end tables I hand-crafted for him to replace the cardboard boxes he was using at the time. He continued to run the imported foods business after the divorce, eventually remarried and supported his second wife in starting a business of her own, as she opened a lingerie shop in San Antonio. But the lingerie business didn't last long, and his wife then joined him and my sis working in the deli. My dad spent years recovering from the financial impact of his divorce from my mom but finally began to enjoy life in his 60s before he was stricken with a severe stroke. Both my parents are gone now, and I wish things could have turned out differently for them, especially in their lives together. To this day, I regret I wasn't in a position to do more for them in their golden years but I made it a point to talk to both of them every day until they passed. I tell that story because their breakup played an important part of my early development. It caused me to grow up at a young age and realize that life isn't perfect. It also taught me plenty of things that I wanted to do differently in my own marriage.

As I mentioned, my sister, Jeannine, followed the family footsteps to A&M and graduated in 1975. She was part of the first class of women to live on campus at A&M in Krueger Hall. When she went for orientation her freshman year, I went with her, and I knew deep-down that I wanted to be an Aggie, too. Unlike a lot of people who grow up with maroon bloodlines, I had not spent much time on campus or attending A&M sporting events as a kid. My father took off one day a week—Sundays—so I had not grown up going to Kyle Field on Saturdays in the fall. Nevertheless, there was something about A&M that I really liked, and after Jeannine was well on her way toward achieving her management degree, I arrived in College Station in the fall of 1975—just in time to watch the Aggie football team roll to a 10-0 record and a No. 2 national ranking following the Thanksgiving Day win over the Longhorns. I attended that game—a 20-10 victory for the Aggies—with my sister, which was a treat. Unfortunately, the Aggies lost their last regular-season game of the year at Arkansas and missed an opportunity to play for a national championship in the Cotton Bowl. But the '75 season was magical enough for me to catch a severe and incurable case of maroon fever.

32 | THE ENTREPRENEURIUAL SPIRIT OF AGGIELAND

I was also serious about my academic pursuits. I didn't have any firm plans about my career when I first arrived at A&M, so I initially decided to major in management simply because that's what my sister had done. But after that first semester, I visited the career placement center and began closely examining the job postings and the salaries. As I flipped through the boards, I noticed that accounting and engineering fields offered the most jobs and the most attractive incomes. I thought momentarily about engineering, but I hated science and figured I better stick to business. I changed my major to accounting after my first semester and became extremely focused on finishing my coursework. I probably inherited my father's work ethic, and I poured every ounce of my energy into earning my degree quickly. I took as many summer classes as possible, remained focused on getting a job as quickly as possible and graduated in three and a half years. I loved college life and had some fun along the way, but I was there for a purpose. With that said, I must admit that one of the reasons I was so anxious to earn enough credits to receive my Aggie ring by the first semester of my junior year was so that I could sit on the floor at basketball games at the old G. Rollie White Coliseum. You had to flash your ring to sit courtside, and the Aggies had some outstanding basketball teams while I was in school.

I loved Aggie athletics, and going to games often served as my only care-free moments. Because of my parents' separation, money was tight. My father paid for my school, but I had to work for my own spending money. During my first semester, I worked at the Commons Halls Cafeteria, and it was some of the most difficult work I had ever done. Making mashed potatoes by the gallon in huge drums was no easy task; nor was scrubbing pots and pans. To keep ourselves entertained, many of my fellow cafeteria co-workers sported huge Afro hair styles. I had quite the massive 'fro and had to wear a hair net while working in the cafeteria. From there, I went to a much easier job as an official for the intramural programs and also served as a resident assistant during my college days. I graduated early in December 1978, although I have always thought of myself as a "Class of '79" graduate. I loved my experiences at Texas A&M, and I sometimes wish now that I had more time to enjoy all the college life. But money was tight, and my reality was that I needed to graduate as quickly as possible and earn a living without any financial dependence on my parents.

PALETTA'S PATH TO ENTREPRENEURIAL SUCCESS

I always had decent grades at Texas A&M, but never great ones. That worried me as I graduated because I knew there were plenty of accounting majors coming out of Texas A&M—not to mention every other university in the country—who could produce more impressive collegiate résumés than me. I knew I wasn't going to merely overwhelm potential employers with my GPA numbers, so I took an extremely proactive approach and targeted two accounting firms: the well-established Arthur Andersen and the more progressive Touche Ross. Even though Touche Ross, which in 1989 became Deloitte & Touche after a major merger, traced its roots to George Touche opening an office in 1898 in London, the firm had a much younger and innovative atmosphere than Arthur Anderson. I was particularly intrigued by Touche Ross because of the many friendly personalities I came across, as well as the firm's focus on significantly expanding its San Antonio office. Ultimately, I believe my connections in San Antonio earned me the job with Touche Ross, and I spent the next eight years in my hometown while performing a variety of roles with the firm.

I was never the typical bean counter, even though I was working for one of the big accounting firms. Virtually any business needs people who can generate new leads and develop marketing opportunities while still possessing some technical abilities. Public accounting fit my people-oriented personality perfectly. I have always loved working and interacting with people, and I have always felt comfortable relating to people of all ethnic, economic and business backgrounds. I also consider myself a Jack of all trades and master of none. I am not an expert in any particular discipline, but I have always been able to adapt and learn on the go, regardless of whether that involves business practices, technology, handyman projects, sports or practically anything else. I grew quite a bit in my business acumen, earned my CPA license, advanced to senior manager and learned from everyone around me during those eight years in San Antonio. I also grew and evolved in my personal life.

After graduating from A&M and going to work with Touche Ross, I married a woman in San Antonio whom I met through my sis. She was outgoing like me, and we had many things in common, but the highs and lows we experienced in our three and one-half years of marriage were almost exactly like what I had watched my parents go through after they moved into the dream house. One day she just decided that she no longer wanted to be married and left. We had bought a house from my sister—the one she lived in when she was first married—and I vividly recall sitting in that house alone wondering what I was going to do and how my marriage had failed in much the same manner as my parents. I also began thinking about where I needed to be on a long-term basis. The firm was going through a critical period in the midst of the savings and loan crisis in the mid- and late-1980s. The economy, particularly in Texas, was not in good shape. I had worked in the San Antonio office longer than anyone else at that point, and when I spoke to one of the partners about my future, he told me he had been looking at an opportunity to transfer me to another office in the firm because there just wasn't enough work in San Antonio to support me. In essence, I was being told I could transfer or likely be let go. I initially considered transferring to offices in Tulsa or New Orleans, but I spoke to a good friend in Sacramento, California, who had transferred from the San Antonio office. He invited me to come to California for Thanksgiving to hang out and talk about my future. Right before I left on that trip, he called back and said he had spoken to the local managing partner, and there was an opportunity for me to work in the Sacramento office at least until the end of the 1986 calendar year. I had done plenty of work with the public sector and governmental entities, and my friend mentioned they worked with a considerable number of governmental clients, as well.

I packed a bag of work clothes and flew to Sacramento for an extended stay—at least a month—without even considering bringing my car. I was 29 years old, reluctantly single and definitely a missed paycheck or two away from being broke. I arrived in Sacramento, stayed at my friend's home and realized I needed a vehicle. I rented a Ford Pinto, a hideous-looking hatchback that Ford had stopped producing in 1980 primarily because of the amount of media controversy and legal cases surrounding the safety of its fuel tank design, for $32 a week. It was white with a red interior that featured a three-speed transmission with a floor-mounted shifter and included—I kid you not—strings of fuzzy little dingle balls hanging from the roof. It was ridiculous, but it served its purpose. One of my co-workers jokingly referred to it as the "Womanizer," assuring me the uniquely decorated vehicle would turn my social life around in no time. As you can imagine, that drew a bit of humor from my new friends in California but perhaps sent a message about my strong commitment to humility and my ability to not take myself too seriously.

I moved into the Sacramento office, met plenty of people and began working my tail off to try to make a positive impression. Before the end of the year, the managing partner said he was happy with my work and asked me if I wanted to transfer to Sacramento. I said I did and never returned to San Antonio. I had my car and my belongings shipped from Texas to California and asked my cousin to sell my house for me. It was a terrific move for me for so many reasons, including the fact that I met my current wife, Wanda, while working in the Sacramento office. She had been working as a word processor in the office for about a year when I transferred, and it didn't take more than a couple of seconds for me to notice her. She was strikingly attractive, always dressed to perfection, possessed a terrific work ethic, and she was—by far—the fastest typist I had ever seen.

I was trying to build a client base to earn my keep and thus began producing as many proposals as possible, and Wanda could knock out the proposals in rapid fashion. We began working on some projects, and inevitably, we would be the last two people in the office at night after everyone else had gone home. I began bringing her some chocolate croissants to show my appreciation for her work ethic and for helping me, and I finally built up enough courage one night to ask her to dinner since I was the reason she was staying so late. She told me she couldn't go out with me that night, but she could the following evening. We went to a Chinese buffet on our first date, then went to see a movie and the chemistry was good. We didn't tell anyone in the office we were dating until there was a function that all the partners and senior managers were asked to attend with their spouses or dates. I wanted to take Wanda, and I asked the managing partner if it was OK to bring her as my date. He looked at me mischievously, grinned and gave me his blessing. That was our office coming-out party, so to speak.

Paletta with a group of students from the Mays Business School

I continued to grow more accustomed to California and more crazy about Wanda in the ensuing weeks. Things were moving along quite well for us until her ex-boyfriend resurfaced after moving to the East Coast. They had dated for seven years and had thought about marriage several times, although he never pulled the trigger. He came from a wealthy family, returned to California once he heard that Wanda was dating me and put a full-court press on her. We had a couple of tense moments about what she was going to do. I told her she had to figure it out, and I just stepped back for a while as she decided what she needed to do. I liked her a lot, and I was willing to do whatever I could to fight for her. But after my first failed marriage I also didn't want to do anything to make her feel pressured into a relationship with me. I wanted her to follow her heart, to go out to her ex-boyfriend's parents' home on the East Coast and also come to San Antonio with me to meet my parents. I wanted to make sure she knew what she really wanted. Eventually—and thankfully for me—she decided that I was the one, although it wasn't really clear to her right away what to do after making both trips. She was confused at first, but she decided she wanted to stay in Sacramento and see how things went with me. I was ecstatic to have the chance to win her heart, and we were engaged in August of 1987.

We were married in Napa—where her parents lived at that time—in May of 1988 and bought a house together to plant roots in Sacramento. We didn't have any money in the bank so putting five percent down on a home that cost $144,000 was a lot of money, especially since my home in San Antonio sold for about half that much. I was on track to make partner at Touche Ross when we were married, but she knew we would eventually be required to move to a larger office such as Chicago, New York or Los Angeles for me to continue to advance in my career. Another big change for us was right around the corner, because in 1989, the accounting firm Deloitte Haskins & Sells in the United States merged with Touche Ross in the U.S. to form Deloitte & Touche L.L.P. Although Touche Ross was one of the "Big Eight" firms when I entered the profession, Deloitte was a much bigger practice, so I was quite nervous about my role because the new managing partner of the Sacramento office was a Deloitte partner. As it turned out, I actually had nothing to worry about, and the merger injected new life into my professional career by presenting me with new clients that offered me an opportunity to enhance my role in the firm.

Again, two of my biggest assets have always been the ability to get along with all types of people and to adjust to changing times and circumstances with relative ease. That was certainly the case with the merger, and the Deloitte people quickly accepted me. I performed many roles with Deloitte & Touche, including attestation, taxation, business reorganization, litigation support and recruiting for the firm. It was on a recruiting trip with a friend that I first learned about an opening at an American Savings Bank. Robert Bass, the president of Keystone, Inc. and one of the legendary Bass brothers who have become well-known for the developments in Tarrant County and their efforts to revitalize downtown Fort Worth, had acquired American Savings Bank.

One of my best friends from San Antonio, Chuck Anderson—the best man in our wedding—had gone to work at American Real Estate Group (AREG) in Stockton, California. The company was owned by Robert Bass and organized solely to manage and liquidate distressed assets that were not included in the acquisition of American Savings. My buddy had been hired to serve as the controller and eventually was promoted to CFO. Since he had been in the banking business for years and was familiar with the Bass organization, I asked him what he thought about an opportunity at American Savings Bank that I had heard about through the grapevine. He encouraged me to pursue it. I did, and I then made the leap from Deloitte & Touche to American Savings Bank, overseeing the day-to-day operations of a large internal audit staff that had about 60 employees. For about 10 months, I commuted from the north side of Sacramento to the south side of Stockton every day—about a 130-mile round trip on Interstate 5—which was no picnic. But the commute was easy compared to one of the first tasks I was asked to perform in my new role: cutting the staff to 35 people in 30 days. Nobody wanted to go to lunch with me back then because I became known as the "hatchet man." Perhaps that experience provided me with my lifelong commitment to always show compassion for others, as well as a deepened appreciation for the opportunity to earn a living and provide for my family.

Fortunately, I was reconnected with Chuck in Stockton, and soon thereafter another close San Antonio friend, Bob Corcoran, who was also in the banking industry, moved his wife, Erin, and family from Texas to north of Stockton to join Chuck at AREG. Bob had been closing down banks for the Resolution Trust Corporation, a U.S. government-owned asset management company that was charged in the late 1980s and early '90s with liquidating assets, primarily real estate-related assets such as mortgage loans that had been assets of savings and loan associations declared insolvent by the Office of Thrift Supervision (OTS) as a consequence of the savings and loan crisis of the 1980s. It was great to have two of my longtime friends from San Antonio living on the West Coast with me, and I was able to stay at Chuck's home from time to time during the week to cut down on a few of the long commutes I had been making on a daily basis. Things were going quite well for me from a personal standpoint with Wanda and a professional standpoint now that I had entered the banking industry.

I probably could have been content to stay on the West Coast for many years to come, but then Chuck approached Bob and me about an opportunity to leave our jobs in Stockton and join a new venture that would replace AREG and be charged with the responsibility of liquidating the remaining assets held by the "bad bank." The plan would be to take 35 to 40 people from California with us and move the operations of the new company to Dallas in connection with the formation of a partnership between Robert Bass and the Federal Deposit Insurance Corporation (FDIC). It sounded like a great opportunity, especially since my two good friends would be part of the move and we'd all be part of the restructuring. All I had to do was convince Wanda, a California girl, to move to Texas. When I explained the opportunity to her, she wasn't particularly ecstatic. But she was willing to move to the Lone Star State as long as it wasn't San Antonio where so many of my relatives and friends were still located. She loved my family, but she didn't necessarily want to be next door to them all. I understood, and we decided to embark on an adventure that seemed remarkably promising. Moving to California in the first place had been such a blessing. God had truly guided and blessed me at one of the absolute low points in my life, allowing me to meet Wanda, as well as to build a strong business foundation and reestablish some longtime friendships. Now, I was ready for the next challenge, which was a pretty big risk. Our task was to basically liquidate a portfolio of non-performing loans and real estate and to work ourselves out of a job in the process. There was no promise of another job or any long-term stability. But the economy in Texas was in good shape, and with my CPA background, I believed we would be fine financially no matter what.

That eventually proved to be the case, as God has blessed us since we made the move to Texas in more ways than we could have ever initially envisioned. But no life journey is ever completely smooth. Inevitably, there are bumps in the road that test you, and sometimes there are huge potholes where your tires blow out and you seem to lose control. But that's where your faith is really tested and you simply must give God the wheel. In my personal life, that had happened following my divorce. In my financial life, that was about to happen when we made the decision to move to the Lone Star State.

PALETTA'S MOST DIFFICULT CHALLENGE

Once I made the decision to move, Chuck, Bob and I departed for Dallas, where we initially lived in a downtown hotel and began working some crazy hours. I barely remember the hotel stays because we were working such long hours. Meanwhile, Wanda stayed back in California to tie up loose ends and sell our house, which was no easy task. But the 10-month wait to sell the house was worth it because we made a nice profit, which we invested into building a new home in the Lewisville area, which is northwest of downtown Dallas.

Paletta (far left) in Paris with fellow 12th Man members on a trip to Europe with the Aggies' men's basketball team

After living in the hotel for a while, Wanda and I finally moved into a 700-square-foot apartment and moved most everything from our home in California into a storage shed in the D/FW area. We really were not necessarily looking to build our own home, but we found a lot in Highland Village right on Lake Lewisville that we really liked. We had the profit from selling our home; we had a moving allowance that we could apply to building the new home; and I really believed we would make out quite well financially as we liquidated the distressed bank's portfolio. Things were going so well that I invested in a nice new home through the same builder that my buddy, Chuck, was using. I was told up-front that he wasn't the fastest builder around, but we were not in any major rush, and we had also been told that his finished product had always been great. I also took out a contract on a beautiful swimming pool through a local pool-builder that needed to be built first because the lot was right up against the lake, and it would have been far more difficult to access the backyard once the foundation of our home had been poured. Despite working long hours at the new business—60- to 70-hour work weeks were commonplace—things were moving along swimmingly, so to speak, when Chuck showed up just before the slab work on the house and said there was a major issue with our builder. He was bankrupt and lost everything, including the roughly $50,000 deposit I had paid him. To make matters worse, I didn't even own the lot that now included a swimming pool that I didn't own. I was an unsecured creditor and was out of luck and money.

Fortunately, a great Christian family owned the pool company, and they didn't come after us. But we lost everything we had invested in the home. I eventually went to the builder, who was a good guy who had made a series of bad financial decisions and investments. I told him about my CPA background and dealing with bankruptcy. I offered him help in working with his creditors, but he passed and walked away from the business. Sitting in that tiny little apartment, Wanda and I looked at each other and turned the wheel over to God. We didn't

LOU PALETTA | 37

know what to do or how things would turn out, but we vowed to trust God and to do everything we could to take advantage of every opportunity that was presented to us. There was no use lamenting the loss of the home, the lot and the pool. We had to push forward, and that's exactly what we did.

We would also see that God brought me back to Texas for another reason when my father had a severe stroke shortly after we had moved from California. Although he survived the stroke and was lucky to be alive, he lost a lot of the movement on his left side and his speech was slowed considerably. Life changed for him in an instant, and because I was back in Texas, I was able to spend much more time with him than I would have otherwise been able to do before he died in 2005. I thank God for the added time I was able to spend with my father. I also thank God for opening a number of business doors for me.

I continued to work long hours in my role as Director of Audit and Compliance for the joint venture with the FDIC, and I was eventually invited to join yet another new company called Brazos Funds that was being formed to operate in the same industry but with a different source of capital. Instead of using the government as our partner, we were going to source institutional money and thus organize as a private equity investment firm. In winding down the old company and selling off assets, I was one of the last guys around because someone had to remain in place to liaise with the FDIC and essentially turn out the lights. I think I was one of the last five people in the original company, which was supposed to be around for three years. But we liquidated the assets so effectively and built such a well-oiled machine that we turned it into a one-year job. We had the recovering economy and low interest rates on our side so people could afford to buy assets from us. Plenty of good things were happening at a rapid rate, but I was actually a little nervous about being left behind when the new company was initially formed in the spring of 1995.

I finally received the call to resign from the joint venture and fly up to Canada and prove my worth to the new company. I arrived in Montreal and pulled an all-nighter on my first full day. Brazos Funds was based in Dallas, but we were buying assets from a Canadian bank, and in this case, we had a hard deadline to submit a bid for a sizable distressed loan portfolio accompanied by a substantial amount of documentation at the closing table. Somebody had to compile the data and paperwork immediately, so my job was to go up there and generate all this documentation. I essentially had 12 hours to do it. I was excited to be on the team, and when my colleagues left for the evening, I kept my head down, worked all night and managed to accomplish what needed to be done. In most instances throughout my professional career, my people skills had made the biggest difference, but I also had my father's old-fashioned work ethic and I was not afraid to work around-the-clock in any circumstances.

I officially joined Brazos Funds in August of 1995, assuming a new role in directing financing and closing activities in connection with all investment acquisitions working side-by-side with the guys who were underwriting the assets and negotiating the transactions. I was excited to be in the new company, and again working really long hours, but I was grateful for the opportunity to have a job. I did that for about a year, although it was completely exhausting and I knew something had to give. I was approaching 39 years old, working as many late hours as when I began my career in public accounting, and I knew I couldn't do that for the rest of my life. Again, I gave God the wheel and I was once again steered in the right direction.

One Sunday I received a call from the managing partner of Brazos Funds, asking me what I had going on that day and if I would like to play golf with him. I knew him, but I didn't really know him well, and I wasn't sure if his invitation was a good thing or not. As I had mentioned previously, I had served as the hatchet man at one point in my life, taking guys out to lunch. I was at least a little nervous that golf was his way of saying it was time to go. Nevertheless, I accepted the invitation and met him at the golf course. He showed up ready to walk the course to discuss business, and I arrived with a golf bag that was so big it would dwarf Rodney Dangerfield's golf bag from the 1980 movie "Caddyshack," which featured a television set, stereo, rotary-dial phone and beer cooler. It was a humorous sight watching me drive a cart while my boss walked beside me carrying his bag on his shoulder, but it turned out to be a very big and beneficial day for me. He informed me of a new position and a new opportunity with Lone Star Funds, a successor organization to Brazos Funds that had been organized when Robert Bass decided to reduce his exposure to North American real estate and discontinue his sponsorship of Brazos. My new role would be to head up fundraising and investor relations. He then offered me the job and told me he planned to bring me into the business as a member of the general partner.

Without diving too deep into the financial details of how it all works, this was the opportunity I had longed to seize, and even though I wasn't technically going out on my own, it invigorated and awakened the entrepreneurial molecules within my genetic DNA. In my industry, you aspire to become involved in the private equity business, reaping your own healthy financial benefits while making money for your partners and investors. And quite frankly, I viewed this as my big break. I was 40 years old and had been extremely loyal and dedicated in my previous roles. I felt like I had paid my dues, treated people the right way and been as patient as possible while maintaining an upbeat and positive attitude. I was absolutely thrilled to receive the opportunity to earn an outstanding income in the most lucratively beneficial position—by far—that I had ever received.

I spent the next 18 years with Lone Star Funds as an Executive Vice President and Director of Investor Relations, traveling the world to places like Europe, Asia, the Middle East, Australia and New Zealand to raise funds and build relationships. In 20 years with Lone Star Funds and its predecessor organizations, I played numerous roles in investor relations, audit committees, fundraising and financing. During that time, I coordinated the formation of 10 private equity funds raising $34 billion of capital commitments from a variety of institutional investors including public pension funds, corporate pension funds, sovereign wealth funds, endowments and foundations. I enjoyed an amazingly rewarding tenure with Lone Star Funds before leaving in February 2013 to team up with a former partner to organize a new investment firm, Kildare Partners. Since then, I have served as the Chief Operating Officer of Kildare, a private equity organization that targets opportunistic, control investments in distressed real estate, as well as related opportunities, including both debt and equity products, exclusively in Western Europe. Kildare successfully raised $2 billion of capital commitments in connection with its first fund-offering, and investments have typically been comprised of portfolios of distressed assets that are either non-performing or sub-performing, meaning that the holders of the assets are often motivated to clear their positions either because of regulatory or other strategic reasons. I'm excited about my future with Kildare and perhaps more than anything, thankful to have an opportunity to control my own destiny while working with colleagues who share my passion for people and commitment to building an organization that values hard work and strong ethical standards.

Quite frankly, I have absolutely loved the adventure Wanda and I have traveled since I first arrived in California in 1986. I have come an awfully long way from that rented Ford Pinto, but I really believe that the key to any success I have been able to achieve was a result of allowing God to steer the wheel in whatever direction He wanted to take us. My unwavering faith and trust in God will remain intact in the years to come as I continue to look for opportunities to expand my business interests and help others in the process.

PALETTA'S ADVICE TO YOUNG ENTREPRENEURS

It's been my experience that far too many people enter any business field or entrepreneurial endeavor so focused on reaching an end destination—typically some preconceived vision of success—that they fail to enjoy the ride. My advice is to thoroughly appreciate every mile of the ride and every step of the journey. My other piece of advice—to borrow the title from an extremely popular Carrie Underwood song that was first released in 2005—is to not attempt to control every twist and turn along life's highway and to instead let "Jesus take the wheel." In my life, it's been absolutely amazing to see where God has steered me and how far He has taken me when I have taken the leap of faith and allowed Him to take me in a certain direction. That's certainly not always easy to do, as it is quite natural for any self-motivated, goal-oriented person to want to control his/her destiny.

It's natural…but not usually possible. As I have grown through decades of ups and downs, as well as devastating disappointments and exhilarating accomplishments, I have realized that you can only free yourself to explore unchartered waters or reach unprecedented heights if you allow God to direct you. I am living proof of that. Going to California was never part of the grand vision I had for myself, but I would have

Sweet Lou is no stranger to the golf course… any golf course

never met Wanda or gained the career experience I needed to succeed in Dallas if I had not first flown to Sacramento for what I assumed would be a one-month stay. And once I had planted roots in California, I had absolutely no plans of returning to Texas unless the right opportunity was presented to me. That opportunity came much sooner than I ever dreamed and led me to financial security that I never imagined I would ever achieve.

Another piece of advice that I would like to share is that you don't necessarily have to start your own business to have an entrepreneurial mindset. My father owned and operated his own business, as did my mother following their divorce. My grandparents were also entrepreneurs in the truest sense. I am much different than them or practically anyone else in this book in that I have never truly opened a new business totally on my own. Yet, in virtually every professional position I have ever worked, I have taken an entrepreneurial approach to my role within an organization. I have been able to work independently, and I have accepted complete responsibility for my own success. I have made it a point to learn from everyone around me, but ultimately, I have taken the approach that "if it is to be, it's up to me." In other words, I would much rather take full responsibility for any project than to merely perform a specific role.

That perspective is rare in the workplace, as so many employees merely want to perform certain tasks or do as little as possible to collect a paycheck. So, taking full responsibility and essentially acting as if you are the CEO of your own career will inevitably earn you the attention of your employers. If you also attempt to treat everyone around you with respect and appreciation—as opposed to only the people above you or those whom you think might benefit you—it will also be noticed and admired. It's really as simple as the Golden Rule: Treat others as you would want to be treated.

Finally, it is extremely important to look at every experience as a learning moment, regardless of whether it is something as potentially demoralizing as a divorce or whether it is as uplifting as finally receiving the opportunity of a lifetime. As F. Scott Fitzgerald once stated so eloquently, "Never confuse a single defeat with a final defeat." Learn from every mistake and everyone around you. And don't just celebrate the victories in life; celebrate and appreciate every step of life's journey.

4.
Dan Allen Hughes, Jr.
President and Owner of Dan A. Hughes Co. LP and Hupecol Operating Co. LLC
Texas A&M Class of 1980

HUGHES' PATH TO TEXAS A&M

Dan Allen and Peggy Hughes on the A&M campus

Perhaps it would be a stretch to say that geology or the oil and gas industry is literally in my blood. It would not, however, be the least bit inaccurate to say that I was likely born with some sort of genetic predisposition to eventually follow in my family's historic footsteps that have traversed oilfields and exploration sites from Beeville, Texas to Bogotá, Colombia, and from Jackson, Mississippi to Perth, Australia. Most people I know explore their ancestry by examining or constructing a family tree. Not the Hughes family, though. Our genealogy is rooted so deeply in geology that an appropriate image of our family tree would look more like an old oil derrick than a Douglas fir.

My grandfather, Dan G. Hughes, began working for the United Gas Company at about the same time the company started, and when my father, Dan, and his twin brother, Dudley, were born in 1929—the same year of the stock market crash and the beginning of the Great Depression—the family was living in the Monroe Gas Field in Louisiana. My grandfather eventually settled in Palestine, Texas in 1936, where he stayed for about 10 years and supervised a network of natural gas pipelines. He moved his family into the United Gas Company-owned home on the property, which was about a mile outside of Palestine. Living on the company's land (a fenced-in compound that also included tool houses, pipe racks, trucks and garages) and in its rent home gave my father and uncle access to some relatively high-tech tools of that era and an abundance of raw materials. When they weren't attending the nearby, three-room, wooden-framed schoolhouse (grades first through eighth), they typically entertained themselves by building and designing whatever their minds could conceive and their raw materials would allow. And when they weren't building tree houses, pipe cannons and so forth, my father and uncle were often feeding their adventuresome personalities by hunting or fishing (two passions that are also part of my DNA). My dad and uncle were the best of friends, although they didn't always agree on oil and gas projects.

Twins obviously share a special bond, and in most families, they are also especially rare. But not in our family, which has a history of multiple births that predates even our oil and gas lineage. Five years after giving birth to my dad and uncle, my grandmother had twin girls, my aunts June and Jane, who also eventually became geologists. Two sets of twins in the same family are rare enough, but my grandfather and my great grandmother also happened to be twins. The family tree/oil derrick can be really confusing to explain, document and follow because, quite frankly, there are so many "Dans" and "Dudleys" in the mix. In addition to my dad and uncle, my grandfather and his brother were also twins named Dan and Dudley, and our family heritage can be traced back further to another set of twins (Dan and Dudley, of course) in Georgia in the 1850s. For the sake of clarity within the family, I've always answered to the name "Dan Allen," and when my wife, Peggy, gave birth to our first child, we honored my family's roots by giving our son the traditional "Dan Allen" family name, but we have always called him "D.A." to help differentiate him from his male relatives.

Obviously, carrying on the family name is extremely important to me, especially since I have so much admiration for how my parents, uncle, aunts, grandparents and so forth built such an impressive legacy. My father and uncle graduated from Palestine High School in 1946, the same year World War II came to an end. Following their graduation, they initially went their separate ways, as my dad went to work in the oilfields for the Magnolia Petroleum Company in Oklahoma and Uncle Dudley went to work for United Gas Company back in Palestine. My grandfather was transferred to Dallas in 1946, where he was a district foreman for the East Texas pipeline system, and my dad and uncle enrolled for a year and a half at North Texas Agriculture Junior College in Arlington, which was a branch at that time of Texas A&M. They were later admitted to Texas A&M College in 1948, enrolling as sophomores. But even though they were sophomores in terms of their academic standing, they were viewed as freshmen—and fresh meat—in the Corps of Cadets hierarchy. They were both assigned to B Battery Engineer Company, and they both endured plenty of hard times and hazing—even though that had technically been banned by the Corps—while surviving some extremely difficult circumstances. My grandfather had borrowed money against his life insurance policy just to pay for my dad and uncle to attend A&M, so they were determined to persist without exception.

They did much more than merely survive, however. They thrived, and they have been forever grateful for the discipline that was instilled during their time in the Corps. Of course, "grateful" was probably not the word they would have chosen to describe those sometimes hellish experiences while they were enduring them. But the toughness and tenacity they developed in the Corps served them well as second lieutenants in the U.S. Army following their graduation from Texas A&M in 1951. While World War II had concluded, it was certainly not a time of world peace.

On June 25, 1950, armed forces from communist North Korea smashed into South Korea, setting off what became known as the Korean War. Korea, a former Japanese possession, had been divided into occupation zones following World War II. The United States accepted the surrender of Japanese forces in southern Korea, while the Soviets did the same in northern Korea. Much like what happened in Germany, however, the "temporary" division soon became permanent. The Soviets assisted in the establishment of a communist regime in North Korea, while the United States became the main source of financial and military support for South Korea. When North Korean forces surprised the South Korean army in late June 1950, the United States responded by pushing a resolution through the U.N.'s Security Council calling for military assistance to South Korea. My father and uncle soon became part of the United States' efforts in Korea. My father was originally commissioned to go to Germany, while Uncle Dudley was sent to Korea. But there was a little-known stipulation in the rules of enlistment that allowed brothers to be stationed in the same locations.

My uncle and dad uncovered the stipulation and requested to be sent to the same location, hoping and praying that they would both be sent into a non-combative situation in Germany. Instead, the two 22-year-old officers were both shipped to Korea in December 1952 and were assigned to separate front-line platoons, manning quad-50 machine gun halftracks. My dad and uncle quickly displayed their resourcefulness and ingenuity, helping to develop techniques that made it possible to fire multiple quad-50s at unseen targets. The effect of the techniques created a wall of fire that terrorized attacking enemy infantry and altered the strategic maneuvers of the Korean War. My uncle eventually wrote a book called, "Wall of Fire: A Diary of the Third Korean Winter Campaign," that details their time and contributions to the war effort (both of them earned Bronze Stars) while also including excerpts from the daily letters written by my uncle to his wife, Robbie.

The Korean War ended almost exactly three years after it had started, and Dan and Dudley returned to the U.S. to begin what would ultimately be viewed as sensationally successful business careers. Before they had even been shipped off to war, the two brothers, while stationed temporarily at Fort Bliss in El Paso, purchased a federal gas lease in Eddy County, New Mexico, the first of many leases they have owned, for .50 cents an acre. After the acquisition, they then swapped the prospect to a local operator for an overriding royalty. At the time of this writing, they are still receiving income from that deal they made in the early 1950s.

After leaving the military for good, the brothers went to work for Union Producing Company, which ultimately became part of Pennzoil and is now Devon Energy. And once they entered the business field, they began distinguishing themselves as quickly as they had done on the battlefields. Dudley and his wife wound up moving to Jackson, Mississippi. Meanwhile, my father, who was not married at that time, was stationed in New Orleans as a geological scout in 1953. My dad was making about $600 a month in New Orleans, which was a pretty decent income at that time. According to Fiftiesweb.com, for example, the average American home in '53 cost $17,400 and the average income was $4,011 a year. At $600 a month, my dad was making a gross annual income of $7,200. But he says it was difficult to save money at that time because there was just too much to do in New Orleans. He requested to be moved to another location and was sent to Beeville, Texas, which is about 55 to 60 miles northwest of Corpus Christi. Rest assured $600 a month went much, much further in tiny Beeville than it did in the "Big Easy."

Once he was in Beeville, my father truly found his niche in geological scouting…and he also scouted out my mother Juanita Jo Wentz, who had grown up in Mathis, which is about 25 miles southeast of Beeville. They were married in 1956, and I was born in 1957. From my earliest recollections, I vividly remember my father working all day, coming home to have dinner with us—my mom, sister, brother and me—and then slipping into his office in the garage. Sometimes he would allow me to accompany him into the garage and would give me a brief explanation of what he was doing. In the most simplistic and generic terms, he was mapping. He was closely examining the existing wells that had been drilled and was analyzing the electric logs that had been inserted into the well. By examining the logs, you can find one formation in one well and then another and another. I think many people not familiar with the oil and gas industry have a misconception about drilling and finding oil and gas. The oil and gas is typically found in just one large reservoir or pool. Oil floats on water, so my father was looking for a high area that is a trap like a fault or a dome. Oil or natural gas would migrate up and trap in those areas, and my father was working diligently to identify those areas and to be able to extract the oil and gas. I would go in the garage and watch him, but he would work into the wee hours of the morning.

My dad was doing well with the Union Producing Company, but in 1963, he and my uncle decided to form a partnership, which was called Hughes & Hughes Oil and Gas. For years, my dad and Uncle Dudley had been independently mapping prospects and cataloguing their own ideas. My dad had targeted a number of prospects in South Texas, while my uncle's projections were in Mississippi and Alabama. Both brothers were still in their early 30s when they decided to go on their own, with my dad opening one office in Beeville and my uncle opening a location in Jackson, Mississippi. Initially, I remember that money was very tight for a while after dad opened his own office, as my mother fed us a steady diet of peanut butter and jelly sandwiches. We were certainly not living a life of luxury or lavishness in those days, but it really didn't matter to us. We had two extremely hard-working parents, a roof over our heads and something to eat at every meal, even if there wasn't a tremendous amount of variety.

In the ensuing years, the company began to grow, as both my father and uncle were exceptional geologists who truly applied science and strategy to what had often previously been the unpredictable and inexact practice of wildcatting. Some of my most vivid and enduring memories of my own childhood involve spending time with my father, who would often allow me to accompany him on business trips to places such as the Laredo oilfields. While he was logging wells—documenting the geologic formations resulting from a borehole—I'd regularly hop out of the truck to open gates, search for arrowheads along the rugged terrain and ask my father numerous questions about the oil and gas business. Without a doubt, I inherited my sincere fascination and fervor for the business from my father. I also inherited my father's passion for hunting and fishing, along with his tremendous appreciation and admiration for Texas A&M.

From left, William, D.A., Dan Allen and Dan Hughes (seated)

My father often credited A&M—particularly his experiences in the Corps of Cadets—for helping him to survive and strategize in Korea and for laying the geological foundation and the discipline principles that propelled him to build thriving businesses. My dad loved A&M, and I grew up dreaming about one day attending Texas A&M, just as he and my uncle had done. I listened to many Aggie football games on the radio throughout the 1960s—mostly lean times for the maroon and white except for the one Southwest Conference championship in 1967—and looked forward to those occasional weekend trips to Aggieland where we'd savor all the pageantry and festivities of game days at Kyle Field. Every time we returned home after those weekend trips—regardless of whether the Aggies won or lost—I was even more determined to one day attend Texas A&M than I had been before making the trip.

I did foresee a significant problem, however. For many years, I really didn't know if I was college material. I struggled to read for as long as I can remember. I was the very last person in the first grade at my elementary school in Beeville to learn my ABCs. Keep in mind that those were much different times than today, and learning disabilities in the early 1960s often went undetected. That was certainly the case for me. In fact, it wasn't until decades later when my own two sons and daughter were diagnosed with dyslexia that I realized I also had that exact same language processing disorder. When my sons were diagnosed with dyslexia, a considerable amount of research had already been done to conclusively determine that the neurological disorder is not a sign of poor intelligence or laziness. It is also not the result of impaired vision. Children and adults with dyslexia simply have a condition that causes their brains to process and interpret information differently. According to the National Institute of Child and Human Development, roughly 15 percent of Americans have major troubles with reading, and many families have multiple cases of dyslexia. As a result, alternative learning methods have been developed and implemented in school, allowing today's students with dyslexia to achieve success in the classroom.

Back in the early and mid-1960s, however, I just felt dumb. I had to work really hard when I was in school, and I had a lot of tutors just to help me survive. In the classroom, many of the other kids would finish a test in 20 minutes or less, and it would take me an hour. I was embarrassed and sometimes ridiculed. It also made it more difficult on me because both my sister and brother were brilliant, and my sister was ultimately the valedictorian of her class. Fortunately, I was blessed with some caring teachers and tutors who allowed me to continue making progress in school. I remember one tutor, in particular, who was also a sixth-grade teacher. She would always stay late after school with me to go over the next day's assignments/tests. She knew I was self-conscious, and she also knew I wasn't dumb because I could answer the questions easily if she asked me as opposed to making me read the questions. By the time I enrolled at Beeville High School, I was better at handling my disorder, even though I was many years from actually being diagnosed with dyslexia.

I coped with the condition in high school by simply working harder than many of the other students around me needed to work. But the countless hours of reading, re-reading, tutoring and so forth eventually paid off when I was accepted into Texas A&M. During my senior year in high school, the 1975 Aggie football team climbed to as high as No. 2 in the national polls after starting the season with a 10-0 record. The student body was also growing rapidly, as more and more women began attending A&M. During the tenure of Gen. James Earl Rudder as president of Texas A&M University (1959-70), enrollment nearly dou-

44 | **THE ENTREPRENEURIUAL SPIRIT OF AGGIELAND**

bled from an all-male student population of 7,500 to a far more diverse group of 14,000 students in '70. By 1975, one-fourth of the student population was women, and by 1980 when I finished at A&M, there were 12,207 women among the burgeoning student body of 33,499. Looking back, those numbers turned out to be quite significant to me personally because one of those women eventually became my wife.

The admission of women was definitely the major driving force in the growth of Texas A&M in the 1960s and into the '70s, but another significant reason for the rapid increase was the decision to make membership in the Corps of Cadets voluntary instead of compulsory. When I arrived at A&M in the fall of '76, I could have chosen not to follow my father's and uncle's footsteps into the Corps of Cadets. America's involvement in Vietnam had ended a couple of years earlier, so there wasn't a tremendous push to leave college as an officer, but deep-down, I felt compelled to give the Corps a shot. I enlisted as a freshman in Squadron 7 along with 20 other freshmen in my outfit. By the midway point of that first semester, however, half of my fellow freshmen had quit, and I was definitely thinking seriously about joining them.

Being a freshman in the Corps was not enjoyable. In fact, it was often down-right miserable. The sophomores were brutal on us, and I think I polished more items—shoes, brass, the floor, toilets, etc.—than I had at any other time in my life. The 5 a.m. wakeup calls were quite rough, too, especially since I was working extra hard—and staying up extra late—just to keep up with my classes. I started college with the full intent of majoring in geology, just like my father and uncle. But the classes were tough and life in the Corps was exhausting. The days were arduous and the weeks were grueling, causing me to rethink my degree plans. Meanwhile, my other friends who were not in the Corps continually told me—perhaps "bragged" would be a more appropriate description—about how much fun they were having every night chasing girls at the relatively new Dixie Chicken (opened in 1974) and other bars in the community. At about the midway point of my first semester of college, I figured I had given it a fair shot, but that I was done with the Corps.

I built up my courage, rehearsing exactly what I'd say and then I called my father. I provided him my long list of excuses and told him, "This Corps of Cadets thing is just not for me." There was no immediate response from the other end of the line. In fact, there was a rather uncomfortable pause. When he finally opened his mouth, my father's ensuing words forever changed my life. "You're an adult now, son," he said. "You can make your own decisions. But let me just say this: The first time you quit, it's a difficult decision. The next time it's a little easier. Before you know it, you're a quitter."

I was absolutely stunned. I tried to think of an appropriate comeback, but nothing came to mind. I certainly did not want to become a quitter or to develop a reputation for giving up whenever circumstances became difficult. I thought about my father's words for several days and ultimately decided to stick with it. I am so glad that I did. Being in the Corps was a great learning experience and taught me more about leadership than I could have possibly imagined or gained otherwise. As a senior, I was the commanding officer of the Second Group in the Air Force. I also made some lifelong friends and overall, things worked out much better for me than I could have ever anticipated.

What I learned at A&M—and I thank my father to this day for his advice—was to never take the easy path. Face your challenges/obstacles head on, and each day the difficulties grow smaller and smaller as your confidence grows bigger and bigger. Besides, sometimes the difficult path leads to much greater things and a better life. That was the case for me.

While I didn't spend much time chasing girls or closing down bars, I managed to have some fun and meet the woman of my dreams while at Texas A&M. My sister, Keleigh Hughes-Sasser, lived at the Treehouse Apartments just a couple of long home runs south of Olsen Field at Blue Bell Park, which originally opened in 1978. One of Keleigh's next-door neighbors at the apartment complex was a strikingly attractive co-ed named Peggy Gorden. My sister introduced me to Peggy in 1979, and we only went on two official dates before I graduated in December of 1980 (I spent four full years in the Corps of Cadets and then explored college life as a "regular student" during my final semester). But even though we didn't have a long dating history together by the time I graduated, we had enough chemistry that I knew I wanted to keep in touch. Peggy graduated from A&M in 1982, which gave me an opportunity to begin my business and entrepreneurial adventures before actively pursuing a long-term relationship with her.

In hindsight, I can clearly see that God was in control of everything—from my future bride moving in next door to my sister to the timing of my graduation, and from my degree plan to my post-graduation plans. Perhaps I could have finished A&M in four years if I had stayed on the geology track from start to finish. But the coursework and the demands of the Corps were too tough, so I switched majors after about two years and earned a management degree from what is now the Mays Business School. I took a number of interesting businesses classes during my time at A&M, but the class that really opened my eyes the most was economics. I had a vague understanding of basic economics, but that class really allowed me to grasp the concept of supply and demand and how those factors affected business. I still considered myself a geologist at heart, but the business courses and management degree were wonderful benefits to me once I began pursuing my own entrepreneurial efforts many years later.

Thanks in large part to following my father's advice, I learned so much in the Corps of Cadets and the classroom settings at Texas A&M. And upon graduation, my father continued to guide me in the right direction, sending me to Perth, the capital and largest city in Western Australia. Perth became known worldwide as the "City of Light" in 1962 when its residents lit their house lights and streetlights as American astronaut John Glenn passed overhead while orbiting the Earth on Friendship 7. Interestingly, Perth is where the light turned on for me, too, in terms of realizing what it would take to lead a business and make some difficult decisions.

HUGHES' PATH TO ENTREPRENEURIAL SUCCESS

While I was attending Texas A&M and working toward my undergraduate degree, my father and uncle were expanding into the "Land Down Under." For quite some time, they had both possessed a passion for expanding internationally, and they initially did some things in Canada in the early- and mid-1970s. In the late 1970s, they expanded their business ventures into Western Australia, which eventually resulted in a significant gas discovery. But when I returned home from college for Christmas in 1980, my father was not pleased with the lack of communication he was receiving from the office he and my uncle had established in Perth.

Keep in mind that communication—especially international communication—was much more primitive than it is today. To communicate with someone overseas, you essentially had two primary options: Pick up the phone and make an extremely expensive call or use the telex network, which was a little more sophisticated than a telegraph, but was still light years away from emails or instant text messaging via cell phones. Telex was state-of-the-art technology in 1980, though, utilizing a switched network of teleprinters, similar to a telephone network, for the purpose of sending text-based messages. The telex exchanges were entirely separate from the telephone system, with their own signaling standards, exchanges and system of telex numbers. But no matter how he attempted to communicate with the office in Western Australia, my father was not pleased with the lack of responses, so on January 2, 1981, I hopped on an airplane bound from Texas to Perth. My instructions from my father were to figure out what was going on and then to address the issues.

I had been to Perth a couple of times previously with my father, and I had also done some traveling on my own through Europe, so I wasn't intimidated about making the trip. On the other hand, I was as green as St. Patrick's Day in terms of my business experience. Nevertheless, I checked into the Parmelia Hilton on a mission to prove myself. I lived in the hotel for about six months, walking back and forth from the Parmelia to the office, as I observed and studied how the office was running. It didn't take long to determine why my father and uncle were not being updated regularly on the progress and productivity of the explorations and drillings. Quite frankly, not much progress was being made because the office manager spent more time each day on his sailboat than studying seismic energy or anything else related to oil and gas, and two or three other employees were following his lazy leadership style. As far as I could decipher, there was only one employee on the staff, Bevan Cook, who was really interested in actually working and earning a living. After about two months in Perth, I met my father in Honolulu and recommended that we keep Cook and fire everyone else. That's exactly what we did. Cook worked for us until the day he died in the early

2010s, and the drilling and exploration in Western Australian turned out to be quite lucrative for us before my father and uncle sold the operations.

That was my first experience internationally, and it provided me with the incentive to eventually run my own business. Of course, I knew there was still plenty I had to learn before ever dreaming of actually going out on my own. I returned from Australia late in 1981 and then decided to finish my geological studies at Texas A&I, which is now Texas A&M-Kingsville. Picking up where I left off at Texas A&M when I changed majors, I finished my geology degree requirements in about a year, making the 75-mile drive from Beeville to Kingsville so many times that I could practically do it in my sleep. I didn't actually graduate from A&I because I never finished the foreign language requirement for the degree, but I finished all the geological, science and math courses that better prepared me for a future in oil and gas exploration.

Then in January of 1982, I traveled to Jackson, Mississippi to work full time for my uncle. My father and uncle decided to dissolve the partnership they had first launched together in the mid-1960s, with my dad headquartering his own operations in Beeville and my uncle staying in Jackson. Working directly for my uncle provided me with some different perspective on how to run a business, even though he and my father both think quite similarly. While working with my uncle, we did quite a bit of drilling in South Florida, particularly in Collier County and the Sunniland Shale formation. The Sunniland is divided into two zones, an upper reservoir and a lower source. Oil had first been discovered in the region in 1943 by the Humble Oil and Refining Company, which became Exxon. And in the early 1980s, we did relatively well in the upper Sunniland, which is a conventional shale play. Back then, I would regularly tell my uncle that I believed there were multiple oil-producing horizons in the lower Sunniland—the rubble zone or source rock—but it was his consensus (and the belief of many others) that the lower Sunniland was simply too tight to be productive. I accepted that conclusion at that time, but more than 30 years later, we returned to the lower Sunniland with new technologies that allowed me to correctly prove my theories. More on that later, though.

Dan Allen and Peggy Hughes at Kyle Field with the 12th Man Foundation's Jacob Green

Overall, I learned a tremendous amount during the year I worked with my uncle, and that's also the time period when I began dating Peggy quite seriously. After graduating from A&M, she had moved to Austin where she was working for the United Way. She flew into Jackson a few times for weekend trips, but we had the most fun while we were dating when she would fly into New Orleans and I would make the drive down to the Big Easy to pick her up from the airport. There was so much to do and enjoy in New Orleans, and I quickly discovered why my father had once struggled to make ends meet on $600 a month while living in the Crescent City. Even in the early 1980s, you could spend that much on a weekend trip. We started dating in January of '83; I asked her marry me in May; and we were married on October 1, 1983. It was a quick courtship, but I'd suspected for years that she could be "the one," and I didn't see any point in wasting time...or in allowing her to possibly change her mind.

While we enjoyed Jackson and I benefitted from working with my uncle, I decided after Peggy and I were married that it was time to do something on my own. I suspect most entrepreneurs possess that internal drive to step out on their own, and I could no longer suppress my intuitions. We bought a little townhome in San Antonio, and I opened my own office. Business was certainly not booming, but I developed some of my own prospects and started making some decent money, although we struggled at times. Looking back at it now, though, I am grateful for those struggles. They made us stronger individually and as a couple. Those struggles also taught us some valuable lessons…like never owning two homes at once. We bought a home at one point without selling the one we previously owned, which placed us in a rather difficult financial bind. Fortunately, I'd spent a large part of my childhood eating peanut butter and jelly sandwiches, so I knew we could survive without any frills.

I'm sure we would have done just fine if we had stayed in San Antonio, but after about five years on our own, my father's explorations manager left. When he left, my father called and said he wanted me to return to Beeville to become his exploration manager. By that time, we had two young boys, D.A., who was about two and William, who was five months old. I was initially hesitant to even consider joining my father's business, the Dan A. Hughes Company, but he had a tremendous early influence on me, and I knew I could learn so much by working alongside him. In 1978, my father was awarded membership in the exclusive All-American Wildcatters Club. And over the years, he has been honored, recognized and saluted by an array of organizations, receiving the M.B. "Duke" Rudman Outstanding Wildcatter Award, the Michael T. Halbouty Geosciences Medal, the Outstanding Citizen of Bee County and so forth.

My father has built his reputation and his thriving business on integrity. He has worked extremely hard; he's invested in people and technology; he has benefited from a number of calculated risks through the years; and he has always operated by the motto that his word is his bond. In assessing the situation, I realized my father was one of the best mentors I could possibly seek, and it would have been rather foolish of me not to join him simply because he was my dad and I was really looking to make a name for myself. I believe it is imperative for young entrepreneurs to find mentors in their field or area of expertise and to learn as much as possible from those mentors. Once I looked at the situation analytically, I realized my father was offering me a golden opportunity to grow as an oil and gas businessman, so Peggy and I packed up our belongings and our boys and moved from San Antonio to Beeville. It was a wise decision for many reasons, and my father presented me with an opportunity to initially be a limited partner. I grew tremendously as a geologist, an entrepreneur and a leader as I started off with a small carried interest and my role within the company gradually increased over time. Our youngest child, daughter Elizabeth, was born while we were living in Beeville, and we spent about five and a half years living in Bee County before making the decision to move back to San Antonio. One of the primary reasons we moved back to San Antonio was because of tutoring and schooling options for our kids. All three of our children have dyslexia—unfortunately, it is hereditary—and there were better options for tutors and teaching techniques in San Antonio, where I established an adjunct office in 1990.

For the most part, though, I stayed in Beeville and did plenty of commuting back and forth from San Antonio (an hour and a half drive). On those long drives, I often pondered what should be our next major business move. By the late 1980s, it had become increasingly difficult to find oil and gas in the United States because the next big technology breakthrough (hydraulic fracturing or "fracking," combined with horizontal drilling) had yet to be fully explored and perfected. By the early 1990s, I was convinced we needed to look internationally to expand our productivity. I considered Australia; I explored South America; I entered into a small deal in Bolivia that never really jelled; and I applied for a bid in Venezuela, but was ultimately told that we did not qualify because we were not big enough to handle the job. Quite frankly, it was all a bit discouraging. But sometimes, it really is darkest just before the dawn. And if you avoid sulking and keep seeking the next opportunity, your big breakthrough may come at a point—or a place—where you least expect it.

HUGHES' MOST DIFFICULT CHALLENGE

Since the late 1990s, business has—at least for the most part—often been booming for the Dan A. Hughes Co., as well as the other ventures I've launched such as Maverick American Natural Gas, which is now called Jonah Energy LLC., and Hupecol Operating Co. LLC. At one point or another, we've done business in Canada, Australia, Argentina, Belize, Italy, Bolivia, Spain, China and Colombia. Thanks to

Dan Allen and Peggy in front of their oil rig in Sicily

tremendous advances in technology, we've also done some great things domestically. I don't want to be excessively technical here, but in the most simplistic and generic terms, hydraulic fracturing—commonly referred to as fracking—is a drilling technique used for extracting oil or natural gas from deep underground. The first experimental use of hydraulic fracturing was in 1947, and the first commercially successful applications of fracking were in 1949. But it wasn't until the 1990s when fracking and horizontal drilling made it possible to extract oil and natural gas from shale plays that were once un-producible with conventional technologies.

In a nutshell, the fracking process starts with a well that is drilled vertically or at an angle from the surface to a depth of one to two miles or more. The vertical well is then encased in steel and/or cement to ensure the well doesn't run the risk of leaking into any groundwater. Once the vertical well reaches the deep layer of rock where natural gas or oil exists, the well curves about 90 degrees and begins drilling horizontally along that rock layer. Horizontal drilling can extend more than one mile from the vertical well bore. After the fracking well is fully drilled and encased, fracking fluid is pumped down into the well at extremely high pressure, which is powerful enough to fracture the surrounding rock, creating fissures and cracks through which oil and gas can flow. In the Lone Star State, the first horizontal well was drilled into the Barnett Shale in north Texas in 1991, but it wasn't until '97 when fellow Aggie George P. Mitchell's group applied the slickwater fracturing technique to make shale extraction widely economical. Mitchell has often been called the "father of fracking" because of his role in applying it in shale plays.

My father and I entered into the Barnett Shale around Fort Worth and did well, building about 15 to 20 wells we eventually sold. That play taught us a tremendous amount about the horizontal drilling process, which we utilized in later plays. We then briefly went into Arkansas and eventually turned our attention to the Eagle Ford Shale in Southwest Texas in 2005-06. Unlike some other Texas shale plays, the Eagle Ford Shale was not just about natural gas. The Eagle Ford is not uniform, as it is essentially divided into three regions, which are described as the "oil window, gas condensate window and dry gas window." But initially, no one realized there was practically an ocean of oil in the Eagle Ford Shale beneath the Austin chalk formation. In the mid-1990s, we had once drilled in Karnes County between Falls City and Karnes City (southeast of San Antonio along U.S. Highway 181), targeting the Edwards Limestone formation along the Edwards Reef Trend. But quite frankly, it didn't make a very good well in the Edwards formation. We had a good oil show while drilling through the Eagle Ford, which lies above the Edwards, and we decided to perforate the Eagle Ford and apply some acid to the formation. The well responded by flowing 60 barrels of oil a day. Years later—following the lessons we learned in the Barnett Shale and the development of emerging technologies—one of my geologists encouraged me to explore Karnes County, which lies at the heart of the Eagle Ford Shale. We ended up leasing roughly 60,000 acres—almost all of it in Karnes County—and eventually drilled roughly 20 wells, some on our own and some in partnership with EOG Resources. It was a great investment, but we would have never made that breakthrough without learning our lessons from the Barnett Shale and the first foray into Karnes County.

We now have plenty of other things going on, as our successes have continued to breed more success. The more we've learned and evolved, the more opportunities we've uncovered. That's also a key point to make to any perspective entrepreneur: Commit to a lifetime of learning.

As technologies have improved, we have also been able to return to plays that were not accessible at one time. Case in point: the Sunniland Shale formation in Florida. Thirty years after my first venture into the Sunniland Shale, we returned with more efficient drilling techniques and acquired the mineral rights to about 200,000 acres, partnering with Collier Resources. We were the first oil company to draw a horizontal well into the lower Sunniland, following up on my hunch from three decades ago. The timing and technologies were not right for exploration in the lower Sunniland in the early 1980s, but some three decades later, things have changed. Lessons have been learned. New strategies can now be applied.

Success in the oil and gas industry—or practically any other field—is often a matter of seizing the right opportunity at the right moment. And as I look back over my career, I believe my biggest break was also one of the biggest risks. As I mentioned previously, I believe success breeds success. In that regard, a company or business can be much like a sports team. With each victory, the team gains a little more confidence and generates a little more momentum. After a couple of wins, the team expects good things to happen. The key, however, is often recording that first big victory, which can kick-start a team's run of greatness.

For me personally, the big victory and the big break probably came in Bogotá, Colombia, long before the Eagle Ford Shale play, the return to Sunniland, the creation of Maverick American Natural Gas and so forth. As previously noted, I believed in the early and mid-1990s that we needed to look internationally to expand our oil productivity. Around that same timeframe, a San Antonio-based partner named John Saunders told me he had met a couple of geologists in Houston who had worked for Chevron in South America. Chevron had drilled a couple of wells in Colombia in the Llanos Basin, but had decided to plug the wells because they didn't seem to be productive enough for one of the giants in the energy and exploration industry. But the geologists were convinced that there was a great opportunity for a smaller, private organization such as the Dan A. Hughes Co. if an entrepreneur was willing to take a risk. The risk, quite frankly, was simply operating in Bogotá, the capital city of Colombia.

Between the mid-1980s to the early-1990s, the population in Bogotá grew substantially, as did violence and crime. For many reasons—primarily drug trafficking—Bogotá was considered one of the most dangerous cities in the world in the mid-1990s. At one point, it had a homicide rate of 80 per 100,000 people, and many of those brutal murders were drug-related. Between 1993 and 1999, Colombia became the world's most prominent producer of coca and cocaine, as well as one of the major exporters of heroin. And the drug barons of Colombia were long considered among the world's most dangerous and most wanted men by the United States' intelligence department. The United States government continually warned U.S. Citizens about the dangers associated with travel to Colombia, particularly Bogotá. As recently as 2007, the U.S. State Department issued this warning: *"Violence by narcoterrorist groups and other criminals continues to affect all parts of the country, urban and rural…Terrorist groups such as the Revolutionary Armed Forces of Colombia (FARC) and the National Liberation Army (ELN), and other criminal organizations, continue to kidnap civilians for ransom or as political bargaining chips. No one can be considered immune from kidnapping on the basis of occupation, nationality, or other factors.… U.S. government officials and their families in Colombia are permitted to travel to major cities in the country, but only by air. They are not allowed to use inter- or intra-city bus transportation. They also are not permitted to travel by road outside of urban areas at night. All Americans in Colombia are urged to follow these precautions."*

Obviously, opening business operations and drilling wells in Colombia came with risks. So did merely traveling to the city. But they were calculated risks worth taking, and John Saunders and I went to Bogotá with one of the Chevron geologists to explore the opportunities. We ended up making a deal and receiving the same block that Chevron had released. We offered the geologist a flat fee of $1,500 or a 2 percent override on this block. He took the $1,500, which proved to be quite short-sighted on his part.

We drilled our first well and made a good discovery. Then we went over to the second well that

Chevron had plugged, and we drilled 15 feet from the original well. Almost immediately, we were making 3,000 barrels a day, and it was still producing 3,000 barrels a day when we sold it three years later. That well continued to produce many years afterward, and it proved to be an incredible business deal for our company. We sold our first deal to a company based in Spain called "CEPSA," which is an integrated energy company operating at every stage of the oil value chain, with more than 11,000 employees. We later sold another deal in Colombia to a China-based, state-owned petrochemical corporation called the "Sinopec Group," which has more than one million employees and was ranked fifth in 2011 on the *Fortune* Global 500. That deal took me to Beijing a couple of times for a whole new kind of negotiating process with the Chinese government. It was an interesting experience, to say the least.

Before either of those sales, however, we invested back into the Bogotá community, making a major and tremendously positive difference for the people who worked for us, as well as their families. We initially had the wrong manager in place in Bogotá, which caused us some unnecessary headaches up front, but we resolved that issue and had such a great experience with the two wells that we have continued working in Colombia. We were originally in an area where there really wasn't a criminal threat, and we employed some good people. We hired local folks and then invested in their lives (as opposed to just paying a salary), building schools for their children, roads for the trucks and pipelines to carry the oil. We bought computers for the schools and paid for teachers to instruct our employees' kids. At the time of this writing, we are still active in Colombia. And the country has improved its image dramatically by reducing crime and investing in legal industries like energy and exploration. We really changed and improved lives in Colombia, and we have operated in the same manner in some of the other international countries where we have drilled, especially in developing countries like Belize. Making a profit is essential to any entrepreneur, but there is no better feeling than making a profit and making a difference in the lives of others.

HUGHES' ADVICE TO YOUNG ENTREPRENEURS

The Hughes family members possess a passion for the outdoors and adventure

Peggy and I both absolutely love adventure. Among many other locations domestically and internationally, we've gone hunting in Africa, Argentina, Mexico, Spain, Scotland and the United Kingdom, while we've fished in Australia, Hawaii, Fiji, Panama, Costa Rica, Alaska, Canada, Mexico and the Caribbean. Peggy climbed the Himalayas in India in 2010, conquered Mount Kilimanjaro (the highest mountain in Africa at 19,341 feet above sea level) in 2012 and walked the Great Wall of China in 2009. We have also shared our love for exciting explorations with our children. We have taken our kids on summer safaris to Africa, and we've fished off the Great Barrier Reef in the Coral Sea off the coast of Australia.

The first date I ever had with Peggy was even an adventuresome hunting trip. Back when my sister, Keleigh, and I were still in school at A&M, she was dating her future husband, Stuart Sasser, and they planned to take my father's plane to Fort Worth to watch the Corps of Cadets march-in prior to a TCU-A&M football game and then to fly into Van Horn (120 miles southeast of El Paso) to go hunting on a ranch roughly 40 minutes outside Van Horn. Since I was participating in the march-in, Keleigh, suggested that I join them on the hunting trip and then mentioned that her friend, Peggy, was no longer envisioning a long-term future with the young man who'd been her boyfriend. I was thrilled at Keleigh's suggestion to also invite Peggy—so thrilled that I even went along with the plan to skip watching the game at Amon Carter Stadium in Fort Worth. It was on that trip that Peggy shot her first mule deer. As fate would have it, we spotted the deer on my side of the vehicle. I told her she couldn't step out of the vehicle because the mule deer would run away. Instead, she had to scoot extremely close to me in order to fire the shot out the window. It wasn't planned, but it worked out quite well.

Ever since that moment, Peggy and I have shared our passion for adventure and the great outdoors with family and friends. Voyages, explorations and outdoor challenges thrill and inspire us. We're not so much "thrill seekers" as we are adventure/adrenaline fanatics. And not just as it relates to hunting, fishing, traveling and so forth, although hunting and fishing are certainly some of our great passions. In fact, I was appointed to the Texas Parks and Wildlife Commission on June 16, 2009 by Governor Rick Perry, and on January 27, 2014, Governor Perry appointed me as the Chairman of the Texas Parks and Wildlife Commission. I served as Chairman until the end of my term, which expired in December of 2015. Those were terrific honors, especially because of my love for the outdoors and adventures.

Here's my point: life is an adventure—not a mundane existence—that is meant to be lived at its fullest. Likewise, business and entrepreneurship are exciting endeavors that are meant to be pursued with all the passion, adrenaline and adventure of a bear or lion hunt. It's all a matter of perspective, and your perspective—how you approach your day-to-day activities—will ultimately determine whether you spend your life chasing a paycheck or pursuing your passions. Speaking from experience, I can assure you that practically any profession can be viewed as either inspiring or draining. You can view each day as a new adventure or the same old drudgery. I've chosen the adventuresome route/mindset, and I encourage you to do the same.

I have such tremendous job satisfaction that I don't really view my career as "work." We haven't always made the right decisions, and we have drilled plenty of dry holes. We've also found oil and gas at times without really making any significant money. But I've tried to learn from all of my mistakes, and I still love the daily pursuit of the next big deal that pushes the needle and revs up our company. Identifying a potential oilfield—whether it's in South Texas or South America—and then transforming the prospect into a producer excites and energizes me. In fact, I love what I do so much that I will probably never retire…much like my father. At the time of this writing, my dad is 87, and he still comes into the office practically every day. I may eventually be in the office far less often than my father because I love being on a boat, visiting the ranch and traveling the globe with Peggy. But the point is that I am still absolutely passionate about what I do, which I attribute to the perspective I have maintained through the years.

Peggy and I are thrilled that both of our sons, Dan Allen III (D.A.) and William, have chosen to follow in the oil and gas footsteps of their great-grandfather, their grandfather and their father, as well as many other family members. But more than just being excited about their decisions to pursue the family business, we're delighted that they, too, are passionate about the profession. Likewise, Peggy and I are ecstatic that our daughter, Elizabeth, is also pursuing her dreams. She is inspired by cooking and culinary arts, and she is ambitiously seeking a career in that field. What I've continually encouraged my children to do is to track down their dreams with the same fervor of tracking an animal on an African safari. Fortunately, the successes we've enjoyed in the oil and gas industry have allowed our family to travel the globe on fishing trips, hunting expeditions and so forth, which have been great teaching moments and metaphors for life and business pursuits. But it wasn't always that way. We still pursued our passions when we were living on peanut butter and jelly sandwiches. The budget was just significantly different then than it is now.

Because of the successes we've enjoyed, I now have an opportunity to speak to many young people in business settings and back at Texas A&M. Inevitably, the subject of advice comes up, and while I am hesitant to offer specific advice without knowing your background or the entrepreneurial field you will choose, there are a few general principles I believe practically every entrepreneur can implement and utilize.

Although there are some people who do it effectively, I typically discourage young men and women from going into business for themselves right out of college or vocational training. For most people, it is much wiser to find a job and gain work experience before starting a business. I understand that many entrepreneurs are born with an insatiable desire to go out on their own as quickly as possible. That internal drive is what often separates entrepreneurs from lifelong paycheck collectors. I felt the drive and was compelled to chart my own course right out of college, as well, but I am ever so thankful that I first learned under the training of my uncle and father. They were great mentors for me, and I think finding mentors is extremely important for anyone.

Whether it is a family member, friend, community icon or complete stranger, I encourage you to identify a mentor who has achieved what you want or is aggressively pursuing his/her dreams. Approach that person respectfully and genuinely and seek his/her time (perhaps a lunch) and advice. I think many young people are hesitant to approach a successful CEO or entrepreneur for fear of being rejected, rebuked, ridiculed or something along those lines. In reality, though, nothing is more flattering to a CEO/entrepreneur than to be approached by a young and ambitious person who is sincerely interested in learning from that CEO/entrepreneur. Obviously, a business owner's time is valuable, so be respectful of the time that person can give you. Learn all you can from a mentor and build up your confidence before taking the proverbial leap of entrepreneurial faith. And once you begin developing your own business plan, bounce your ideas off a mentor whom you trust before going out on your own. Doing so will likely save you thousands upon thousands of dollars and plenty of headaches, as well.

Another positive associated with going into the work force right out of college—as opposed to immediately pursuing your entrepreneurial dreams—is the ability to gain a grasp of how a business operates at all levels of a company or organization. Too many young people go into the work force and focus only on their own jobs and daily roles. But if you truly have a dream of running your own organization, study every department and talk to other employees in sales, marketing, finance, technology, human resources, etc. View your initial jobs as paid training in preparation for one day leading your own venture. Even if you have to change jobs early in your career because you discover that a particular field is not what you want to do, that is perfectly OK. But view each job and each position you hold within an organization as a golden opportunity to learn what you want to do as a business owner and also what you want to avoid. And no matter how tedious, boring or miserable some of your initial jobs may be, stick with them for a while…and learn. Remember, it's all about perspective.

I also encourage you to embrace challenges in the work place and volunteer for new roles. So many employees merely want to do as little as possible to earn their paychecks. But again, if your dream is to one day run your own business, don't be afraid to take chances and to step outside your comfort zone. You may fail from time to time and you will likely struggle when performing new roles. But be grateful for the struggles. As I look back on my own career, those times when I struggled and failed also represent the greatest growth periods in my professional development. It's never easy to welcome struggles when you are in the midst of them, but heed the instructions of the Biblical verses found in James 1:2-4, which state: "Consider it pure joy, my brothers and sisters, whenever you face trials of many kinds, because you know that the testing of your faith produces perseverance. Let perseverance finish its work so that you may be mature and complete, not lacking anything." That's applicable to virtually anything in life, regardless of your faith/denomination/religion.

As you gather ideas, learn lessons from mentors and develop perseverance through trials and obstacles, I encourage you to begin working on writing and perfecting your business plan. When the time is right, you will need that business plan to acquire start-up funding. I always try to encourage young people to seek marketers and investors instead of trying to fund projects on their own. And I also encourage you to seek funding from sources other than a bank loan or conventional line of credit. As I mentioned in the paragraph about mentors, I think many young people are hesitant to approach successful businessmen, entrepreneurs and individuals about investing in their start-up organizations for fear of being rejected, rebuked or ridiculed. But the reality is that a successful entrepreneur is far more likely to recognize a great idea and well-structured business plan than a typical bank loan officer. I am always interested in looking for new investment opportunities. In fact, I have a man who works for me and a big part of his job is looking at other opportunities.

The key to piquing the interest of a potential investor is to have a game plan. If you want me to invest in your vision, you must show my why it is a good investment for me. Give me an idea of the return on investment that you project five and 10 years down the road. Make sure you have all your ducks in a row before sitting down with a potential investor. Return to your mentor(s) and make the presentation first to him/her. Run ideas by successful businessmen you know and ask them if they see any obvious deficiencies in your presentation and business plan. Who knows? Your mentor may be so impressed that he/she will invest in your vision first. Most successful entrepreneurs are quite willing to help young, motivated and enthusiastic young men and women who truly want to pursue their entrepreneurial dreams with great passion.

Quite frankly, that is one of the primary reasons why I invest so much time and money back into Texas A&M. My father and uncle credit Texas A&M for much of their success. Peggy and I both are extremely grateful to Texas A&M, as well, for providing us with a great foundation for success. That's why we've supported Texas A&M academically and athletically for many years. In 2009, for example, my father, my uncle, my wife and I provided the lead gift for A&M's Berg-Hughes Center for Petroleum and Sedimentary Systems. My father also made a significant gift to renovate Military Walk—the pedestrian greenway that links Sbisa Dining Hall to the Memorial Student Center Complex, and our family has previously endowed faculty chairs in geosciences. Peggy and I have also invested in the $450 million redevelopment of Kyle Field, as well as making financial contributions to the Davis Player Development Center at the south end of Kyle Field. And we love returning to A&M to speak to aspiring entrepreneurs like you.

Trust me when I say that you are in the right place to develop and grow your entrepreneurial dreams. Texas A&M University has a long history of producing great men and women in practically every business field imaginable. There are literally thousands upon thousands of remarkable stories involving Aggies who have gone into business for themselves, overcome great odds in various industries and accomplished great things. I encourage you to be bold, to be assertive, to treat every day as a new adventure, to learn from every experience and to maintain a positive perspective about your own dreams and visions. You can write the next chapter in a book like this, and I look forward to reading it and celebrating your success.

5.
Terrence Murphy
CEO/Broker/Founder of TM5 Properties
Texas A&M Class of 2005

MURPHY'S PATH TO TEXAS A&M

**Terrence and Erica Murphy with their children:
Teryn, Tatiana and Terrence, Jr.**

Looking back on my childhood and my route to Texas A&M University, I probably didn't fully appreciate the difficulty of the journey. That's not a misprint. I know some people look back on their childhood as a carefree time in their lives, and they long for those simpler, easier times. I am not one of those people.

Growing up in Chapel Hill, a small rural community a few miles east of Tyler, made earning a scholarship to Texas A&M difficult. It was not a particularly carefree time in my life. Not having a great relationship with my biological father, watching neighborhood friends fall victim to drugs and crime, seeing my mother battle for her life following a heart attack, flipping burgers at Dairy Queen, sacking groceries at Albertsons to help make ends meet and attracting college recruiters while playing on a football team that went 1-19 my first two years on the varsity did not make for an easy path to Aggieland. Besides, my high school had not produced a major, Division I scholarship player in almost 10 years, so the odds of being noticed were stacked against me. These are just a few obstacles I encountered, which combined to give me the chip on my shoulder at the time…and one I still carry to this day. It wasn't my choice to do things the hard way; it was just my only option. I would have changed some things about my story, but to be totally honest, that's life and it produced grit, substance and a never-ending desire in me to work hard at an early age.

I truly give thanks for obstacles now. A muscle grows stronger when it encounters resistance; diamonds are formed because of high temperatures and pressure; trees grow deep roots and develop the stress wood they need to remain upright in response to battering winds; and people develop strength, character and courage when encountering and overcoming challenges. Every person in this book and practically every successful person on the planet has faced adversities that have strengthened them. We all know that trials test, toughen and train us for greater triumphs. It's just that in the midst of storms and adversities, it is not easy or natural to embrace the difficulties. But once you see the rainbow after the storm, you can appreciate the journey.

Fortunately for me, I can clearly see now that the difficulties and challenges I faced in my past shaped me into the man I am today. Without a doubt in my mind, I wouldn't be where I am without all the difficult circumstances I've faced. I say that not to pat myself on the back or to make my story seem more entertaining or heroic. I say that to encourage you if you are going through difficult times. And chances are that if you are not going through challenges and hurdling obstacles right now, you will be in the near future or may have already dealt with them in your past. That's just the nature of life and entrepreneurism. But my hope is that my story can be a source of encouragement to you as you encounter the inevitable struggles of life or if your blueprint for success doesn't go as planned. The bottom line is that—sooner or later—life is probably going to send you to the school of hard knocks. When you're there, make sure you earn your education. Learn from hard times, make the most of difficult circumstances and remember that the biggest challenges will ultimately prepare you for the biggest growth and success. I feel like I am living proof of that and I want to encourage anyone reading this chapter with this simple reminder: It's not where you start that matters; it's where you are going.

Throughout my life God has continually allowed me to face enough trials and tribulations to prepare me for greater triumphs than I could have imagined in endeavors that I could have never envisioned. I never fathomed, for example, that before my 30th birthday I would rank among the top one percent of realtors in the Bryan-College Station market or that I would be one of 50 finalists in the country for the National Association of Realtors' prestigious 30 under 30 Award. To think that my real estate brokerage, TM5 Properties, would make the Aggie 100 in our first year of being eligible or that we would have roughly $250 million in sales in our first few years as a group of realtors still boggles my mind. Quite frankly, my original plan never involved returning to Bryan-College Station, winning real estate awards or becoming an entrepreneur. In my early 30s, I figured I would still be helping the Green Bay Packers win Super Bowls en route to what would hopefully be a Hall of Fame-caliber career in the NFL.

But for reasons I will detail later, the Hall of Fame career in the NFL was out of the realm of possibilities before even the midway part of my rookie season. I had to find another way to achieve my dreams. In fact, I had to find entirely new dreams and passions for my life.

I was born prematurely on December 15, 1982 to a wonderful woman named Brenda Lee in Tyler, Texas. Unfortunately, my father did not play a significant role in my childhood after my parents divorced. Even when he did make an effort to see me, he was completely unreliable. One of the things from my childhood that is emblazoned in my mind is sitting with my older brothers and sister while we all waited for our fathers to pick us up (I had a different biological father than the other older siblings). Their dad came and picked them up, but many times I would be left behind waiting on the front porch or being told some excuse by my mom. My father's lack of involvement in my life and inconsistency taught me at an early age to learn how to navigate problems and figure out how to watch other people's actions and how they interacted. I truly believe God wired me a certain way, but this produced a drive within me to depend on myself and not make any excuses for what may have been perceived as adverse circumstances in terms of economic status, background, neighborhood, etc. Those things lit a fire in me and ultimately fueled me to be extremely independent and driven. Like practically every other kid, I wanted my father to be a role model, my hero, my biggest fan or to be told that he was proud of me. When it became obvious that was not going to happen, I dreamed a different dream.

While I didn't have a biological father to lead, encourage or inspire me, I did have a great mother and teachers, coaches and principals who saw something different in me as child. I also had sports, and I channeled much of my energies and frustrations into becoming the best athlete possible. From a young age, I could do things on baseball diamonds, basketball courts and football fields that others could not. I also realized that talent alone could not take me where I wanted to go. So, I worked, trained, studied, prepared and prayed as if my entire future depended on the progress I made the next day.

Baseball was actually my best sport, but ever since my mother bought me a Doug Williams/Washington Redskins uniform as a young child—it was a Christmas present that she hoped could double the following fall as a Halloween costume—football became my primary passion. It also didn't hurt that that my older brother, Kendrick Bell, was an exceptional all-around athlete who led Chapel Hill High School to the 1989 Class 4A state championship, beating A&M Consolidated in the title game and rushing for more than 1,500 yards during the season. While Kendrick was admired by many football fans in the community, he was absolutely adored by me. Kendrick was more than just my brother; he was my first hero, taking the place of my biological father. When my mother was forced to work nights, it was Kendrick who would pick me up at the daycare after his football practices, take me home and feed me. On many of those nights before I went to bed, Kendrick would allow me to watch game film with him as he studied an upcoming opponent.

After his stellar high school career, Kendrick went to Baylor, where he played running back his first two years and cornerback his final two seasons. From time to time, I was even able to hang out with Kendrick in Waco, spending a couple of nights at a time with him and his teammates in their apartment. I grew to love Baylor football and further admire and appreciate Kendrick. Watching my brother and my hero win a state championship and earn a college scholarship made me want to do the same thing. I knew collegiate athletics could serve as my ticket to a much brighter and better future.

My total focus on becoming a scholarship-worthy athlete helped me to avoid many of the pitfalls and temptations that derailed some of my friends and other teenagers in the area. Following my mother's heart attack—an ordeal that nearly took her life—I spent virtually all my time working, going to school, playing sports or working out. At 15, I was sacking groceries, flipping burgers and mowing yards to earn my own money and ease the financial burden on my mother and step-father. I certainly wasn't the coolest guy in the neighborhood when I was dropping fries in the hot grease. But even then I wasn't just enduring those tedious jobs; I was paying attention and learning from everything and everyone around me. I knew then it was all a test and God had a greater plan for my life. Not once did I believe that I was destined for hourly jobs with little room for growth. I knew there was more. I just needed to be patient, pay my dues and be prepared for an opportunity if it presented itself.

I have always been a chameleon in my ability to blend into an environment and to learn as I watched others. Way back at Dairy Queen I figured out that there are people with an employee mentality, and there are people who are meant to lead or to be creators. There is absolutely nothing wrong with an employee mentality, and I know many friends and colleagues who can/will happily spend 45 years in the workplace working for others. I think it is very important to realize that if you have that mentality, entrepreneurism is probably not right for you. But if you are a risk taker, believe in yourself at all times, are driven to control your own destiny and are OK with no guaranteed salary, then you're reading the right book.

Honestly, I didn't really know what entrepreneurism was at 15, but I knew I had something deep within me—a gene or something within the core of my being—that made me always step to the front of the line and to step out of the crowd, as opposed to following the "cool kids." Obviously, I didn't immediately demand to take over the managerial role at Dairy Queen, but I did figure out relatively early in my life that I wanted to eventually call my own shots and set the course of direction in the workplace instead of merely following instructions and working for someone else. While I couldn't immediately do that in the work setting, I found another outlet.

In the late 1990s, 7-on-7 football started gaining strong popularity across the state of Texas. Nowadays, there is a Texas State 7-on-7 Association, and the whole process is a well-oiled machine. But during my high school days things began taking shape, and teams were competing around the state in the spring and summer. Because of various UIL rules, coaches from the high schools couldn't actually coach the teams, couldn't oversee practices and couldn't officially do a lot of other things. Our coaches at Chapel Hill had designed some plays and a basic offensive system for us to run that we would then carry into my senior season at quarterback. But after glancing at the plays, I called a mandatory practice with all the skill position guys from the football team at Chapel Hill. We spent about 45 minutes to an hour running the plays our coaches had designed. After practice, I told the guys, "We are not running this crap." Instead, I had my own plan that would make our offense unstoppable.

I went home that night and designed a new offense, with new formations and a new system in which to call the plays. Then I called my top guys and told them on the phone the game plan. We had more than 30 new plays from scratch. I taught those plays to my guys; we practiced them regularly; and we set off to win games against other teams in East Texas in hopes of making it to the state 7-on-7 tournament at Texas A&M. Sound like a risk taker to you?

Nobody figured we had a prayer because of how poorly the Chapel Hill regular-season football teams had been in recent falls. To make a long story short, though, we almost went undefeated through East Texas. We not only made it to College Station for the state tournament; we also made it to the final day of competition at A&M, and we were among the top 15 teams. My teammates were thrilled, but our regular high school coaches were essentially pissed off that I had changed their plays. My hope was that our coaches would see the effectiveness of my offensive system (it was similar to what Mike Leach was doing at that time at Texas Tech) and that we would implement that offense into the Chapel Hill system in the fall. That never happened, and we continued to stumble. All the success from the 7-on-7 fizzled.

During my sophomore year—my first on the varsity—we went 0-10. The following year when I took over as the starting quarterback, we made some dramatic improvements, but we still went 1-9. During my senior year, though, we quadrupled our win total. While that sounds good, it actually means we went 4-6 and didn't have a single winning season in my high school career. During the final two years, I passed for more than 2,500 yards, rushed for over 1,100 yards and contributed to 25 touchdowns. Despite our win-loss record, those numbers helped me to win the District 16-4A Offensive MVP in 2000 in a district that produced over 20 Division I signees in one year.

I think those numbers and my overall play should have helped me earn the attention of many college coaches and recruiting services. But I simply didn't receive any help from my high school coaches in terms of promoting me to college suitors. I don't know what any of my high school coaches said or didn't say to college coaches, but I do know that I had to produce my own highlight films to send to college coaches… and this was long before the simplicity of digital video technology that practically anyone can compile into a collection of plays. Fortunately for me, there was a teacher at Chapel Hill who ran what we called "Bulldog TV," and she had all the audio and video equipment, as well as the actual footage from the games that I needed. I told her I would sweep her floors, clean her room and perform any necessary grunt work in exchange for some access to the video recorders. I was able to piece together my own highlight tapes. Then I wrote letters to college coaches, following up with phone calls and more phone calls.

The point is—and this also applies to entrepreneurism—that even if you don't know exactly what to do, take action. Doing something is far, far better than doing nothing. If I had merely waited on my high school coaches to take any initiative in my recruiting efforts, I might have never played big-time college football. I was not going to let my problems become bigger than my dreams. I could focus on the problems or focus on the opportunity at hand (a scholarship to a major university), which at the time was the biggest opportunity of my life.

Primarily because of my familiarity with Baylor, along with the school's knowledge of my brother's accomplishments in green and gold, I initially committed to play for the Bears, who were then coached by Kevin Steele. I had also taken a recruiting trip during my senior year to A&M to watch the 2000 game against No. 1-ranked Oklahoma, and even though the Aggies lost a close game to a team that eventually won the national championship, I was extremely impressed with the electric atmosphere of Kyle Field. I was not a five-star recruit, but this was the time where desire and a never-ending work ethic opened the door of opportunity.

Texas A&M head coach R.C. Slocum had commitments from many big-time recruits in that particular signing class and had a few scholarships left. Assistant coach Tam Hollingshead convinced him to watch the highlight tape I had spent countless hours making, and it was an instant success.

Coach Slocum called an immediate coaching staff meeting and they called me from a speakerphone to offer me a scholarship. When Coach Slocum offered me a scholarship after reviewing my highlight film, I took a few weeks to come around to make sure A&M really wanted me. Then I leapt at the opportunity to build a football future and to earn an education in Aggieland. This was truly a life-defining moment, and it was the opportunity I had spent countless hours dreaming about and working toward. The road to that successful moment in my life was very lonely at times, because I was on a mission that no one around me thought was remotely possible. But I believed it was possible, and I did not let anyone talk me out of the dream. It may seem cliché, but looking back at the odds that were against me, it was only remotely possible with God's favor and a never-ending work ethic.

Once I received the opportunity, I vowed to make the most of it. I only thought I had worked hard in high school. When I arrived in College Station in the summer of 2001, I slept on a couch of some guys on the team, and I was a man on a mission. I busted my butt in the weight room and during voluntary workouts, and I made quite an impression on my teammates, including veteran quarterback Mark Farris, who had a spectacular season in 2000. The reporters asked Farris about the younger guys who had impressed him, and he mentioned me prominently. In making a position switch from quarterback to wide receiver, I also benefitted from some great coaching, as A&M had just hired a talented and tremendous teacher of the game named Kevin Sumlin as the wide receivers coach.

The hard work paid off right away. In my first collegiate game, I caught four passes for 79 yards and a touchdown in a 38-24 win over McNeese State, a game we trailed by two touchdowns in the third quarter. I caught the game-winning touchdown in the fourth quarter and was overwhelmed with emotion because I knew the journey I had traveled to reach that point. That was the start of a strong debut season for me in maroon and white. Farris trusted me right from the start, Coach Sumlin mentored me, and I learned from the veteran receivers on the roster. By the end of the season, I led the entire team in receiving yards and average yards per catch, and I finished second behind only Jamaar Taylor with 36 receptions. Even though I dealt with a number of injuries and missed the season-opener in 2002, my sophomore season was even better from an individual standpoint. My overall numbers were better, and in the biggest win of the year and one of the biggest in school history, I caught five passes for 128 yards and two touchdowns in our 30-26 upset victory over No. 1-ranked and previously undefeated Oklahoma. Unfortunately, after the amazing victory over the Sooners, we dropped the next two games and Coach Slocum was fired after the season. It was extremely difficult to say goodbye to him, as well as Coach Sumlin, whom I trusted tremendously.

Murphy left A&M as the school's all-time leading receiver

A&M hired Dennis Franchione as the head coach for that next season and following the devastating 2003 season for our team— it was actually my best year statistically to that point—I did plenty of praying, soul-searching and deliberating. I received plenty of calls about leaving Texas A&M early for the NFL Draft, but I could not leave a university that had done so much for me in the state that the program was headed going into my senior season. I decided to return for my senior season and I resolved to carry Texas A&M's football program and its proud history on my back. On one hand, it wasn't my job to pull the team back together. But the reality is that my senior year was on the horizon. I believed that if I didn't take the lead—with my actions and my words—the dysfunction, doubt and disgust would continue to increase while the team chemistry would continue to disintegrate. In essence, I decided that I was going to do everything I could to unify the team, with or without any input from the coaching staff.

My solution was to work even harder than ever before. Not just in practices or mandatory workouts, either. When other guys would go hang out, I would go out to the practice fields to work on my quickness, conditioning and commitment in the dead of night. It didn't matter if it was 10 p.m., midnight or 12:30 a.m.,

I was going to put in the work to lead by actions. It didn't take long for guys—especially younger players—to begin trying to emulate my efforts and dedication. And whenever the opportunity presented itself, I used my words to encourage my teammates to push themselves beyond their comfort zones. The turnaround in 2004 certainly was not a result of only my efforts. Many other guys contributed and helped us to rally the troops, generating the unity we needed. Despite a tough start at Utah, we rolled to six straight wins and finished the regular season at 7-4 overall. It certainly wasn't a championship season, but we did earn an invitation to the 2005 Cotton Bowl.

My senior season was the best of my career, as I caught 56 passes and earned first-team All-Big 12 honors. I departed A&M as the leading receiver in school history in receptions and receiving yards, and I was a three-time member of the Big 12 All-Academic team and a two-time All-Big 12 first team selection. Most of all, I was proud of how I was leaving the football program. Practically every senior class wants to leave a legacy, and I believe the senior class of 2004-05 restored some of the luster that was completely lost during the humiliating 2002 and 2003 seasons. I was proud to have played a prominent role in turning things around and placing the Aggies back in a New Year's Day bowl game for the first time since 1998. I hadn't enjoyed playing for Franchione, but I had made the most of my senior season and placed myself in position to fulfill my childhood dreams of playing in the NFL. As I looked toward the 2005 NFL Draft, my football future seemed bright. I had positioned myself as a lock for being selected in the first two rounds of the NFL Draft.

MURPHY'S MOST DIFFICULT CHALLENGE

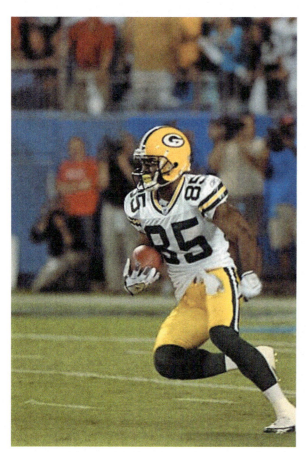

Murphy was a second-round draft pick of the Packers in 2005, the same year his career was cut short by a neck injury

As long as I live, I'll never forget the night of February 6, 2011. I wanted to be happy. I also wanted to feel some sort of satisfaction. But I couldn't even fake a grin because, at the core of my being, I was miserable. Across the country and around the world, millions upon millions of people had spent the day celebrating with friends, family and fellow football fans at Super Bowl parties. But now that the game was over, I was holding a pity party in my bedroom. The Green Bay Packers had beaten the Pittsburgh Steelers in Super Bowl XLV before a capacity crowd of 103,219 at Cowboys Stadium in Arlington. Not only had my former team captured the biggest prize in professional sports, but one of my best friends from my time in Green Bay—quarterback Aaron Rodgers—had just been awarded the MVP.

In 2005, the Packers used their first selection in the NFL Draft to take Rodgers with the 24th pick. They chose me after Nick Collins in the second round with their 58th choice. The three of us came into the league together, with Rodgers and Collins both playing huge roles in leading the Packers to a championship on the biggest stage in professional sports. I really was pleased for Aaron, Nick and many other guys I still knew on the team. The Packers invited me to attend the game and to stand on the sidelines. I appreciated the offer, but I declined. Instead, I watched the Super Bowl from my home in College Station, hoping I could merely be happy for all my former teammates.

When it was all said and done, I just felt sick to my stomach. I literally went to bed that night with tears in my eyes and a gut-wrenching emptiness in the pit of my stomach. Again and again, the thoughts that raced through my head were: "Why God? Why not me?

Hadn't I earned the right to be on that field with them?" It had been more than five years since my life changed in the blink of an eye on the night of October 3, 2005. During a kickoff return that night against the Panthers at Charlotte's Bank of America Stadium, I suffered a severe neck injury. I was momentarily paralyzed, and because of the severity of the neck injury, I never played another down and later retired from the NFL in 2007.

More than five years after the injury as I prepared to watch the Super Bowl, I thought I was done lamenting what might have been if my football career hand not ended. But the Packers' win in Super Bowl XLV brought all of those emotions—and many others—to the forefront of my consciousness. I went to bed that night with a heavy heart.

I thank God, however, for the life-altering, eye-opening transformation he provided me when I woke up the next morning. With the arrival of a new day, my eyes were opened to a new perspective. While my football career had ended more than five years earlier, I was obviously still holding on to the pain associated with having the game taken away from me. And quite frankly, I was holding on to other wounds and scars, as well. For example, after my injury, I returned to A&M and began working toward a postgraduate business degree with a specialty in real estate. The problem was that my heart wasn't completely in real estate; my heart was still in football. I figured the only way to satisfy the desires of my football-focused dreams at that time was to go into coaching.

I initially interviewed with Mike Sherman, who was then the head coach at Green Bay, but he didn't offer me a job. The collegiate program that offered me a coaching position right away was Trinity Valley Community College (TVCC) in Athens, Texas. I took the offer and moved into a dorm room on campus, where I coached for a year. I eventually received job offers from Green Bay and the Seattle Seahawks and turned them down in 2008 and 2009.

Looking back now, I realize God was speaking to me and through me, but I wasn't fully embracing the peace that transcends all understanding. At least I was focused enough on serving and honoring God that I made some good decisions that led me to where I am today. One of those decisions was to commit to pursuing a relationship with a beautiful woman—inside and out—named Erica Calabrese, whom I had first met while in college at Texas A&M. Erica, a graduate of the University of Texas, and I started off as mere acquaintances. We then developed a friendship, began communicating often and began thinking about taking things to another level. She supported me after the injury, and our relationship developed to the point that I was first committed to dating her exclusively. Soon afterward, I asked her to marry me.

We were engaged when I was at TVCC, and we were planning a future wedding when I attended a national coaches convention in Anaheim, California following that season at TVCC. I still believed coaching was the career of my future, and I was honestly pretty frustrated that I couldn't land a job on Mike Sherman's A&M staff after Franchione had been fired. Think about this: Sherman had been at Green Bay, my former team, and he was going to A&M, my alma mater, where I was still the leading receiver in school history. When Sherman was hired in Aggieland, I had a great interview with him. I thought it was meant for me to be on his staff…until I was told I was just too young. Even my mentor, Kevin Sumlin, didn't have an opening on his staff when he was hired at the University of Houston.

Obviously, God had different plans for me, and he began revealing those plans when I attended the coaching convention on the West Coast. Late one evening I was in my hotel room, falling asleep with the TV still on, although I was not paying much attention to what was airing. I awoke to an infomercial that featured entrepreneur Robert Kiyosaki talking about financial education and generating passive income by means of business and investment opportunities, such as real estate investments. It was just background noise at first, but as I began to hear Kiyosaki, the author of the book *Rich Dad Poor Dad*, discuss financial education and achieving financial independence through investments rather than seeking a paycheck, I sat up in bed and began to take notes. Some people may call it coincidence, but I really took that infomercial with Robert Kiyosaki as a sign from God. It just so happened that I had the TV on a channel that featured Robert Kiyosaki's infomercial. That infomercial was like the match that started an internal fire within me for the real estate industry. It should be noted that, while the Kiyosaki infomercial truly did serve as a spark, it did not yet light an inferno.

God truly blessed me in my commitment to Erica, and we were married on February 18, 2008. On our honeymoon, I told her that I felt like God was calling me back to College Station. She looked at me in stunned disbelief and said: "College Station? You didn't get the job at A&M. Why College Station?" Quite frankly, I couldn't explain it, but I definitely felt a calling to begin a real estate career in College Station. Fortunately, my bride supported my decision. Against the better judgement—and the stern advice—of my financial advisor, I also took most of my money that I had and began making my own real estate investments. One thing I learned about start-up companies or entrepreneurships is that you can read books all day long, but there's something extremely important about making the leap and going for it in the real world. It was kind of like me putting high school tapes together all over again. I didn't know exactly what I needed to do, but I knew it was time to take action.

At about that same time, the coaching job offers began pouring in from both the NFL and collegiate levels. But we had bought a house, and I really believed that entrepreneurism—not football—was my future. One of the first things I did once we returned to College Station was to visit a local bookstore. As I browsed through the real estate, finance and personal investment sections, I was drawn to a Robert Kiyosaki book called *Who Took My Money?* I had never been a particularly fast reader, but that book piqued my interest from the opening page, and I finished it in two days. Kiyosaki's book stoked my entrepreneurial flame. I conceived the name for my business—TM5 Properties—and eventually bought a couple of duplexes near Kyle Field that were run-down, drug-infested messes. Erica began teaching at an elementary school in College Station and I began studying the real estate market. I didn't have my real estate license, but I began calling realtors asking them to show me houses. I needed to network and make contacts; I needed to learn the market; and I needed to begin renovating the duplexes I had purchased. My original vision was merely to buy distressed properties, renovate them and sell or lease them. Eventually, I bought an entire block on Welsh Street off of George Bush Drive, tore down the dilapidated houses and built six or seven homes that made the street look like an entirely different neighborhood. This urban development raised a lot of eyebrows in town and catapulted me to the forefront as a serious player in the real estate market.

I generated some momentum, began producing profits and turned plenty of heads. I then shifted my attention toward possibly building custom homes, and in 2008, I decided to buy a small retail business. The goal for the retail business was to get it up and running and then turn it into passive income. I also liked the idea of income diversification. But after about a year and a half of pouring my time, energy and money into the retail business, I was miserable. I discovered that retail was a 24-hour-a-day, seven-days-a-week headache. After two years in retail and lots of discussion with Erica and my accountant, I closed the business. Our first child was born in September 2010, and I shut down the store in December. At that point, I decided I really needed to pray for God to reveal my future course of direction. I needed a true passion, and I felt like a failure in many ways, because of the way my NFL career ended and my failing in the retail business. I don't pretend to know the mind of God, but my suspicion is that, as I prayed for career direction, God must have been wondering, "How many times do I have to show you that real estate is your future?"

Fortunately, my frustration with the retail business had driven me to earn my real estate license. I initially started working at a major real estate office in the Bryan-College Station area, and I did well, but I also wasn't pouring all my efforts into it. I owned eight or nine houses that I was leasing, and I was still looking for investment homes while I was working as a realtor. In other words, I was selling homes, but I was not sold out to my career as a realtor. Looking back, I needed something to jolt me out of my half-hearted approach and my semi-depression regarding lost opportunities. That "something" I needed occurred on February 6, 2011 when the Packers beat the Steelers to win the Super Bowl. I went to bed thinking, "Why me?"

After my morning prayers, however, I finally understood what God was trying to tell me: Real estate could be my passion, fuel my competitive drive and lead me to a business "Super Bowl" of sorts. That morning, with tears in my eyes, I told Erica that I recommitted myself to her and to lead our family because I was working so much in the retail business and had drug her through the ups and downs of retail entrepreneurship. I also wrote "Real Estate is my Super Bowl" on a piece of paper and vowed to dominate the Bryan-College Station real estate market going forward. That injury could have haunted me for the next 40 years if I allowed it. I realized I couldn't live in the past like that. I realized my greatest achievements were not meant to be on a football field; I realized I had achieved a lot of amazing things by the age 22, but my best days were still ahead. I was meant to be an entrepreneur and to provide a service to others.

MURPHY'S PATH TO ENTREPRENEURIAL SUCCESS

Once I made the decision to truly become all that I could be in the real estate industry—as opposed to continuing to be haunted by what might have been as a pro football player—my ultimate success was practically predetermined. Let that statement sink in for a moment. It may initially come across as incredibly cocky or arrogant, but it's really one of the fundamental principles of success in any industry.

Success is often dependent on focus and determining exactly what you want. Perhaps there are some exceptions, but from my experience, it is virtually impossible to haphazardly enter a profession, dabble in it—as I initially had done in real estate—and become a major success in it. In that regard, life is much like a camera in that the clarity of your focus determines your overall development. Throughout history, many wise men and women have eloquently reached the same conclusion. For example:

- "There is one quality which one must possess to win, and that is definiteness of purpose, the knowledge of what one wants, and a burning desire to possess it." – Napoleon Hill
- "Once you make a decision, the universe conspires to make it happen." – Ralph Waldo Emerson
- "You can have anything you want if you want it badly enough. You can be anything you want to be, do anything you set out to accomplish if you hold to that desire with singleness of purpose. Determine that the thing can and shall be done and then... find the way." Abraham Lincoln

My favorite author, Robert Kiyosaki, agrees that focus is a critical component to achieving any goals. His memorable acronym for f-o-c-u-s is: Follow One Course Until Successful.

TM5 Properties continues to earn honors and blaze new trails

No matter how you say it or recall the principle, I highly recommend that you not only commit it to memory, but also put it into practice in your own life and career. So many people go through their entire careers without any real passion for their profession or focus on their goals…other than reaching the end of the day or the week. They merely put in the time and expect—perhaps magically—to rise to the top of their profession. But if making it to the end of the week is your primary goal, your end results are likely to be quite weak. And if you are merely going through the motions, don't expect to be going to any special heights in your career or to build anything of value.

Fortunately for me, I realized at a fairly young age that I was, indeed, going through the motions in my life-after-football endeavors. I had entered an entrepreneurial profession by purchasing properties, but I didn't view myself as an entrepreneur, a realtor or anything of the sort. I still viewed myself as a football player who had been forced to retire. Furthermore, I initially figured that my name—Terrence Murphy, the football player—entitled me to entrepreneurial success, especially in College Station, where I had been a record-breaking wide receiver.

But the sense of entitlement, combined with my lack of focus, passion and commitment to entrepreneurism, practically assured me of being nothing more than a mediocre entrepreneur. Deep-down, I was still missing the sweat, hard work, pushing-yourself-to the-limit frame of mind that football provided me. But once I finally made up my mind that real estate could be my passion—or my Super Bowl—I began taking some major strides in the right direction.

For one thing, I began doing the things I needed to do, even the tedious, tiresome things I didn't want to do, in order to grow and prosper as an entrepreneur. When I was a football player, nobody worked harder in the weight room or after practice than me. I practically lived in the gym, pumping iron and pouring sweat to develop a chiseled physique that helped me succeed on the field. What most of my teammates and friends never realized, however, was that I hated the weight room. I loathed lifting weights, but I did it passionately and purposefully because I knew it would give me the advantage I needed on the field. It was the necessary evil I needed to learn to love in order to be a great football player.

The same goes for reading about entrepreneurism, finances, real estate, etc. When I decided to devote all my energy and efforts toward becoming a great realtor, I knew I needed to acquire a tremendous amount of knowledge. I didn't have a father, older brother or even a mentor to show me the real estate ropes or to help me avoid making multiple mistakes. In fact, I went to work for one of the larger brokerage firms in the Bryan-College Station area thinking that I would learn plenty about the industry from some of the experienced realtors in the office. You can't start your own brokerage until you earn your brokerage license, and I truly believed that I would receive plenty of training, advice and education from the proven and established realtors on the "team" I had joined.

I figured wrong. Most of the members of my new team viewed me more as a threat or adversary than a teammate. They didn't want to help or train me because they didn't want me to potentially cut into their sales or commissions. While that initially bothered me, it also propelled me to gain the industry knowledge I needed to succeed. With no other place to turn, I became a voracious reader, even though I really hated to read as much as I once hated to lift weights. From the time I was in kindergarten until I entered Texas A&M as a student, I read one book, cover-to-cover. Just one! I would skim through a book if it was an absolute necessity, but I would go to great lengths to avoid really reading a book. Reading has never been enjoyable for me, but I realized that in the world of entrepreneurship, you are on your own unless you have partners or co-founders. I wanted the advice of great entrepreneurs who had authored books, so I committed to stepping outside my comfort zone and doing what was necessary to succeed.

As a football player, that meant working out on my own when others had gone out to party or studying my playbook and film long after others had called it quits. As an ambitious entrepreneur, that meant reading 45 books in a span of about 18 to 24 months. And I didn't just skim through those books. I read them cover-to-cover, re-reading key chapters and making notes throughout the text. As I committed to learning and digesting as much knowledge as possible, my perspectives changed, my horizons broadened and I even began to enjoy—at least somewhat—reading on a regular basis. I was already inspired to make real estate my Super Bowl, but reading gave me definitive strategies, techniques and game plans to take me where I wanted to go. I earned my brokerage license in 2012, but I was already hitting the ground running, which is exactly what I did, becoming, among other things, one of 50 finalists in the country for the National Association of Realtors' prestigious 30 under 30 Award.

From the time TM5 Properties was founded in 2010 until November 2016, we completed more than 2,350 transactions, and we had one of the highest transactions per agent ratios in the market. Along with the success and growth of TM5, I personally completed 75 transactions for a total sales volume right at $20 million in 2012, 90 transactions for total sales of $22.5 million in 2014 and more than $30 million in total sales in 2016, ranking me in the top one percent of realtors in the Bryan-College Station market. I also found a knack for listing and selling farm and ranchland, and I was one of the only realtors in the BCS market to close four or more transactions that were minimum of 500-acre tracts in one calendar sales year. Overall, I completed more than 350 transactions totaling $100 million in total sales volume in my first 6.5 years as a realtor. I do not tell you that to brag. Those numbers should clearly show you that anything is possible with hard work, passion and the desire to learn and achieve.

In the fall of 2015 I was honored by Texas A&M by being chosen among the Aggie 100. The Aggie 100 identifies, recognizes and celebrates the 100 fastest-growing Aggie-owned or Aggie-led businesses in the world. The Aggie 100 not only celebrates their success, it also provides a forum to pass lessons to the next generation of Aggie entrepreneurs. It was created in 2005 by Mays Business School's Center for New Ventures and Entrepreneurship (CNVE). CNVE solicits nominations from around the world through the Aggie Network. To be considered for the Aggie 100, a company must have been in operation for five years or more; must have verifiable revenues of $250,000 or more; must be owned or operated by a TAMU former student or group of former students; and must operate in a manner consistent with the Aggie Code of Honor and in keeping with the values and image of Texas A&M. TM5 was ranked No. 37 overall in the 2015 Aggie 100, and we were the No. 1 residential real estate brokerage on the list, which was a tremendous honor. Then we made the Aggie 100 again in 2016. I celebrated by taking my wife—of course—to the luncheon, along with staff and friends.

People who do not know me well or do not know my story have often complimented me or commented about me being on the fast track to success. Many others have asked me about my secret to success, hoping that I might provide them with some shortcut to success. But the keys to success aren't so secretive, and they don't involve taking any shortcuts. Start by determining exactly what you want, sharpen your focus and begin working toward your dreams by taking action even if you aren't exactly sure how to begin. Take matters into your own hands. Move forward. You cannot generate any momentum without movement. I was always told God cannot steer a parked car. You've got to pull the car out the garage and start moving.

MURPHY'S ADVICE TO YOUNG ENTREPRENEURS

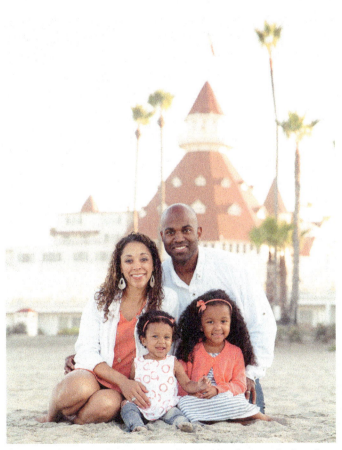

The Murphy crew loves to spend time together on the beaches

Humility is especially important in this day and age because it is so rare. From a young entrepreneurial/young professional standpoint, the lack of humility and the abundance of self-importance have created unrealistic expectations for so many young people who are just entering the marketplace or who are just opening their own business. As I have documented, I was not immune to those feelings despite my extremely humble, East Texas roots.

When I first left football, I believed I was entitled to a big-time job in football because, well, I deserved it. That was my mindset because of what I had done on the field at Texas A&M and the NFL. And when I first entered real estate I figured that my name alone would deliver me business and a long list of clients. In any endeavor, however, you must start at the bottom and earn your right to be heard or for people to give you an opportunity. I always encourage young people to find their passion, study, learn their craft, become an industry leader in your field and then success will follow. So many times we start this process backward. What's the first thing graduates ask?

How much am I going to make? Who cares? Find out if it's your passion. I know some people who are highly successful who initially worked for free just to get a foot in the door.

It wasn't until I humbled myself and began taking responsibility for my past and present that I began progressing toward reaching my dreams. So, I think my first piece of advice to any young entrepreneur is to humble yourself and to understand that entrepreneurial success, prosperity and financial independence are not your birthright and are not likely to be gained right away. When I hire young people—especially young college graduates—one of the first things I do is to give them grunt work. If they are huffing, puffing and complaining about menial paper work, they obviously aren't willing to humble themselves. I know plenty of aspiring, young entrepreneurs, particularly realtors in training, who want to see a picture of themselves on business cards, for-sale signs and billboards. Those are some of the "sexy," high-profile components of the industry, but none of those things will generate an ounce of business—in the real estate industry or practically any other—unless you are first willing to be a servant to others. It's extremely difficult to be any kind of a servant without humility.

Secondly, you need to find an industry or profession that truly ignites your passions. I think that is the foundation of success at any level. Much wiser and more successful men than me have said the same thing. For example, Steve Jobs said, "Your work is going to fill a large part of your life, and the only way to be truly satisfied is to do what you believe is great work. And the only way to do great work is to love what you do." Similarly, Warren Buffet said, "There comes a time when you ought to start doing what you want. Take a job that you love. You will jump out of bed in the morning. I think you are out of your mind if you keep taking jobs that you don't like because you think it will look good on your résumé. Isn't that a little like saving up sex for your old age?"

That does not mean, however, that you cannot develop a great passion for what you might not initially consider your dream job. I am living proof of that. My dream job was to be an All-Pro wide receiver in the NFL, who was regularly playing in Pro Bowls and Super Bowls. The only real estate that ever stirred my passions as a child, teen and young adult were 100-yard patches of green grass or artificial turf. But when that door was closed, I placed all my energies into helping others through real estate. I became absolutely passionate about my profession. I think you need to put all your energy on blooming where God has planted you. If you still don't enjoy it after a couple years of genuine effort and pouring yourself into a career field, then it might be time to move on and move forward. But there is something about making the best of every situation that builds character. Positive thinking generates positive results.

As an Aggie, I also really believe you must understand the "Aggie network." Going through school, all I heard was: "Aggies take care of Aggies." That set me up with some false expectations because I didn't realize I had to work the network. I didn't realize how to integrate myself into the network. I just figured I would flash my ring and send out a résumé or two and I would magically be taken care of by Aggies who wanted to hire me. But it takes more than that. It takes genuine relationships.

When I returned to College Station, I took on the challenge of going to every event I could where I might network. I wanted to trade business cards with anyone I could meet. There was nothing going on locally involving networking among Aggies that I didn't attend. On one hand, that taught me how to have a conversation and how to interact with people, but after a couple of months, all I had to show for my networking focus was a stack of business cards in my room. I wasn't doing anything with them, but I had them. I thought that was what networking was all about, and I couldn't understand why it wasn't working for me.

It took me a while to realize that if I didn't follow up to build an actual relationship with these people, they were just going to say, "Hey, I met Terrance Murphy. He is a nice guy and a good Aggie." But there is no relationship-building in that scenario. I was nothing more than an acquaintance. What I learned about that experience is you must work the network, but then you have to build genuine relationships with people. You must have a goal in mind and you must have a purpose. There has to be a specific thing. For me—and this is the secret to many industries—my goal became to develop a relationship. It wasn't about asking them for my business; it was about genuinely connecting with that person. That made all the difference for me, because I took the focus off of myself and placed it on building a relationship with others. Personal development coach Zig Ziglar stated it this way: "If people like you, they will listen to you. But if they trust you, they will do business with you."

As a result, the Aggie network began working for me, because there is no stronger network in America among college graduates than the Aggie network. I truly see that now. I didn't see that at 22 or 25, but I see it now because I know that Aggies want to work for Aggies and with Aggies. Also, I am not just reciting clichés. Of our 26 employees at TM5 Properties at the time of this writing, 19 are Texas A&M graduates. But the key to working the network is that there first must be a relationship. My advice now is to go to the networking opportunities and to focus on making a couple of great new friends, not collecting business cards. Make friends, develop bonds and see how God blesses your focus on being a friend instead of just trying to generate business and get your name or start-up idea out.

Finally, never lose your faith, your hope or your belief. Adversities will come your way. Trials will stop you in your tracks. Road blocks and detours will blindside you. But as you encounter difficulties remember my story and others in this book. Remember that a muscle grows stronger when it encounters resistance; diamonds are formed because of high temperatures and pressure; trees grow deep roots and develop the stress wood they need to remain upright in response to battering winds; and people develop strength, character and courage when encountering and overcoming challenges. You may not want to hear that in the midst of your struggles. But persevere. God is just strengthening you for the road ahead to make an impact in the lives of others and not just to be successful. Let me leave you with this quote by Zig Ziglar:

"Don't be distracted by criticism. Remember the only taste of success some people have is when they take a bite out of you."

Keep Pushing. Keep Dreaming. Keep Living. Keep Loving. Define Yourself. Let no one put you in a social box. We only get one shot at this life, so we have to live like it is our last week on earth.

6.

Artie McFerrin

Founder, President & CEO, KMCO, LP
President and Owner, South Coast Terminals
Author of *The Executioner: Implementing Intangible, Elusive Success Principles*
Texas A&M Class of 1965

McFERRIN'S PATH TO TEXAS A&M

Artie and Dorothy McFerrin on their wedding day and a "few" years later

As a seventh-grader in mid-November 1955, I traveled on a bus from my home in Beaumont, Texas to Houston's Rice Stadium to attend my first major college football game as part of a school-sponsored field trip. Although I could not have possibly predicted it at the time, attending that football game shaped my future in ways I could have never imagined.

I entered the stadium on November 12, 1955 with no allegiances to either team playing that day, Texas A&M or Rice. But I was captivated by the pageantry of the game-day experience, from the 68,000 fans inside the stadium to the music of the Fightin' Texas Aggie Band. The game was rather uneventful for much of the day, as Rice outplayed the Bear Bryant-coached Aggies and led 12-0 midway through the fourth quarter. Then A&M, led by Loyd Taylor on offense and Jack Pardee on defense, rallied furiously to score 20 points in two minutes and nine seconds. A&M's stunning, 20-12 comeback victory ended Rice's 10-game winning streak in the series and sent me back to Beaumont as a dyed-in-the-wool Aggie fan. It was just Bryant's second year as head coach at A&M, but he had already put his winning stamp on the program, and I was mesmerized by what I had just seen.

From that point forward, I started actively following the Aggies, who went 7-2-1 in 1955, 9-0-1 in '56 and reached No. 1 in the national polls in 1957, the same year John David Crow won the Heisman Trophy. I fell in love with Aggie football, Bryant, Crow, Pardee, Gene Stallings, Dennis Goehring, Charlie Krueger and many other Aggie players during those years, and that was the start of a lifelong passion for me. Six years after I attended my first Aggie football game, I became a student at Texas A&M, which at that time was still a predominantly male, military-affiliated school. I'd like to tell you I arrived at A&M and made as much of a positive impression in a relatively short time as Bryant, Crow, Pardee and so forth. But the reality is that I showed up at A&M and was as ineffective as the Aggies had been in the first year under Bryant, when A&M went 1-9 in 1954.

I've often wondered how shocked some of my old A&M classmates must have been when they first discovered that I managed to build successful, specialty chemical manufacturing companies around the world. I can only imagine their disbelief if they read I was awarded the Texas A&M Association of Former Students Distinguished Alumnus Award in 2008 or if they happened to notice that my name is featured prominently on several facilities on the A&M campus. My wife and I have been able to make some significant donations to several athletics-focused capital campaign projects, and the 12th Man Foundation arranged for our name to be placed on the buildings. Overall, my wife, Dorothy, and I have been able to donate more than $40 million to Texas A&M for education initiatives, the chemical engineering department and athletics. Dorothy and I have also spent over $70 million thus far on our Faberge collection that is featured in the Houston Museum of Natural Science.

I mention those things not to brag, but instead to encourage everyone—no matter where he/she may be right now—regarding the unlimited financial possibilities that exist in the future. I've spent countless hours studying successful people and the success principles they've implemented in their lives, and I've come to realize that anyone is capable of gaining control of his entrepreneurial future and soaring to remarkable heights by learning to think and act in the most effective ways. And I do mean "anyone." I am living proof of that. The people who knew me when I was a student at A&M must be dumbfounded that I would be featured in a book like this that celebrates successful entrepreneurism, because when I first arrived at A&M in the early 1960s, I could have easily been voted "Least Likely to Succeed" in my freshman class.

I was tall, but woefully short on valuable assets. I was about as mentally tough and physically menacing as a newborn Labrador puppy. I regularly thought about running back home to Beaumont during my first two years as a member of the Corps of Cadets. I probably would have returned home with my tail between my legs except for the fact that I knew my working-class, blue-collar parents would send me back to College Station. My father dropped me off at A&M in 1961, and he wished me good luck before driving home. I had never been in College Station previously, and I was totally unprepared for college, being on my own or enduring life in the Corps of Cadets.

Upperclassmen began barking orders and yelling at me. I essentially responded by shriveling into a corner like a scolded puppy. I already lacked self-confidence before I arrived in College Station, and the boot camp-like conditions of those early days at A&M turned me into a weak-kneed wallflower. I thought about transferring to an easier school—one without military training—and I probably would have left town if I had owned my own mode of transportation. I quickly concluded I was not cut out for the Corps or for A&M because I was softer than all of those leatherneck boys who'd been raised on farms. I was certainly not alone in that conclusion. The name on my uniform said: "McFerrin." It may have been more appropriate at the time, however, if it had read: "MeekFerrin."

Surviving those first two years in the Corps of Cadets was not easy, but those experiences taught me valuable lessons about myself—lessons I would file away and reference years later when I started my own business. I gained some much-needed courage from being in the Corps. It toughened me up, and I realized I could handle a high level of adversity by developing some tenacity. I also learned great lessons about responsibility, teamwork, values and confidence from being in the Corps of Cadets, as have many hundreds of thousands of other young people who have been trained in the Aggie Corps and other service academies.

Along the way, I realized that if I could juggle the rigors of the Corps with school, I could handle anything. I also had a breakthrough discovery of sorts, as I noticed the people who were most enthusiastic about the military training at A&M had a much better time than I did. The training was difficult for everyone, but a few guys figured out they could choose to have an attitude that actually made the training more tolerable. I resolved to be enthusiastic about whatever I did from then on, regardless of the level of difficulty of the task I chose to tackle. I had unnecessarily made it much tougher on myself than it needed to be by just trying to survive. I discovered that if you embrace a challenge—as opposed to merely enduring it—you greatly enhance your chances of success. I still didn't know how to be a leader or how to achieve success, but I did learn discipline, toughness and how to work as a team.

I stayed in the Corps of Cadets for two years and then spent the next two years focusing on my schoolwork. Despite my early doubts and deep-seeded insecurities, I gained a sense of accomplishment by earning a degree in chemical engineering. With that said, when I graduated in May 1965, my "self-esteem tank" was still closer to empty than full. I was apprehensive about entering the workplace…so I decided to stay in College Station and attend graduate school. I claimed I wanted an advanced degree in chemical engineering, but I was not ready to leave my comfort zone. The "real world" scared me, so I delayed facing it.

I earned my graduate degree from A&M in 1967, and I accepted a job—I finally had to face the real world—from Shell Oil in Deer Park, Texas (far southeast Houston area). Six years of higher education, including two years of military training and two years of post-graduate work, had elevated my self-worth barometer from an embarrassing low to a medium. I earned a couple of degrees to hang on my wall, but my greatest lessons in "success training" were still ahead of me.

McFERRIN'S PATH TO SUCCESS

In decades of studying what makes people thrive in their business and personal endeavors, I have come to realize there are really no "overnight" financial successes. Sure, there are lottery and jackpot winners, but there is a reason why many of those people—even after winning millions of dollars—typically wind up with nothing to show for their winnings. To truly change your financial circumstances, you must first change the way you think about money, entrepreneurism and success. If someone thinks poorly, he/she will most likely live in constant poverty, failing to become all that is possible because of self-limiting thoughts. Likewise, a person will never truly become an entrepreneurial success by thinking "conventionally" like a manager or an employee. Entrepreneurism is unique. It's an area of business that no one outside of an accomplished entrepreneur is likely to understand.

While it's true that even a blind squirrel will occasionally find a nut, no one will consistently achieve peak levels of success until he/she is able to consistently think in a successful manner. After all, we are what we think. Change the way you think, and you can change your world. That's been the case for me, as I have practiced and believed in a type of entrepreneurism that is based on the universal principles that are explained in Napoleon Hill's classic success book, *Think and Grow Rich*, originally published in 1937. Hill's book and my entrepreneurial foundation are based on a positive mental attitude (PMA), CEO thinking, goal setting, creativity and intangible success principles.

It's important to distinguish that my journey toward entrepreneurial success and my definition of entrepreneurism is much different from the conventional thinking that is prevalent in government and large business. That form of conventional thinking is based on intellectual knowledge that is typically taught in a classroom, verbal ability, politics, relationship building, organizational abilities and managerial qualities. Those things, while extremely valuable and desirable in the opinion of many people, contribute to a more linear form of success than I am referencing. Most large business organizations and government agencies practice the conventional, manager type of success. On the other hand, most of the highly successful entrepreneurs I have encountered or studied have typically implemented "CEO thinking" and universal success principles in building their entrepreneurial capabilities.

One thing I have noticed in common about both types of success is that it is basically up to you, as an individual, to determine how to become successful. Unfortunately, most universities and businesses do not teach their students or employees the specific life skills needed to ensure either type of success. We're mostly all on our own to learn, since society at large—or the education system—is primarily intent on enslaving the masses to meet the specific objectives of a select few.

That's why I am excited to be part of this book that covers a gamut on entrepreneurial backgrounds. In this book, you will see various entrepreneurial types and success methods with each chapter. You are free to choose the examples or methods that appeal to you the most…or to not make a choice at all. Most people do not realize they can make a choice. Instead, they simply plod forward in life and allow circumstances to dictate their future.

I chose a success principle-based method that offered me more freedom, opportunity and personal growth and allowed me to keep from being enslaved by others. However, my method doesn't fit everyone's strengths. For me, changing the way I think has changed my life. At every point in my career, I've discovered that when my attitude, thinking and perspective were right, everything worked at lightning speed. Until that point, however, nothing really "took off." The big breakthrough in my business life occurred when I finally learned how to think like a CEO/entrepreneur. But it took many years of programming my mind for success before I experienced a transformation from conventional thinking like a manager to thinking like a CEO.

According to Malcolm Gladwell's book, *Outliers: The Story of Success*, it takes 10,000 hours over 10 years of feeding your mind the "right stuff" before a real transformation occurs. I believe this rule applies to everything, from universal success principles to conventional thinking. It basically takes the human mind 10,000 hours of the right mental conditioning and the right confirming action to transform the brain into a higher state. No one has done it in less time. And no one starts out in life or in the work force with the "right stuff." Likewise, no one initially knows what the right stuff is or where to find it.

Artie and Dorothy McFerrin at a book signing

But trust me on this. If we do not transform ourselves, we'll never obtain a mastery of the way we think. Thinking like a CEO/entrepreneur can benefit you immeasurably, regardless of whether you plan to eventually run a *Fortune* 500 company or whether you are looking for ways to more effectively run a small business. The book I wrote, *The Executioner: Implementing Intangible, Elusive Success Principles*, uses the concept of learning and performing the high-level duties of a CEO to develop successful CEO thinking.

Unfortunately, most people never embark upon a career with an understanding of how important it is to learn how to think like a successful CEO. And most people never grasp the concept that we are all CEOs of ourselves and our own lives. Coming out of college or starting from scratch, most of us merely want to land the best job we can find, start a family, continually make more money with each paycheck and live happily ever after. But that way of thinking will often lead to a life of entrapment and limited achievement. Typically, something dramatic or catastrophic must happen to us to find the courage to explore new opportunities and ways to change how we think.

That was the case for me as I entered the "real world." After leaving A&M and landing a job with Shell, I gradually began to grow more comfortable in my career. My self-confidence kept growing when I met the woman of my dreams. I eventually worked up enough courage to ask Dorothy to marry me, and she accepted in 1966. Three years later, Dorothy gave birth to our first child, son Jeffrey. We had money in the bank, we had a sense of security, and we had peace of mind. Life was going along smoothly, but then it slapped me in the face. In 1971, when I was 28, I was laid off by Shell. I was a victim of budget cuts and economic hard times.

It could have been an ego-shattering, confidence-crippling time. Instead, it was one of the greatest blessings that ever happened to my career and my confidence. As the late Walt Disney once said, "You may not realize it when it happens, but a kick in the teeth may be the best thing in the world for you." Losing my job forced me to grow and program my mind for success in the future. I was already thinking about what else I could do that offered me more opportunity, but I had yet to come up with any answers. While I was collecting paychecks in my job routine, I had already asked myself—even if I had not vocalized it to anyone else—"Is this all there is to my career?" I had landed a nice, conventional job, and it paid well. But it really didn't offer any exciting opportunity for me. I had yet to discover entrepreneurism, and now—suddenly and unexpectedly—I was out of a job.

In need of employment, I turned to a company that had nothing to do with engineering, chemicals, the oil and gas industry or anything of the sort. I took a job with Success Motivation International, Inc. (SMI), which was based in Waco, Texas. It was run by Paul J. Meyer, who'd started his career as a top-producing insurance agent. Meyer later became a sales executive with Word, Inc., a firm that distributed religious books and records. He built a national sales organization and increased its business 1,500 percent in 24 months. And in 1960, he launched SMI, followed by Leadership Management, Inc. and Family Motivation International. Meyer, who died in 2009, is considered by many to be the founder of the personal development/self-help industry. He was the first person to condense books and record them on records and cassettes. His product line expanded to include nearly 30 full-length courses and programs in leadership development, goal setting, attitude, management training and more. All of these programs use spaced repetition, which has been the key to success for millions of people in more than 60 countries.

I am one of Meyer's success stories, although I was a major flop as a sales agent with SMI. My job was to sell the management, sales and success programs. While I was enthusiastic in my approach, I was not a good salesperson. I could not close deals, and I could not persuade people. I spent nearly two years with the company, and I was such a lousy salesperson I almost drained my personal savings I had put together in four and a half years with Shell. But those two years with SMI were invaluable. I'm convinced those two years as a struggling salesman paved my way to success in other ways.

As I crisscrossed greater Houston in an attempt to sell SMI materials, I listened to the best motivational speakers on cassette tapes in my car. I read and studied great philosophers and thinkers of our time and attended numerous seminars. I became a student of success. I read the books. I listened to the tapes. Then I read the books and listened to the tapes over and over to program them into my thinking. I became totally engrossed and completely immersed in the study of success, and I began to learn how to think more effectively.

Meanwhile, I continued to be a lousy salesman. Even though I was not making much money as a salesman, I was programming my mind for long-term success. Honestly, my mind hadn't grasped or internalized all the concepts I was hearing and studying. I didn't know yet about the concept of needing 10,000 hours of the right stuff to obtain mastery of anything, and I was missing a lot of the "right" 10,000 hours. Nor did I gain the confidence from successful action, which I learned later to be just as necessary for implementing the principles. But I learned the lesson that, in the world of the truly successful, intellectual knowledge (the kind of information we often learn in schools) means very little. And I later realized I had not yet overcome all my lingering self-doubts or transformed my thinking.

It wasn't until nearly a year after I left SMI and went into independent engineering consulting that all of those concepts and principles finally clicked. After conditioning my brain with the right stuff for about 3,000 hours and another 7,000 hours of the "right action," my mind started functioning more in the success mode. Once it all clicked, it was as if I had stepped out of the darkness and into the light. The fog of self-doubt had lifted. The black, foreboding clouds disappeared. Once the gloom lifted, I realized I had lived much of my life like "Joe Btfsplk" the character in the satirical newspaper comic strip, *Li'l Abner*. Joe, the creation of the cartoonist Al Capp, was well-meaning but he continually brought misfortune into his life, as a small, dark rain cloud perpetually hovered over his head. The reality is most of the world's workers actually have that cloud of self-doubt hanging over them from the time they enter the business world until the time they retire. It isn't visible, but it is there.

Once I left that cloud behind, I knew what I wanted to do. I was suddenly filled with enough confidence to realize I could actually do it. I had developed a strong positive mental attitude with the elimination of self-doubt. I believe less than one percent of the population ever accomplishes that kind of mind mastery. For me, the transformation was mainly the result of the mental programming I did at SMI. Seven years of work, leadership action and development helped, as well. Four years of strong leadership development in the Jaycees and my years in the Corps of Cadets at A&M also played a large role in the 10,000 hours of the right stuff required for mastery in any field. All of that prepared me to open my own business.

Without getting too technical, I decided, after having worked in chemical consulting with small businesses for a year, that I could start making my own, specialized custom chemicals. I believed my company could fill a niche. Large companies make large volumes, and sometimes it is much more economical for them to have smaller volumes of chemicals made by outsourcing them. I decided I could start a business that outsourced those chemicals, and for the first time in my life, I had a strong mental attitude.

I eliminated self-doubts and started seeing how things could be done instead of worrying about how I might fail. Overcoming negative thinking is wonderful and liberating. I was able to see the whole picture, and I was only concerned about how to achieve results. Once a person has a conversion to a positive mental attitude and mastery, he/she can clearly see opportunities that didn't initially reveal themselves. This concept is quite difficult to conceive if you haven't turned the corner and made the conversion, but it is exactly what has happened to people who have achieved the greatest breakthroughs. A positive mental attitude conversion is much like being an Aggie. As the old A&M saying goes, "From the inside looking out, we can't explain it to others, and from the outside looking in, it can't really be understood."

As I started my business, I continued reading self-help, management, business and psychology books. I joined the book summary club, and I immersed myself in success principles. I discovered it takes being exposed to a concept or theory 100 times—and sometimes 1,000 times—for it actually to become a part of you. Let me repeat that because it is so important: *It often takes about 100 times or more of hearing something, reading something or visualizing something for it to become a part of who we are and how we think.* Improving our mind requires plenty of proactive, repetitive conditioning to offset the tens of thousands of hours of negativity we are exposed to on many fronts. That's why we see TV commercials over and over, and why companies pay billions for repetitive exposure through advertising. Repetitive messages—good or bad—become a part of who we are, which is why it is important to program your mind with positive images and the right information. Read a book once for information, but if you want transformation, you need to review it and study it over and over again.

Most people aren't willing to make the commitment it takes for a positive transformation, but they might if they believed in the principle. That's why most people don't see their lives changed by books they purchase with such high hopes. I had listened to about 3,000 hours of positive, success-principle conditioning before I was able to change my thinking. Before I completed 3,000 hours of programming, I did not see any improvement, even though I was intellectually convinced these were the right principles for success. Then my thinking changed instantly.

On January 1, 1975, I decided to start my own company. I was going to build a chemical processing facility that would run seven days a week, 24 hours a day. Once I built the first one, I was going to build another. I finished my consulting work, found a partner and started the business with a shoestring budget—frayed and fragile shoestrings, at that.

My partner, Bob Keenan, and I each contributed $5,000 from savings, and we worked for free until the company started making a profit. We found a piece of land with a run-down, closed research plant in Crosby, Texas that would serve as our headquarters. The courts had taken it over, and it probably should have been condemned. It featured weeds that resembled small trees and enough corroded, flaking metal to fill the rust belt. But I saw potential, and I agreed to a six-month lease with a purchase after the lease deal. I obtained a Small Business Administration guaranteed loan six months later to buy the plant for $77,000.

Believe it or not, I also became quite the salesman, convincing people to loan me equipment I could not afford to buy. I found six or seven retired or part-time welders, laborers and crewmen and convinced them to work for free until I could pay them. Obviously, I had come a long way from the days when I was such a lousy salesman at SMI. Now I was only selling a vision, and I was able to convince people to work for free. It had everything to do with my passion, positive mental attitude and years of programming.

The McFerrin family photo that appeared on the cover of *12th Man Magazine*

Shell Chemical needed chemical processing done for a government job. It was a nasty chloride stream that nobody else would touch. Even though I had virtually nothing, Shell gave me a chance because I was willing to do it. I started plant production on March 15, 1975, and I vividly remember the first check I received for about $10,000. I paid off some bills and started paying the people who'd bought into my vision. As time went along, we began to make more money, turning a bigger profit each month. We upgraded the plant, replacing the leaky tin roof and the sheetrock that was falling off the walls. We paved the driveway and replaced the weeds with plants and trees. I knew right away the business was going to prosper, and by the end of the first year I already had started building another unit.

Every week, I bought more tanks. My vision and boldness scared my partner so much that I eventually bought his interest in the company. But things were going so well and happening so fast my only focus was to drive the business full speed ahead. I hired a super salesman, Steve Bordelon, to help our sales, and he did just that. Business was booming. I wasn't just pursuing my business dreams; I was living them out.

McFERRIN'S MOST DIFFICULT CHALLENGE

Former British Prime Minister Benjamin Disraeli once said, "There is no education like adversity." I believed that before 1978, and I thought being laid off by Shell in 1971 represented the biggest dose of adversity I'd encounter on my career path. That changed on January 8, 1978, when our plant burned down during the coldest winter in the history of Houston. The fire was a test of my faith, and it cost me more than $500,000 to rebuild the plant. It was the kind of event that could have ruined my business, especially since I had no insurance except for the office building that the SBA made me insure. But as author William Hazlitt once said, "While prosperity is a great teacher, adversity is a greater."

I whole heartedly agree. It took us about three months to return to full operation after the blaze, so I can say we were quite literally tested under fire. It took us another year or two to return to some level of stability, as nearly all the employees quit after the fire. It was a huge mess, and I still owed my partner about $300,000 for his half of the company I had bought two weeks before the fire, which put me $800,000 in the hole. Despite the obstacles, we eventually came back stronger than ever before. All that mental

74 | THE ENTREPRENEURIUAL SPIRIT OF AGGIELAND

programming paid off many times over. By the late 1990s, I was netting several million a year, and we were doing quite well.

We've always done well financially despite all of our other challenges. Nevertheless, it was a battle for me personally every day as the leader of my company because it seemed like I always had 40 problems to resolve. I would handle a crisis situation here, run to see a client there and never complete my expanding to-do list. Consequently, my company wasn't expanding as quickly as I wanted, either. Every time I took two steps forward, we'd end up taking a step or two backward. I was running the business on pure effort and trying to do everything, but not like a good CEO. I was a leader, but perhaps a fairly defective one in many regards.

So, I returned to what has been the foundation of all my business success: Mental programming and studying the science of success. I continued to read and to seek expert opinions by joining Vistage, the largest CEO organization in the world. Vistage helps build better CEOs, teaching entrepreneurs to avoid being enslaved by their business. When I first joined Vistage, I listened to Walt Sutton, a former CEO who became an entrepreneurial author, coach and consultant. While speaking about the duties of a CEO, Sutton's information helped me to organize my business in a way I had never envisioned. I became a master of my day instead of being a slave to it. I started performing the high-level duties of a CEO, as outlined by Walt, instead of trying to do all the manager and worker chores that were killing my day.

Artie McFerrin poses with Johnny Manziel's Heisman Trophy

Once I made changes to the way I led the company, business skyrocketed. My progress in applying the universal principles of success improved perhaps as much as 16 times what it had previously been, even though I had been successful running the business before I made these changes. We developed new rivers of profit, and the flood gates opened. Business began pouring in, as everything clicked once again. I became a much better CEO and my company prospered beyond my wildest dreams when I quit attempting to be a "Jack of All Trades" and focused exclusively on being "Artie the CEO." I was able to eliminate 80 percent of the non-CEO duties and non-success principles I was previously performing, which were enslaving me and creating very little return.

Instead, I focused on the 20 percent of duties that produced the most results. I tapped into the 80/20 principle, a universal truth that is applicable in practically every area of life. This principle states that 20 percent of our actions produce 80 percent of our results. All success principles and the best business practices that correlate to success are the 20 percent that produce 80 percent of results. The most successful people spend most of their effort each day on the most productive 20 percent of actions. Of course, very few people understand what the important 20 percent is…or they would be doing it. This 80/20 formula is not my rule. I didn't create it, but by finally grasping it and making it a fundamental part of the way I think and run my business, I became much more effective and my companies have exceeded my wildest expectations.

The key to my success as an entrepreneur has been my commitment to continuing my education in the universal principles of success. The 80/20 formula is the second chapter covered in my book, *The Executioner*. The other duties use the 80/20 principle. I learned to think and act like a highly effective entrepreneur/CEO by encompassing the CEO duties that conform to the 80/20 principle.

McFERRIN'S ADVICE TO YOUNG ENTREPRENEURS

For the most part, entrepreneurism is a "black hole" of understanding for non-entrepreneurs. But I believe entrepreneurism is the best route to opportunity and success for those who wholeheartedly commit to it. Entrepreneurism places us in complete control and responsibility, which is needed for real and significant personal growth. As an entrepreneur, you will experience constant action, opportunity and adversity, which will force you to grow, innovate, solve problems, evolve and change to become successful. Others in conventional jobs will rarely be able to experience all of this action and opportunity that is necessary for entrepreneurial success. But entrepreneurs develop rapidly by putting themselves in "harm's way." They develop more in one year from the action, opportunities and adversities they encounter than most people do in 20 to 30 years on a regular job.

This is the magic of entrepreneurism that few understand. Millions of people have become successful through entrepreneurism who wouldn't have otherwise because of the courage, confidence, positive mental attitude, determination and so forth that entrepreneurs must develop. I didn't understand this when I became an entrepreneur. I was just trying to make money.

I believe the real magic of entrepreneurism comes when a lone entrepreneur takes the responsibility of CEO duties directed at achieving high results. And I believe the best way to experience the true success principle form of entrepreneurism is to start at the bottom with the bootstrap method (i.e. pull yourself up). In this way, you'll learn it from the bottom up and you'll be in control with total responsibility. You'll bring out the creativity and genius you never knew you had.

Therefore, my advice to aspiring entrepreneurs with big dreams is to simply start your entrepreneurial career by finding something others will pay you for, and go for it. It is best that you start with only a small amount of startup money. The success rate of this startup method is much greater than starting a business with a large amount of money. It's been my observation that most people who start with an abundance of money fail, and the ones who survive never are forced to develop their creativity and never learn the business from the ground up. They tend to become more investors and managers and they don't experience as much of the magic that is entrepreneurism. Starting as a lone entrepreneur, on the other hand, will expose you to more than you can imagine and will put you into enough action to develop your business, to gain confidence and wisdom and to set and achieve high goals. This is the entrepreneurism that drives economies of the world, and it works.

Artie and Dorothy McFerrin

Upon first glance, this may sound easy. It isn't. The success principle-based entrepreneurism is essentially all mental, and the success is dependent on the development of the mind of the entrepreneur. The more independent entrepreneur will need a lot of courage to take this leap of faith. The great majority of want-to-be entrepreneurs never spring toward the "leap of faith" because everything is never just right. On the whole, these people are just as capable as the people who succeed. But they never jump into the action. You must start the process with a simple jump in the right direction. This is why success in this form of entrepreneurism depends on personal growth and implementing the universal success principle thinking, such as the principles taught in *Think and Grow Rich*.

The foundation of these principles is developing a positive mental attitude (PMA) with a strong enough mixture of belief, faith, discipline, confidence, courage and determination to get into a strong action mode. Good goal-setting and CEO-thinking techniques need to go along with this PMA. It also requires a person to do 10,000 hours of the "right stuff" over 10 years to acquire the mastery to achieve at a long-term high level. But don't wait to obtain this mastery to start. You'll achieve mastery along the journey. Any of us can learn any business practice or principle, and you will master many as a lone entrepreneur…as long as you commit to taking that first leap.

I also encourage young entrepreneurs to commit to a lifetime of learning. Success is a lifelong process, not a destination. I heard that same thing when I was young, but I never really believed it until I was old. We only succeed to the degree of our personal growth, thinking, action and goals. It's not due to our business schemes, intelligence, knowledge and luck like most of the naive think. That's why we need to keep working on mastering success principles and refining the way we think.

Success is not a one-time scenario. It's like dieting in that if a person loses 50 pounds over a six-month period, it won't make any long-term difference if the 50 pounds is gained back in the next year. The same principle applies to success. There's no doubt in my mind that many other people I know in my industry could have done as much or more than I have by using the principles I have applied to my life and career. But only a few people I know learned the "right stuff" and chose to make the necessary commitment and stick to it.

Ever since I went to work with SMI in the early 1970s, and was subsequently exposed to the magnificent self-help books and audio programs, I pondered writing a comprehensive book designed to help goal-oriented people apply success principles to their own lives. But back then, I hadn't used the principles that I had intellectually learned very well. I'm an engineer and entrepreneur, a technical type of guy whose mind works in concepts and processes, not words. Inevitably, as soon as I would seriously think about writing a book, I realized I wasn't ready. What could I offer that others—real-life, experienced authors—hadn't already done? What great value could I provide to businessmen that wasn't already available? How could I possibly condense the massive amount of information in my mind into a book that didn't rival Leo Tolstoy's *War and Peace* in terms of sheer size? And since I was enslaved in my business, how would I have the time?

After decades of doubt, the proverbial light turned on for me, clearly revealing that I needed to narrow my focus in order to deliver the right stuff I've learned the hard way…things that aren't found in other books. As I narrowed my focus, I became acutely aware of a real need in the marketplace for a blueprint to better implement the intangible, difficult-to-implement universal success principles with the right best business practices for personal success. Implementation has always been the weakest link in utilizing the universal success principles, and working on these duties makes the implementation process so much easier. Ultimately, I resolved to finally write the book, *The Executioner*.

In that book, I cover in great detail the specific duties that every leader—regardless of whether he is the top executive of a Wall Street corporation or running his own one-person business on Main Street—must understand and perform in order to reach his full, success principle-based potential as the CEO of his organization or his own life. Mastery of every duty is certainly not necessary…or even possible. But identifying and implementing each duty can, over time, generate a domino effect that can transform a person and/or business from good-to-great and can forever alter the professional status of an individual entrepreneur from surviving-to-thriving.

Obviously, I do not have the space here to cover all of those duties. So, I will be concise in my advice. The fact that you picked up this book and have read this far into my chapter is proof you have an entrepreneurial spirit. I encourage you to always nurture and protect that spirit. It is much easier to graduate from college and merely pursue a career working for someone else than it is to be a true entrepreneur. But entrepreneurism has proven to be the most effective way to test and stretch us, as it constantly puts us in the position of having to take CEO responsibility and be in action. It's a proven fact that personal growth only happens when a person changes his/her thinking and is in meaningful action achieving competitive results. Entrepreneurism does this in ways that working for others will not. At some level, probably every self-help book that has ever been written addresses that. I'd strongly encourage you to continue considering entrepreneurism for yourself, as it has proven to be the most effective route for most to financial freedom and success. And it forces us to think like a CEO. I've found that successful entrepreneurs are mostly people who would not be as successful at a high level in a conventional job setting. Entrepreneurs are often forced to be "whole brain" thinkers, opening up a realm on new possibilities.

My other piece of advice here is simply this: Develop a positive mental attitude. As American philosopher and psychologist William James once said, "The greatest discovery of my generation is that a human being can alter his life by altering his attitudes of mind."

We've all heard countless stories throughout our lives about the power of positivity. We've heard how developing a positive attitude—and maintaining it—has helped patients overcome terminal diseases that science and medicine could not cure. We've read stories and articles about how adopting a positive mental attitude transformed individuals for the better and rescued fledgling businesses. The world of sports is also filled with one story after another about how athletes have used a PMA to build their careers. One of those stories involves Stan "The Man" Musial, one of the greatest hitters in the history of Major League Baseball. In 22 seasons with the St. Louis Cardinals, Musial produced at least a .300 batting average 17 times. He also won seven batting titles and three MVP awards.

In the book *Living Joyfully*, author Brian Harbour recounts the story of a pregame interaction between Musial and one of his former teammates, Wally Westlake, a career .272 hitter over the course of 10 seasons (1947-56). Shortly after batting practice one afternoon, Westlake approached Musial and informed the future Hall of Famer of how good he was feeling on that particular day. "I slept great last night," Westlake told Musial. "My breakfast this morning was great. I hit a couple of home runs in batting practice. Coach has me in the lineup, and I feel like I could get three hits today. Stan, do you ever feel that way?" Without hesitation, Musial replied, "Wally, I feel that way every day."

Think about that. Musial played 3,026 games in a career that spanned more than two decades and went to the plate 12,712 times. He failed to produce a hit in 9,082 of those trips, but "The Man" never stepped into the batter's box without the expectation that he was going to deliver a hit, which he did 3,630 times. Even in the midst of thousands of failures, Musial's confidence never wavered and his positive mental attitude was never shaken.

From personal experience, I've found that great achievement and "mastery" never happens for anyone until he/she can fully develop a PMA like Stan Musial. None of the dynamic CEO duties I described in my book will work effectively without a strong PMA. And in developing a strong PMA, you are removing self-doubt and self-limiting thoughts. Most ambitious people believe they have a strong PMA. I certainly did when I was young. Between the ages of 21 and 31, I was a high-energy, enthusiastic and generally positive person, and I was optimistic and convinced that I owned a PMA. I did not! Not even close.

I can assure you a true PMA and mastery is an extremely important factor in success, and it's what you need to work on to obtain mastery in your field. As Thomas Jefferson once said, "Nothing can stop the man with the right mental attitude from achieving his goal; nothing can help the man with the wrong mental attitude." A true PMA will allow you to achieve great success. Just being optimistic will only take you part of the way there. Achievement and happiness only occur to the degree a person has developed his mind, thinking and attitude to the proven ways of the successful and not the linear and less positive "conventional ways."

To cover positive mental attitudes comprehensively and to provide an in-depth view into the power of positive thinking, it would require several books. But for the sake of brevity, I would simply encourage you to commit to a lifelong learning and training. Remember, there are no "overnight" success stories, and it requires years of training with the right information to experience a transformation.

Listening to audio programs will infinitely help in the process, as they will condition your thinking positively. Listen to them repetitively for thousands of hours so that they will positively program your thinking and help keep the negative from beating you down. It takes no time away from other activities if you listen to them in your vehicle while you travel or listen while you exercise instead of listening to "going nowhere" music. The personal and financial rewards are great in entrepreneurism if you are a person who is committed to doing whatever it takes in pursuit of entrepreneurial dreams.

Keep reading. Keep listening to PMA audios by the many great speakers, writers and entrepreneurs who are willing to share their secrets to success. Most drivers around you on the freeway or the people with headphones on next to you at the gym are listening to music to pass the time. Don't be like those people. Make the most of every minute and prepare yourself for success.

Believe you have what it takes to be successful and commit to experiencing a transformation. Where we are in life today is because of our thoughts. To improve our lives, we must first improve our thinking. Goal setting also helps in creating a PMA. For most people, goal setting is extremely tough to do, and very few people manage to do it well. But as self-help guru Brian Tracy once said, "Success is goal setting; all else is commentary."

Listening, reading and programming your mind for so long without much progress is frustrating. In fact, it makes it very difficult for most people to keep the faith and stick with the program. If it could be done in 100 hours, everyone might attempt it. But it rarely can be done in such a short amount of time. My recommendation is to listen to Brian Tracy's Ultimate Goal Setting Program, Richard Koch's *80/20 Principle* and *As a Man Thinketh* at least 100 times before even considering any other audios. Then listen to Brian Tracy's *Universal Laws of Success and Achievement* as much as you can. These provide great positive mental conditioning. So does listening to Napoleon Hill, Jack Canfield, Wayne Dyer and other Brian Tracy audios.

Management programs, business seminars, investment strategies and such may be educational, but they're mostly not positive conditioning. Other self-help programs are educational, but some are not necessarily the "right" positive conditioning. If you are willing to invest the time, trust the proven conditioning programs I have suggested. While there are masses of success and motivational audios, there aren't many positive conditioning audios. And remember that if you want to be a professor, read and study a thousand books. But if you want to achieve greatly, internalize a handful of the "right" books that will transform you and program you to think successfully.

Whenever you are tempted to give up—and there will be times when you will want to quit on yourself, your dreams, your mental programming, etc.—think about me, the kid at A&M who wanted to quit school in my first year; the young man who was laid off from his first job and nearly went broke in his second because he was such a lousy salesperson; and the guy who was roughly $800,000 in the hole after his business burned to the ground. Know that if I can transform myself, you can, too!

7.
Lyle Eastham
President of Big E Drilling Co.
Texas A&M Class of 1994

EASTHAM'S PATH TO TEXAS A&M

Lyle and Andrea Eastham with daughters Madelynn, Bella and Aspen

The last thing I remember was fumbling around momentarily with the rotating pedals on my bicycle, trying to quickly gain my balance and generate enough forward momentum to propel me safely to the other side of the street. I was 6 years old; I was playing "follow the leader" with a little girl who was four years older than me and was watching me while my mother took a shower; I was right in front of my childhood home in Houston's Memorial Village area; and I would have made it to the other side if I had not fumbled with my footwork. Instead, the next thing I remember was being loaded into an ambulance, as my mother and many other neighbors breathed a sigh of relief when I finally opened my eyes.

I never heard any screeching tires or screams. I didn't see what hit me, either. But I was later told that the red Mercedes I had seen at the far end of the street (I really did look both ways) clipped me as I was riding to the other side. The female driver was drunk and going too fast in a neighborhood setting. I don't think she was practicing for the Indianapolis 500, but she was going too fast in a house-lined, kid-filled subdivision. When she hit me, I flipped off my bike and into the air, landing on the side of the road where my head literally bounced off the curb. That knocked me out immediately. Fortunately, the driver did stop suddenly because after I bounced off the curb, I rolled back onto the street and came to rest with my head lying underneath the car and just in front of one of the tires. When my mother heard the commotion, she threw on her clothes and raced out of the front door. At first glance, I must have looked like I was dead. But by the time the ambulance arrived and the paramedics placed me on the gurney, I had regained consciousness. I was later diagnosed with a severe concussion—the first of many—but there were no cracks in my skull or broken bones.

The funny thing is that my most vivid memories from that near-death experience were eating Jell-O and watching TV in the hospital, where I was kept overnight for observation. As best as I can recall, I had a good time in the hospital as all the doctors and nurses cared for me. Nevertheless, I was extremely lucky, and I genuinely thanked God for allowing me to celebrate my seventh birthday.

I was just as lucky to survive that year and to see my eighth birthday. While playing with a friend one day at his home, we were running from room to room and into the foyer, where there was a sliding glass door that led to the backyard. My friend knew it was a door; I did not. I went right through the door and sliced my wrist wide open. I cut the ulnar artery in two and also severed the volar carpal ligament. Blood spewed from my wrist like an old oil well gusher, and as I looked toward my friend, his face was as white as a sheet. Fortunately, his father literally saved my life. While I bled all over the kitchen, my friend's father tied a beach towel around my arm, using it as a tourniquet. He then wrapped a towel around my gaping wound and placed me in the family's Suburban. By the time we reached the hospital, the beach towel was soaked in blood and dripping like a leaky faucet onto the floorboard carpet. I was extremely lightheaded due to the amount of lost blood, but I never completely lost consciousness until we reached the hospital and they prepped me for emergency surgery. I woke up with a cast on my arm, but at least I woke up.

In the span of a year, I nearly died twice. I suppose those two horrific childhood episodes could have easily left some terribly haunting emotional scars or debilitating physical wounds. But I actually think those events impacted me positively. I have always had a healthy appreciation for my life, trying to never take the blessings of the next day, the next hour and even the next breath for granted. I believe God spared me—or protected me—because He had further plans for my life. His purpose for my life had obviously not yet been fulfilled. As such, I've lived most of my life with an optimistic outlook, seeking ways to make a positive difference, embracing challenges as opportunities and chasing my dreams.

One of the dreams I fulfilled was receiving the opportunity to attend Texas A&M on a football scholarship, which opened many doors for me in other areas of my life. It's actually rather miraculous I was able to play sports as long as I did because of those early injuries and some of the lingering effects of them. After slicing my right wrist in 1978, doctors and medical personnel didn't think I would ever be able to throw a football or baseball again. There was extensive damage to my artery and cartilage, and I vividly recall looking down at my wrist when they wheeled me into the operating room and unraveled the blood-soaked towel. It was mangled and I remember seeing white cartilage sticking out of the wound. I don't know how they put me back together, but the surgeons did a remarkable job. When the cast was removed months later, they made no promises, warning me that I might not ever have the same strength in my hand and lower forearm that I previously possessed. But on the first day after the cast came off, I picked up a baseball, wrapped my hand around the laces and fired away. I didn't need any rehabilitation or special therapy. I had to build up the muscles in my injured arm because of a lack of use for several months, but there was no long-term damage. In fact, I returned to my Little League baseball career without missing a beat, using the talents that God gave me and playing with more purpose and passion than ever.

Now, don't misunderstand. I certainly wasn't one of those natural-looking athletes who seem so graceful and fluid in their effortless motions. Those descriptions would be so much more fitting for my brother, Albert, who is two and a half years older than me. Conversely, I was one of those plodding and heavyset (that's a nice word for "chubby" or "dumpy") boys who often seemed to be running in quick sand as I trudged from one base to another on the Little League fields. But God did bless me with great hand-eye coordination…and some power. I quickly discovered that I didn't need to be lightning quick or blazingly fast in running the bases if I simply knocked the baseball over the fence, which I often did in Little League. I was one of the larger kids in my elementary school, and even though I didn't make things look as easy as my older brother on the athletic fields, I had plenty of success in youth sports such as baseball, football and even golf. I obviously inherited some great athletic genes from my parents. My mother, Eileen, was a really good athlete, who once won the Beaumont Country Club individual tennis championship even though she was six months pregnant with me. My father, Gerald, was also a tremendous athlete who starred as a football player and discus thrower at Beaumont Central High School.

In hindsight, I might have had an even brighter athletic future if I had stuck with baseball, golf or some other non-contact sport, because I believe the severe concussion I suffered as a 6-year-old probably made me susceptible to other concussions. Of course, the concussion I endured two years after the drunk driver hit me probably didn't help, either. As an 8-year-old, I was on the playground at my elementary school on a cold, winter morning and didn't pay enough attention to the ice that had formed at various places on the blacktop. I slipped and hit my head hard on the pavement. I don't remember what happened next. It wasn't until I was in the middle of math class later that afternoon that I began to be aware of what was happening around me. Even though I had entered the schoolhouse, gone to lunch and taken a seat at my desk, I had essentially blacked out for hours without ever losing consciousness. I didn't remember a thing that happened for hours after slipping on the ice. Nowadays, I realize such lengthy blackouts can be extremely dangerous. I could have fallen into a coma at school or later that night. But at the time, nobody noticed at school and I didn't even bother to tell my parents about my headache that evening.

Many people have jokingly accused me of being brain damaged through the years, which may not actually be too far from the truth. I am fairly certain that if the medical professionals had known as much back then as they do now about the long-term effects of concussions that I would have been more strongly discouraged from playing football. But that never crossed my mind as I grew up, and even though I developed into a really strong pitcher and all-around baseball player, football was my first love. I gave up baseball as a freshman at Houston's Memorial High School to focus on my football career. That seemed like a really good decision at the time, as I grew to become a 6-foot-5, 250-pound lineman. I made a name for myself initially as a defensive lineman, but prior to my senior year, the offensive line coach at Memorial, Rick Hoffman, told me my future would ultimately be much brighter on the opposite side of the line of scrimmage. I was somewhat reluctant at first, but it proved to be a good move, as I began receiving recruiting letters and attention from numerous colleges across the state and throughout the region. *The Houston Chronicle, Dallas Morning News* and *Fort Worth Star-Telegram* also listed me among the top 100 recruiting prospects in Texas for the 1990 signing class.

My brother, whose athletic career ended prematurely when he broke his femur during his junior year in high school, was attending Texas Tech when I was being recruited, and I definitely gave some consideration to joining him in Lubbock. I took a visit to the South Plains, and Texas Tech had a cute girl who had baked some chocolate chip cookies for me, but I was definitely more impressed with Texas A&M and the Aggies' recruiting efforts. Former A&M head coach R.C. Slocum and former recruiting coordinator Tim Cassidy had called me at home from the locker room following one of the Aggies' victories during the 1989 season, and I remember being particularly impressed that they were using something called a mobile phone. The bulky phone had a huge antenna, and it probably emitted more radiation than a nuclear power plant meltdown. Practically every middle school kid in the country now owns a smart phone, but in the late 1980s and early '90s, talking to coaches on a fancy "handheld mobile device" was just cool.

A&M assistant coach John Pearce was assigned to recruit me and others in the Houston area, and he was a prince of a guy. A&M also had an advantage with me because my father had attended school in Aggieland for three semesters before joining the Marine Corps. My father didn't graduate from A&M, but he spoke glowingly about the university, its traditions and its military background.

I visited other schools, but I was sold on A&M for numerous reasons, including the friendliness of the campus and the genuine nature of practically everyone I met on my recruiting trip. Beyond just visiting campus, Coach Pearce took several recruits into the country where we were eating barbecue and shooting skeet. I didn't know what to expect on the trip, but Coach Pearce approached me and offered me a scholarship to Texas A&M. I jumped on that offer as fast as a kid leaping into the pool on the first day of summer vacation. I didn't call my parents; I didn't think it over; and I didn't hesitate. I just said, "Sign me up." I didn't want to give the coaches any chance of changing their minds.

I eventually called my girlfriend and my parents and told them I committed to attend Texas A&M. I remember my mom being startled that I had decided so quickly. Honestly, she tried to convince me to take a little more time to think everything through, but I was sold on A&M. I know my parents were proud of me, too. Being a former Marine, my dad wasn't the kind of person who would sit me down and shower me with a bunch of warm, fuzzy and sentimental praises, but I could tell he was really pleased I had chosen a place with the tradition and disciplined culture of Texas A&M. We ended up hosting a big National Letter of Intent Signing Day party at my house in February 1990. Although I was certainly not one of the most high-profile recruits in the A&M class, my party was covered by Bob Allen and Dave Ward of KTRK (Channel 13) in Houston. Ward, the longtime anchor of the station's weekday Eyewitness News reports, was friends with my girlfriend's mother, so the TV cameras showed up at our home, along with hundreds of friends and family members. Our garage was overflowing with people in a celebration that I will remember for the rest of my life.

A&M's 1990 recruiting class was ranked among the nation's best and featured so many great players, including future MLB pitcher Jeff Granger, future NFL players Greg Hill, Eric England and Mark Wheeler and future strength and conditioning coach Larry Jackson, among others. It was an honor to be part of such an incredible class, and I felt like I belonged when all the freshmen reported to campus in July of '90. We opened the season at Aloha Stadium against Hawaii on September 1, so the freshmen reported especially early. We had some intense practices, but I believed I was making a positive impression on the coaches and my teammates. I even remember thinking to myself, "I belong in this stadium and at this level."

Then reality hit when the upperclassmen arrived, and that feeling disappeared faster than a pizza in a room full of offensive linemen. The guys I was facing in practice—future NFL draft picks like Mike Arthur and Keith Alex and future All-SWC selections like Matt McCall and John Ellisor—were in a different league from anything I had previously seen.

I was constantly beaten, battered and bludgeoned by those veterans, and I was also being pushed and tested mentally by our great offensive line coach Mike Sherman, who would eventually become a head coach in the NFL and at A&M. Coach Sherman was a brilliant tactician, who could easily put all of the offensive linemen, especially the younger guys, in a brain cramp with his lectures and legendary film-session discussions. He had a mind for the game and a Massachusetts accent as thick as clam chowder. He was a tremendous coach, a superb man and a great Christian influence. Football is a violent game that often produces plenty of explicit trash talk and vulgar locker room language. But I remember Coach Sherman really trying to clean up his own language, and in his effort to serve as an even better role model, I vividly recall him putting a $1 bill inside a jar every time he let a four-letter word slip out of his mouth. I think he ran out of money fairly quickly, but he was always striving to improve himself and those he coached. I certainly believe I improved as a player under his guidance, and perhaps I could have eventually developed into a starter on some really good A&M teams…if only my body would have cooperated.

I redshirted during the 1990 season and didn't play in any games, but the pounding in practices took a toll on my body, as the concussions returned. Throughout my high school career, I had endured several other concussions. On Saturday mornings, I would watch game film from the previous night, and there were many times I didn't remember long stretches during the games. My body was on the field, but my brain was on autopilot. Obviously, the collisions are even more intense on the college level, and toward the end of the season, I began sitting out some practices after suffering concussions. I was then sent to a neurologist in Houston, where a variety of tests were performed. I told the neurologist about the childhood concussions, but after being checked out thoroughly, I was permitted to return to football practices the following spring. Thank God I wasn't seriously injured, because it became fairly obvious to me that I was especially susceptible to concussions.

At that time in my life, however, I wasn't going to allow anything to prevent me from chasing my dream of playing college football. After a good spring in 1991, I did, indeed, appear in a game during the fall of '91. On November 23, 1991, we were pounding poor SMU into oblivion at Kyle Field. The '91 Mustangs were only in their third year back from the NCAA-mandated "death penalty," and they had only won a single game the previous year. We rolled out to a 65-0 lead, and it could have been much worse. But our coaching staff didn't try to run up the score, and I was one of the 75 Aggies to see action against the Mustangs. It was an absolute thrill for me to have the opportunity to make my college football debut on a day when we clinched the Southwest Conference title.

We finished the regular season in '91 by whipping Texas, 31-14, on Thanksgiving night in College Station and then began preparations to play Florida State in the Cotton Bowl. During practices for the bowl game, I was blocking defensive end Kefa Chatham and I took a power step to my right. My right knee didn't collapse underneath me, but something definitely did not feel right. It felt loose and unstable, but I stumbled around long enough that it popped back in place…temporarily. On the next play, my knee again popped out of place. I didn't want to take myself out of practice, but I had no choice. My knee felt so wobbly that I figured something was wrong. My concerns were confirmed when doctors examined it and informed me that my ACL was essentially gone and I would need surgery right away. I initially planned to have the surgery in College Station and to stay on campus during much of the Christmas break, but I called my mom and dad the next day and found out that my father had undergone a cardiac catheterization and was then required emergency open-heart surgery. At my mother's request, I decided to come home to be with my family and to have the knee surgery after the Cotton Bowl.

I eventually rehabilitated the knee and came back stronger than ever the following summer. But on the first day of practice in preparation for the '92 season, I suffered a meniscus tear in my right knee that marked the beginning of the end of my football career. I continued to play through knee pain, icing the knee every day. I also was battling back issues and endured yet another concussion during the 1992 season, which resulted in splitting headaches. As I attempted to continue playing through all the ailments, I became addicted to pain medication. I felt miserable, and by the end of the '92 season, I talked to the doctors and trainers and then reluctantly informed Coach Sherman that I could not continue playing. I vividly recall taking off my pads for the final time following the 1993 Cotton Bowl. I didn't cry, but it was an emotional moment, signifying the end of an era for me and the beginning of a much different way of life in college.

Lyle and Andrea Eastham at Kyle Field

I loved representing Texas A&M as a football player, and I would have happily continued playing if my body wouldn't have deteriorated. But being part of the football team at a big-time university is extremely time-consuming. When I quit playing, I realized the typical college lifestyle can be leisurely and laid back. Without the practices, meetings, weight workouts and so forth, I hardly knew what to do with all my free time. Fortunately, that free time did lead me to the Tap (a popular bar on Harvey Road) on the right night in January 1994 when I met my future wife, Andrea. I noticed her—a strikingly beautiful blonde—right away, and I immediately concluded that she was way out of my league. But I've always been the type of person who isn't afraid to fail, so I decided I would at least try to meet her. Andrea certainly wouldn't have been the first attractive woman to tell me to "get lost," but to my pleasant surprise, she was as engaging as she was captivating. We talked for almost two hours, and I was further entranced by her when I discovered she was a biomedical sciences major. She was beautiful, brilliant and—most baffling to my buddies—apparently interested in me. Or, at the very least, she was not perturbed by my interest in her.

We became friends that night, and I learned that her roommate was friends with one of the trainers from the football team. The four of us went out a couple times, and then I finally found the courage to ask Andrea out on a real, one-on-one date. On that date, which started at a restaurant called Bullwinkle's Bar &

Grill on Texas Avenue, I discovered that practically everything about her fascinated me. We hit it off at the restaurant and then I completely fell for her when we went to hit golf balls later that evening at the driving range. She was good, and she looked really good swinging a golf club.

I must admit I am a complete "competition addict," and at that time in my life, golf became my competitive outlet. I first started playing golf when I was nine, but I really enjoyed the camaraderie of team sports so much more as I was growing up. When football was no longer an option in college, however, I returned to golf and I became enamored with the idea of competing in what was then known as the "Chrysler National Long Drive Championship," which became a big deal in the early- and mid-1990s. The long drive championships originated in the mid-1970s, and they are still going on today (RE/MAX World Long Drive Championship). But the popularity of the long drive competitions was at its best in the '90s. I had first competed in the Houston qualifiers when I was 18, but I was built for football at that time, and I didn't have the flexibility or range of motion to hit a golf ball as far as some of the top long drivers. After I quit playing football at A&M, I lost some weight and began hitting—or pounding—as many as 500 balls per day.

My father even allowed me to fly to California to take a two-day lesson from Mike Austin, a former engineer, who developed a power swing and hit the longest recorded drive in a professional tour event, with a 515-yard shot while playing in the U.S. National Seniors Open in 1974. Austin was 64 at the time, and the *Guinness Book of World Records* confirmed that distance. Austin picked me up at that airport, and we nearly crashed three times while he drove me to my hotel. But his methods were effective, and I returned to College Station to begin practicing as I worked toward completing my degree in business communications. I began my college career by majoring in petroleum engineering, but some of the math classes led me to pursue business management and then communications. During my last semester at A&M, however, my two primary focuses were Andrea and long-distance driving. I knew I wasn't a good enough all-around golfer to pursue a PGA career, but the long-distance competitions fueled my competitive fires, and they paid well if you could compete at an elite level. I spent plenty of time perfecting my ability to crush a golf ball, and I also devoted as much time as possible developing the "crush" I had on Andrea. The time investment I made in Andrea eventually proved to be so much more valuable than the golf pursuit.

I graduated in May of 1994, and Andrea graduated in December of that same year. We continued to date, and in my ultimate sales job victory, I convinced her to marry me. God blessed us immensely when our first daughter, Madeline, was born in August of '96, and our second daughter, Bella, arrived three years later. Our third daughter, Aspen, was born in 2003, which was about the same time my father was diagnosed with Leukemia. Andrea also had some health issues following the birth of Aspen, and it just made sense at that time to give up the long-distance drive competitions, which were always held on weekends. Following my graduation from A&M, I had given the long-distance driving a legitimate shot. I entered numerous qualifying events in the fall of '94 and began competing later that year. I initially performed rather poorly, but I improved in 1995 and '96, when I began winning some qualifier events. I continued to improve and eventually made it to the World Finals in Las Vegas twice (only the top 60 in the world qualify to compete in Vegas), finishing in the top 20 in 2001, the same year I won the Texas state title.

I enjoyed all of the competitions, and Andrea was quite supportive of the abundance of time and travel the sport required. But in 2003, I knew it was time to hang up the competitive golf spikes. In building my business in the ensuing years, I still played golf with customers, and my success on the long-drive circuit opened some doors for me that may have otherwise been shut. But much like giving up football was the right decision, giving up the competitive golf was also the right decision. I knew it was time to pour my competitive juices into business interests, which leads me into the reason I was asked to be part of this book project.

EASTHAM'S PATH TO ENTREPRENEURIAL SUCCESS

Lyle Eastham has never shied away from big obstacles

In 2013, our family business celebrated its 100th year of operations. Whenever I inform people of that historic fact—particularly people who are unfamiliar with my background—I suspect this thought likely crosses their minds: "Lucky Lyle must've inherited all of his family's money." At least that's the G-rated version of what I imagine is running through their minds. The more forthright, blunt version probably starts with, "Lazy Lyle" and includes terms like "S.O.B." and a variety of four-letter words.

I suspect that because big inheritances and mounds of old money are common in the oil, gas and drilling-related industries. In my particular case, however, inheriting the family's business fortunes is certainly not part of my life story. In fact, following my graduation from A&M, my father strongly encouraged me to run as fast and as far away from the family business as humanly possible. But in hindsight, perhaps all those football knee injuries were actually a blessing in disguise. After all, I couldn't run too far, and I've never been able to run too fast. Even though we've endured some extremely difficult times, God has most definitely blessed our business and has allowed me to build upon the foundations that my father, grandfather and great grandfather established decades before me. Perhaps it's best to begin the story of my entrepreneurial journey with a short history lesson of my family's business background.

On January 10, 1901, the Lucas Gusher at Spindletop Oil Field exploded, revealing the natural resource that lay below much of Beaumont and the surrounding area. Within days of the explosion, approximately 40,000 sightseers, speculators and job-seekers came to Beaumont. The new oil field soon produced more than 100,000 barrels of oil per day, and the strike at Spindletop represented a major turning point for Texas and the United States. No oil field in the world had ever been so productive. The ensuing frenzy of oil exploration, along with the economic development it generated in the Lone Star State, became known as the "Texas Oil Boom." My great grandfather arrived in Beaumont as part of that boom. In 1913, he and several partners opened an oilfield service-oriented business called Beaumont Well Works that manufactured steel-forged equipment that was essential to the burgeoning oil industry.

Forging is one of the oldest known metalworking processes, and it is still a major worldwide industry that has evolved tremendously with advancements in technology. Nowadays, industrial forging involves presses, hydraulic-powered hammers, elaborate computer systems and so forth. Back in 1913 when my great grandfather was a 20 percent owner of the small business, workers used hand-held hammers and anvils to produce, among other products, surface connectors to tie pipes together from the oil wells that were being drilled.

My great grandfather did well, and he bought more of the company from his partners in the ensuing years. He survived the Great Depression in the 1930s, and my grandfather took over the Beaumont-based business from his dad in the 1940s. My father, Gerald, was honorably discharged from the Marine Corps in April 1955, and he began overseeing the operations of the company in the late 1950s. My father was a great businessman, and he grew the company through a countless array of highs and lows in the oilfield industry. He built a major plant in Houston and continued to build the company throughout the 1960s and most of the '70s. In 1977, however, a large competitor approached my father looking to buy the business. It was more of a threat than a business proposal, because the competitor made it clear that if my father didn't sell, he was going to be run out of business. Reluctantly, my dad sold a portion of Beaumont Well Works in 1977, but he kept the rights to the property.

He started Big E Drilling Company in 1981, which is when he moved our family to Houston. He initially bought two old Canadian rigs and ordered a new rig as he transitioned optimistically into the land-drilling business. Unfortunately for my dad, it was not a good time to begin an oil-related drilling company. In fact, in terms of really bad business timing, it was about like investing in one-hour photo developing storefronts just as digital cameras were being introduced. It wasn't completely impossible to make a living, but it was extremely difficult.

A widespread recession in the United States reached its lowest point in 1982, severely dampening energy demand. By 1983, oil prices dropped below $30 a barrel, and in 1984, the U.S. savings and loan institutions started to fail. Throughout that time, my father was essentially generating no income of any significance with his three rigs, and as you might imagine, he was edgy and irritable. First, he'd been forced into selling the family business in Beaumont, and all the money he'd invested from that sales transaction was yielding nothing in Houston. We basically stopped operations for a few years, but somehow, he managed to keep the doors open and never shut the company down.

He started operations back up again in the 1986-87 timeframe, which was an even more disastrous year in the industry. Texas reported 366,200 jobs related to oil and gas extraction and oilfield equipment in the early 1980s, according to the Federal Reserve Bank of Dallas. By 1987, only a year after the great oil price collapse of '86, 175,000 of those jobs had vanished. Like the Ford Pinto or the AMC Pacer, they were everywhere one day and practically gone the next.

According to a 2006 article in *The Explorer*, a publication of the *American Association of Petroleum Geologists*, the state of Texas lost more than $1 billion in oil and gas severance taxes in 1986. The standard oilfield joke then was that the biggest employer of petroleum engineers after 1986 was Safeway grocery stores. The industry was in terrible shape, as people were stealing from each other in a wild, wild West mentality. But my father used the desperation of the times to hire some good people desperately in need of work, as he started our really big drilling foundation. Also in 1987, my dad started Eastham Forge on the same property in Beaumont that the family business had originated in 1913. The competitor that forced my father to sell Beaumont Well Works in 1977 had gone belly up, and my father bought back the surface equipment from the bank that repossessed it.

When the dust settled in '87 and '88, my brother and I questioned my dad's intelligence several times because business was terrible. But somehow, he kept things afloat and managed to keep food on the table. I worked in the oilfields throughout the summers during many of the difficult years. It was hard work, and I did just about everything with the exception of working the oilfield tongs, which are large-capacity, self-locking wrenches used to grip drill-string components and apply torque. My father was worried I'd lose a finger working the tongs, and he wanted me to have all 10 fingers so I could still hold opposing defensive linemen on the football field.

I learned so much about the industry and developed an even stronger work ethic by toiling in the summertime heat in the oilfields. I was paid the lowest rate among my dad's employees, but I learned that rig managers, drillers, derrick hands, lease hands, floor hands and so forth typically earn every dime they make. I couldn't have imagined it at the time, but the summers I spent out there provided me with great insight that I would one day use in leading the company. Today, I understand the importance of every position, and I believe I treat the oilfield guys with more appreciation and respect than many other business leaders in my position. Because of my personal oilfield experiences, I also tend to pay those workers better than some others within the industry, which makes for an overall happier organization.

I consider it a blessing that I was able to work in so many oilfield roles during the summers while I was in my teen-age years, and as an added benefit, I was always in great shape for the start of two-a-day football practices in high school and in college. Oilfield work can be dirty, grimy, grueling and punishing, which was perfect training for being an offensive lineman.

After I graduated from A&M, my father instructed me to interview for other jobs instead of merely entering the family business. My brother graduated from Texas Tech a couple of years before me, and he was overseeing the operations of Eastham Forge in Beaumont when I graduated from A&M in '94. To this day, my brother is still running Eastham Forge, and he has always done a great job. He has handled many challenging business times and circumstances, and I knew I would have to tackle some huge obstacles, as well, if I chose to ignore my father's advice and join the management team at Big E Drilling Company. I interviewed for a sales job in the pipe-fitting industry, and I was offered a position that paid a minimum of $70,000 per year. It was a great entry-level offer, and it would have initially been far more financially beneficial if I had simply accepted it. Instead of following the money, however, I followed my heart and chose the family business.

My father had not been feeling well during the latter part of my time at Texas A&M. We have a history of heart problems on my father's side of the family, as both my great grandfather and grandfather died in their mid-50s from the same heart defect that doctors fortunately discovered in my father in the nick of time. As I mentioned previously, surgeons cracked open my father's chest in the early 1990s and performed eight hours of open-heart surgery on him while I was at A&M. Surgeons saved his life, but the heart condition, the surgery and the recovery took a toll on my dad and the business. In my father's absence, Big E Drilling had taken a big nosedive and was figuratively on life support.

After I graduated from A&M, I took a short trip with Andrea and then began working at Big E less than a week after my graduation. I'd arrive at the office at 5:30 in the morning to review drilling reports, which at that time were still faxed to our office in Houston from the drilling rigs. In the ensuing years, we were on the leading edge of technology in our utilization of computer software to analyze reports and handle payroll, but in the mid-1990s we were still studying blurry fax reports.

You didn't need to be a rocket scientist to look at our overall financial numbers and see that we were not generating enough revenue to pay our bills. We had some bad equipment. We had some unreliable clients who weren't always paying us. We had a couple of questionable business practices. And although we generally had great people on our staff, we had one sour lemon in a managerial position.

I started with Big E making a salary of $30,000 a year, which was less than many of the lower-level oilfield workers. I lived in a small apartment near the office, while I studied every business practice, analyzed every report I could find and reviewed our staff members and our equipment. Safety was initially a big issue for me, and I spent a great deal of time studying our equipment, our day-to-day operations and our oilfield practices. We were a small company, with 80 to 90 employees, and I knew we could not afford to lose work time due to injuries, malfunctioning equipment, workman's compensation issues and so forth. Focusing on safety issues and investing in preventative maintenance for equipment does not dramatically affect the bottom line in the short term. But over the long haul, it proved to be extremely beneficial. I also made a concerted effort to invest any profits—and they were very limited in those early days—into equipment, purchasing drill pipes, upgrading engines, repairing mud pumps and so forth.

That wasn't necessarily a popular move with our employees, who would have much rather seen me invest any income in bonuses and increased compensation. But I stuck to the plan, even if I didn't win any popularity contests. I was 22 years old, and I felt like I had been thrown into the lion's den of the oilfield, which can be an awfully scary, corrupt and decadent atmosphere. In addition to the emphasis I placed on safety, I knew we also needed to make some aggressive moves to generate new revenue streams (like taking business to Mexico two years after I graduated in a very risky venture that paid off), as well as eliminating any counterproductive practices or employees.

My dad was an invaluable resource to me as I contemplated moves and strategies, and initially, he had the final veto on any major moves. But for the most part, he allowed me to gradually make more of the significant business decisions. As I look back on those times, I realize how quickly I grew as a business leader because my father allowed me to make so many calls. I made plenty of good ones and some bad ones, but I learned from every maneuver. It wasn't always easy to work with my father, but it was a blessing.

One of the more difficult decisions I made right away was terminating the "sour lemon" in a managerial role in 1995. He held a key position in the company, but he and I were not on the same page. He was in his mid-50s and I was in my early 20s, and he did not take kindly to being fired by a man less than half his age. Of course, I faced plenty of other age-related scrutiny in those days. Practically everyone I encountered in the oilfield during those days was 20, 30 or 40 years older than me. As I made sales calls, I was often harassed for my lack of experience. Even though I am 6-foot-4, many people often talked down to me. But I never showed any frustration and I never pretended to know something that I didn't. In many cases, I think being sincere and genuine eventually won me favor—and business—from the significantly older clients I was contacting. In many other cases, it was probably the Cotton Bowl ring I proudly displayed whenever I was meeting with an Aggie.

I definitely used my A&M background to get a foot in the door and as a conversation-starter once I was in front of a decision maker with maroon blood. There are plenty of Aggies in the oil and gas industry, and my Cotton Bowl rings usually bought me at least a little time to state my case in person. I will admit there was one Longhorn whom I was pitching, and at the risk of angering the ghosts of E. King Gill (the original 12th Man), John Kimbrough (hero of the Aggies' 1939 national championship team) and Joe Routt (first-ever A&M football All-American), I turned the Cotton Bowl ring and my Aggie ring around so the prospective client wouldn't notice. I bleed maroon and I despise burnt orange, but we desperately needed the green.

Fortunately, we did enough things right in 1994 and '95 that we actually turned a profit in 1996. I recall jumping up and down at the end of '96 because the bottom-line figure didn't have a parenthesis around it indicating that we were in a deficit. Our total profit in 1996 was a whopping $68,000. It wasn't going to change my tax bracket, but it was definitely a change for the better. The following year was a good one, too, as natural gas prices spiked up. I continued to invest back in the equipment, although it was tempting to "live it up a little." Fortunately, I resisted the temptation. In this industry, things can change quickly, and they did much sooner than I could have anticipated.

EASTHAM'S MOST DIFFICULT CHALLENGE

The Eastham family with daughters Madelynn, Bella and Aspen

Former United States Army General George S. Patton once said, "Success is how high you bounce when you hit bottom." That's probably applicable in every walk of life, but it seems particularly fitting for the drilling/energy industries. If you stay in the business long enough, you will likely gain an intimate familiarity with rock bottom. For various reasons, 1998 and '99 were extremely difficult years within the industry, and it often took a balancing act just too keep the doors open and my head above the water. Nevertheless, we continued to invest every penny we could back into the company in hopes of riding the roller coaster back up to more profitable peaks.

Thankfully, that happened in 2000 and 2001. We made some good decisions to sell some older equipment, and we turned down a couple of offers to sell the company. Instead of pocketing a big chunk of money, we chose to keep moving forward, and we were rewarded with good years in 2000-01. At that point, I invested the profits into the company more heavily than ever before and expanded from four rigs to six. In 2000, I also took a risk by investing in a full-time safety manager.

We were still a small company, but we had an increasingly big presence. By 2003, we looked at selling Big E again because, quite frankly, running the business was wearing on me…and even demoralizing me. Andrea had just given birth to our third daughter, and even though I had only been in the business for about 10 years, it often felt more like 30. The highs and lows of the business were taking their toll on me, and we spent about a year researching the possibility of selling Big E Drilling. Thank God we didn't, and thank God I began to rely more and more on the consistency of Jesus Christ's assurances instead of being physically and emotionally drained by the volatility of the drilling/energy industries. I've discovered that maturation is often one of the keys to gaining perspective, and as I began focusing on my spiritual maturation, it gave me greater peace and assurance in all other areas of my life, including my business.

I won't pinpoint just one specific challenge that has tested, shaped or defined me as an entrepreneur. Quite frankly, there have been so many that it is difficult to choose one. But perhaps my greatest growth as an entrepreneur came around 2003 with yet another downward turn. During every previous down cycle within the industry, I often found myself fretting and worrying unnecessarily about so many issues that were absolutely beyond my control. After roughly 10 years of overseeing the business, however, I took a step back and assessed how blessed we had been. I've learned to give the credit to the Lord and to rely on His timing. That doesn't mean I merely sat back and waited on God to deliver me business or to change the energy prices. I continued to work as hard as I could and prepared as diligently as possible to seize opportunities when they arose. But I realized God had blessed our business over and over again, and every time I thought we were on the verge of becoming nothing more than a tumbleweed, something good would happen to turn our fortunes around. Some people may call that coincidence, but I believe it has been God's timing. I've gained great assurance now that, as long as we continue to do things the right way and to operate with great integrity that honors God, everything will ultimately work out for the best.

We will still endure difficult times and great challenges, but my faith has given me a better perspective. I also give a ton of credit to my employees, to my father and to my wife for their support and composure during intense business times. Virtually every family deals with financial issues, but when you are working for a family-owned company and you have major issues, it can multiply the stress level because it becomes so much more difficult to separate your personal life from your business. Fortunately, many key people have stuck by me as we've grown the company, and good times have always followed difficult ones.

That was again the case following the difficult times in 2003-04. The Atlantic hurricane season of 2005 rewrote the United States record books on many levels, including most tropical storms (28), most hurricanes (15), most Category Five hurricanes (4) and most financial damage (an estimated $150 billion). The biggest storm of '05 was Hurricane Katrina, which was determined to be the costliest natural disaster, as well as one of the five deadliest hurricanes, in U.S. history. It was a tragedy of mammoth proportions, as at least 1,833 people died in the hurricane and subsequent floods, and total property damage was estimated at $81 billion. The storms destroyed or damaged numerous rigs and disrupted natural gas wells throughout the Gulf Coast region.

We put our rigs to work, and we were highly productive. I then made some proactive moves by selling three of our older rigs for more money than I could have ever envisioned and investing in new technology rigs that allowed us to drill horizontally and deeper than ever before. The new rigs were extremely expensive, and my father worried aloud, telling me several times, "Lyle, I hope you know what you are doing." You never know with absolute certainty in this industry, but I had a strong hunch, and I prayed continually. We invested millions upon millions in new technology rigs, and by the end of 2006, I had replaced all three old rigs with state-of-the art new ones. The new rigs were about three times the price of the old ones, but it began to pay off in a big way. Fortunately, my father was able to see the company begin to thrive in 2008 before he lost his courageous five-year battle with leukemia on November 3, 2008, at the age of 75. Interestingly, my dad died on the day that Barack Obama was elected as the 44th President of the United States. I've always thought he chose a good day to check out.

Losing my dad rocked me, as we had been talking about our future plans right up until the day he died. We were always talking about the next move and where to deploy the capital we generated most recently. I know my father would be proud of where we are today, because I have continued to reinvest in the company at every opportunity. As I write today, we are still a relatively small, six-rig company. But we have replaced the old rigs with new-age drilling equipment. During the years of transition, we had a great operations manager, who was an expert on drilling equipment. He provided us with an invaluable edge as we invested in the latest technologies. Today, I would estimate that our rigs are worth as much as $20 million apiece, which is about four times more than what we paid to build the first new ones in 2006 and '07. We made some wise decisions, and my employees played a huge role in those decisions.

This has never, ever been all about me or even just about my family. Another way God has blessed us is in allowing me to assemble a terrific team that now includes roughly 250 employees, all of whom have a specific role to perform in making us a great company. We have definitely invested in equipment and technology through the years, but we have also poured our resources into people. We've been blessed to hire great people, but for the most part, we have kept them with us by making them realize they are vital to our success. We've done that by paying them fairly, investing in their retirement accounts, providing them with great benefits and so forth. I am proud to say that my lowest-paid employee, as of this writing, earned more than $75,000 per year. That's a far cry from the $30,000 I took home in my first year with the company… and my father was the owner.

Keeping up to date with equipment and keeping our team intact has allowed us to continually seize opportunities in the marketplace. We did that in the aftermath of Hurricane Katrina in 2005, and we did again in 2009 when we made a concerted effort to move from natural gas drilling to shale drilling. That was a prosperous decision, as well, thanks to the Eagle Ford Shale, a hydrocarbon-producing formation that became the heart of economic activity and development in Texas due to its capability of producing both gas and more oil than other traditional shale plays. The Eagle Ford Shale is situated primarily in South Texas, but it is 400 miles long and 50 miles wide, touching the Mexican border and reaching all the way up to East Texas. Hydraulic fracturing or "fracking" is typically used in the Eagle Ford, where wells are drilled deep underground vertically, then moved horizontally into shale beds. The first well to produce oil and gas from the Eagle Ford was in 2008 in LaSalle County, and we began drilling in 2009, which was a great move for our company. The Eagle Ford Shale became one of the most actively drilled targets for oil and gas in the United States, but we were only able to take advantage of the investment because of the state-of-the-art equipment we had acquired.

EASTHAM'S ADVICE TO YOUNG ENTREPRENEURS

Lyle and Andrea Eastham

Adapt. Reevaluate. Adjust. Reassess. Get the picture?

Your plans for the future may now seem so perfect, and they may, indeed, lead you straight to your ultimate dreams. But from personal experience, I believe that one of the keys to success in life and entrepreneurship is being flexible enough to reexamine your goals based on the circumstances life delivers. After all, I was going to be a professional football player or perhaps a pro golfer. When those things didn't work out, I was going to make mounds of money in the steel business, which was a family tradition. Or maybe I'd make my money in oil.

Quite frankly, none of my grand plans worked out exactly according to my own visions. But I believe God has a plan for my life, and after spending many years worrying about my future, I finally realized God was leading me in the best direction all along. So, the very best advice I can offer any young entrepreneur is to trust in the Lord with all your heart and lean not on your own understanding

(Proverbs 3:5). I realize this is not a spiritual book, so I will not preach. But whether you are a Christian or not, I believe you must have faith to be successful.

One of the biggest keys to my success has been honoring God and doing things with integrity and honesty. When I decided to stick with the family business—as opposed to taking more than twice as much annual salary and going into sales right out of college—I knew it was vital to continue building on the strong and positive reputation my father, grandfather and great-grandfather worked to achieve. Even more than that, though, I worked to represent my heavenly father. I often fall short; I frequently make mistakes; and I have done so many things wrong. But I have always worked toward making amends for the errors I've made and worked toward making a positive difference in the way we operate.

Integrity can never be taken away. You can take the money away, but integrity never wavers or fades with changing times, oil prices, the economy and so forth. In my particular industry—especially in lean times—there is plenty of corruption. I've seen competitors try to influence prospects by taking them to strip clubs, buying them table dances, arranging for the female dancers to have sex with the prospective clients and so forth. Basically anything was made available—sex, alcohol, drugs, hunting trips, vehicles, cash kickbacks, etc.—to prospects. There was a time where that element existed in our company, as well. But I put an end to that, and I am so glad I did.

I realized we might lose some customers to competitors in the short-term by not compromising our values, but I believed we would ultimately be blessed in the long-term for operating with integrity and dignity. God blessed us, while some of our competitors were sued for breaking up families, providing sex as a favor (basically prostitution), arranging for drugs and alcohol and so forth. We made a commitment to do things the right way, and whether you are a Christian or not, operating a business with integrity and honesty will eventually pay off. It certainly did for us.

Another piece of advice that has been helpful to me—especially in more recent years—is to always keep the big picture in mind. I was tempted many times to sell our company and to go public because of difficult circumstances created by the volatility of the drilling/energy industry. It would have been easy to sell. It would have made sense to sell at various times. But every time I seriously considered unloading the business, God allowed me to see the bigger picture. I am so thankful we never went public and never sold out.

I've also learned—reluctantly, at times—that you must rely on others to be successful. When I was younger, I believed I could tackle the world on my own. But over time, I realized that in business—like football—you must rely on your teammates to be successful. You may start a wonderful business on your own, but you will only build a great entrepreneurship by hiring good people, empowering good people, trusting good people and retaining good people.

Remember also that you are not capable of being all things to all people and that you can't accomplish everything at once. I have seen so many potentially great entrepreneurs crash and fail because they have tried to take on too much responsibility on their own. Develop your ideas and build your business gradually. Be patient with yourself and your employees. You can't do everything in a day or a week or a year. And stick to one thing at a time instead of trying to juggle 10 things at once. You will discover that you are so much more effective doing one thing than attempting to do too much.

Finally, don't wait to chase your dreams. If God has planted a dream in you, nurture it, water it, develop it and pursue it. Be flexible enough to change when circumstances demand change, but also be determined enough to follow your dreams through good times and bad. And remember, that if you are still living, God still has a plan to achieve through your life. Whenever you are tempted to think otherwise, remember me. I should have been dead long ago, whether the cause of death was being hit in the street by a drunk driver or almost slicing my wrist in half. But God obviously wasn't through with me yet. Perhaps part of the reason I am still here involves sharing my story with you. Be encouraged, be persistent and be all that you can be.

8.
Neal Adams
President/Partner
Adams, Lynch & Loftin, P.C.
Texas A&M Class of 1968

ADAMS' PATH TO TEXAS A&M

Neal and Sonja Adams with daughters Marti and Paige

Growing up in East Texas, there was never, ever a doubt that my brother and I would eventually attend Texas A&M. My father and uncle both entered Texas A&M in 1941 as freshmen in the Corp of Cadets, although my uncle is actually about two years older than my dad. Nevertheless, they entered college at the same time, with my father enrolling at just 16 years old. Sixteen! That's hard for me to even fathom now, but those were obviously different times across the country and around the world. By 1941, Adolf Hitler had already begun his maniacal mission in a quest for global domination, and by 1943, both my father and my uncle—along with most of the other upperclassmen at A&M—had departed College Station to join the Allied Forces' war efforts.

Seniors were commissioned and juniors received a conditional commission based on finishing training. Dad and my uncle were juniors at that time. They ended up going through training and eventually became officers, with my dad serving in the Air Force and my uncle in the Army. My dad came back in '46 and finished at A&M in '48, becoming the first member of my family to ever graduate from college. My uncle never came back to A&M, but he bleeds maroon and white like anyone else who wears the Aggie ring. And those two brothers certainly shared their maroon pride and passion with their kids. My dad had two sons and my uncle had three boys. Three civil engineers and two lawyers came out of that quintet. All five of us wear Aggie rings, and we all have Texas A&M diplomas hanging on our walls. Obviously, we were brainwashed in the purest sense. I've been told that I actually attended my first Aggie football game when I was 11. That's 11 months, not years. Kyle Field has been a prominent part of my life since that time.

My father and uncle reinforced the importance of earning a college degree by making sure all of us worked extremely hard in manual labor jobs. They wanted us to use our heads, not our backs and hands to eventually earn a living. My first job came at age 6 or 7, as I was working on my grandfather's ranch west of Tyler. My brother, Ron, and I lived with my grandparents for a year while my mother was in the hospital, and I was put to work feeding the cattle, which wasn't too bad, and cleaning the chicken coup, which was absolutely awful. I also carried water to the African-Americans who worked on my grandfather's ranch. We had big, glass gallon jugs that my grandmother had sewed burlap around to serve as primitive insulation. When the burlap was wet, it kept the water cool. I would carry those water bottles to the ranch hands who were working in the fields. I grew up around African-American kids whom I liked and respected, so I didn't have the prejudice that was so prevalent during those times in East Texas, where the Tyler schools were still segregated throughout my adolescence.

I also worked in middle school and throughout my time at Robert E. Lee High School. My father believed it was important for his kids—as well as his nephews—to have a strong work ethic and to also possess a good understanding of money. In fact, when I bought a brand new bicycle in junior high, my father made me borrow the money from Tyler Bank and Trust Company so I gained an understanding for banking, installment payments, interest, etc. During a couple of summers in high school, my cousins, brother and I worked our ever-lovin' butts off by hauling hay, and I also worked at my father's car lot throughout the school year washing the vehicles he had for sale. We certainly didn't have much excess money in our middle-class home, but we didn't lack for anything, either. Life was good, and we all worked hard. We played hard, too, as I grew up participating in every sport I could, depending on the time of the year. I played golf and football, but baseball was my best sport. I was a switch-hitting centerfielder, and I was the fastest player on my team, which certainly helped me to hit .500 during my senior season.

I had such a good senior season at Lee High that I actually earned a partial baseball scholarship to Texas A&M. I had injured my right (throwing) shoulder while playing football in high school, and while it didn't really bother me during high school, the wear and tear caught up with me in college. Even if I had been completely healthy, I was probably never going to be a star for A&M head coach Tom Chandler, who had guided the Aggies to the College World Series the same year (1964) that I graduated from Lee. But the injury sealed my fate before my collegiate baseball career ever really began. In hindsight, though, that was probably for the best. If I had continued to play baseball throughout my college career, I may have never run for yell leader, which was one of the greatest things I have ever done.

I had obviously grown up around Kyle Field, and I had always been impressed by how the yell leaders worked the crowd during A&M games. But I probably didn't decide I actually wanted to be a yell leader until I watched Joe Bush, a junior yell leader in 1964-65 and the head yell leader in 1965-66. He just had a real presence. Joe probably had more influence on yell leaders and students in the 1960s than anyone else I have ever met because he was such a class Aggie and represented everything A&M stood for. He was our role model. According to John Adams' book, *Keepers of the Spirit: The Corps of Cadets at Texas A&M University, 1876-2001,* Bush was named the outstanding cadet among more than 1,800 young men who attended camps in the summer of '65 in both the Fourth and Fifth Army ROTC training regions. He was beloved and admired by older and younger students at A&M, especially as a yell leader, and he possessed a captivating charisma. After graduating from A&M, Bush left for Southeast Asia on April 21, 1968, which is the traditional date for Aggie Muster. Unfortunately, he became the first reported American to die in Laos on February 10, 1969 when he was just 25. But he certainly left a legacy and made a great impression on me.

When I first arrived at A&M in the fall of '64, I joined the Corps of Cadets and began a degree path that would eventually make me a civil engineer. I chose that major because I had been really good in math and chemistry in high school. But after taking engineering physics during my second semester at A&M, I realized becoming an engineer was not for me. There were 11 guys and one female in that engineering physics class. She made an A in the class, while all of the boys made Ds and Fs. I switched my major to marketing and business, and it turned out to be a really good move for me.

Another really good move for me came toward the end of my freshman year when I agreed to take a co-ed from Baylor to the Tyler Rose Festival, which is a major deal in East Texas. One of my really good friends from Tyler, Elaine McKay, was going to Baylor, and one of her roommates was a young lady from Fort Worth named Sonja Moreland. During high school and early in her time at Baylor, Sonja had been dating another future A&M yell leader, Dick Carey '67. But to make a long, convoluted and rather confusing story short, Elaine had been chosen to serve as the Rose Queen, and she asked Sonja to be her duchess from Fort Worth for the weeklong festival. Sonja and Dick had been on rather thin ice, and besides, she figured it would be far more enjoyable if her escort was from Tyler and knew many of the people who would be participating and attending the events. Sonja asked me to be her escort, I accepted and we had a good time together. We experienced some chemistry, and we began dating, although not exclusively at first.

From time to time, we would simply meet along Highway 6 in Marlin and stroll around the park as we grew to know each other better. It was certainly nothing fancy, as I was having to work my tail off just to keep enough gas in my car so that I could meet Sonja every once in a while for a picnic. It didn't take me long to realize that Sonja was a keeper, and we decided to stop dating other people and to only date each other. As time progressed at A&M, I also decided I wanted to run for yell leader. Unfortunately, I did not have the opportunity to run for yell leader entering my junior year because I missed the academic cutoff by one-tenth of a point. That engineering physics class was still haunting me.

But I continued to work hard in the classroom, and it paid off. Not only did I run for yell leader in the spring of 1967, but I also was elected. And because one of the two junior yell leaders from 1966-67 was not able to run for election and the other was defeated, I was chosen as head yell leader for my senior year. That was quite significant at the time because the tradition at that point was for the head yell leader to go through two-a-day workouts with the football team. And the 1967 A&M football team was loaded with stars such as quarterback Edd Hargett, running back Larry Stegent, wide receiver Bob Long, linebacker Billy Hobbs, defensive back Tommy Maxwell and punter Steve O'Neal. Despite narrowly losing the first four games of the season, that group of guys helped the Aggies win their first SWC title since the mid-1950s. It would have been an incredible experience if I had been able to work out with those guys, but I had to go home for the summer to work. I had no other choice, so I gave fellow senior yell leader Wayne Porter the opportunity to go through two-a-days. But I did get to know many of the players and coaches on that team because I was permitted to travel with the team.

Neal Adams as the head yell leader at Texas A&M

I have so many great memories of those times. Prior to the 1967 game against the Arkansas Razorbacks, for example, head coach Gene Stallings warned all members of the traveling party to exit the field after the game as quickly as possible, especially if the Aggies won. Stallings told everyone that it was not uncommon for Arkansas fans to hurl empty whiskey bottles onto the field and in the direction of opponents after the game. The Aggies rallied from a 14-7 halftime deficit and seized control of the game with 19 points in the fourth quarter to beat the Hogs, 33-21. In the excitement of the fast-paced fourth quarter, I forgot momentarily about Stallings' warning.

I remembered rather quickly, though, when an empty Jack Daniels bottle went flying right by my head, so we high-tailed it to the dressing room. Aside from that, another thing I remember about that trip was that I had to go to the bathroom in the airport terminal in Arkansas after the game and in the excitement of getting on the plane I left my books in the terminal. As the plane pulled away from the terminal, I had to go ask Coach Stallings if there was any way I could go get my books. Thank God we won because I wouldn't have even run the chance of making him mad with my request if we had been outscored. Gene Stallings was as impressive and as imposing as former A&M President General James Earl Rudder to me. He was a big guy with a very deep voice who had played for Bear Bryant. He went to the pilot and told him what was going on, so they dropped a rope out of the cockpit and shimmied my books up. Stallings has never forgotten that memory, either.

Being a yell leader at the Cotton Bowl at the end of that year, where Stallings and the Aggies upset Bear Bryant and the Alabama Crimson Tide was an incredible experience, as well. I was right next to those legendary coaches after the game when Bryant picked up Stallings and gave him a "Bear" hug. That was a memory I will forever cherish.

NEAL ADAMS | 95

The best thing about being a yell leader, however, was how it prepared me for future success. At that time, the yell leaders were still in charge of building bonfire. Organizing bonfire was a huge endeavor, and we built it in three weeks. When I had run for yell leader, I had a pretty good idea of the time commitment it would take to be a yell leader, but I had no concept of how much time and attention bonfire would require of me. We started organizing in July, but once we had our first cut, it was cut and stacked in three weeks. We located the cutting area, which was the very first thing we had to do. Then we had to organize the cut, and the one thing that made it easy back then in the Corp of Cadets was that you were either a stack outfit or you were a cutting area outfit. This was good because learning the ropes and safety issues were all under a chain of command, and I had that at my disposal as head yell leader.

Then we had a junior yell leader and senior yell leader who were in charge of the stack and a junior yell leader and senior yell leader in charge of the cutting area along with people under them who had been active sophomores and juniors, helping them with the stack and cutting area. I learned more out of that experience in developing organizational skills and anticipating what needed to be done to meet the objective to build bonfire than any other thing I have done in my entire life. I gained skills through that process that I use today and have forever in my law practice regarding how I approach something. Back then, 85 percent of the student body was in the Corp of Cadets, so I had the chain of command at my disposal, which made a huge difference because we didn't have discipline issues. Looking back on it now, it was really an incredible operation from start to finish. Being in charge of that was very difficult, but it was also very rewarding.

Similarly, being required to speak in front of crowds, adapt on the fly and think quickly about what I was going to say and develop those thought processes before I did something have been huge skills for me as a lawyer. Those are skills I use regularly in my law practice, standing in front of a jury, a judge or a group of people. Depending on the circumstances, being able to improvise and react, especially at an athletic event such as a basketball game or on Kyle Field, was great preparation in teaching me how to be flexible and versatile. I think the leadership skills I developed as a yell leader helped me in many ways later in life. In respecting that position and the responsibility that comes with it, you understand the importance of representing your school and others at all times in a high-profile role. You learn to think on your feet.

ADAMS' PATH TO ENTREPRENEURIAL SUCCESS

Neal and Sonja are longtime donors to the 12th Man Foundation

After earning my business administration in marketing in 1968, Sonja and I were married on June 8, 1968. I then received my commission from the U.S. Army, and I went to Baylor School of Law to work on my juris doctorate. While I was going to law school, Sonja, who had earned an education degree from Baylor, took a position at the dean of admissions office with what used to be known as Texas State Technical Institute (now Texas State Technical College) at the old Air Force base in Waco. She earned a whopping $129. Not a day or a week; we actually lived—or at least covered a majority of our expenses—on $129 per month for several months.

After I had been accepted to law school, I went to see Mr. Harry Stringer in East Texas at the bank where my father had done business for most of his life. As previously stated, my father believed everyone needed a strong relationship with a banker, and one of the things I have stressed with my own children and the lawyers who have worked for me is that business success in virtually any endeavor is ultimately about building relationships. I had a relationship with Mr. Stringer, and I went to see him and told him I wanted to go to law school. The problem was I didn't have the funds to pay for law school. Neither did my parents. Mr. Stringer, who had recently taken over as president of the bank, told me about an interest-free loan program to support young men and women who wanted to purse higher education in the fields of medicine, dentistry, veterinarian medicine or law school. He offered me the loan, and I vowed to pay it back as quickly as possible. That meant not wasting any time in completing law school.

I put my nose to the grindstone at Baylor, reading as much as I could for as long as I could keep my eyes open. I also clerked for former State Sen. Murray Watson throughout law school, and Sonja received a big break when she was hired full-time as an elementary school teacher in the Waco Independent School District, bringing home more than $300 a month. With the dramatic increase in pay, we thought we had died and gone to heaven, and we saved as much as possible to pay back the loan Mr. Stringer had approved. We were rolling along with our initial plans until we received a major surprise in May of 1970. Although it certainly wasn't planned, Sonja discovered she was pregnant with our first daughter. On one hand, we thanked God for the blessing. We also did some unnecessary worrying, as well.

At that time, the public schools did not allow teachers to continue working when they were pregnant. So naturally, we didn't tell anyone aside from our own family members about our surprise. My goal was to finish law school in November, but until then, we really needed Sonja to continue working and bringing home those paychecks in September and October. Fortunately, she didn't show too quickly, and my mother provided Sonja with the fabrics and materials she needed during the summer to sew very loose-fitting work clothes for the fall. As far as we know, only one janitor questioned another teacher about whether Sonja was pregnant. She finally told the principal the truth at the end of October, and 27 months after starting law school, I earned my juris doctorate in November 1970. It was a whirlwind journey, to say the least, and more chaotic times were on the horizon.

We lived briefly with Sonja's parents in Fort Worth and then I received word that I was going on active duty with the U.S. Army in Indianapolis on January 10. That created a couple of concerns. First, the airlines wouldn't allow pregnant women to fly back then, but fortunately, Sonja had enough loose-fitting outfits that she was able to make it through airport security (which was much different in those days than it is now) and fly to Louisville, Kentucky, where she lived with one of her grandmothers while I went to Indianapolis for office observation. The second and much bigger issue was that when we finally arrived in Indianapolis together in early January with everything we owned in the back of a trailer, I was told by the nurse at the hospital on the Army base that Sonja could not be seen by a doctor until I had actually gone on active duty. At that point, I went into full-fledged "angry lawyer mode," creating enough of a commotion that one of the doctors came out and said he would be glad to see my wife. We weren't in a courthouse, but unofficially, that may have been the first time when my cross-examination skills delivered the verdict we desperately needed.

Sonja gave birth to our first daughter, Marti, on January 15, 1971 in Indianapolis, and unfortunately, neither one of our mothers could be there to help because they were both back in Texas working. We were on our own with a new baby in a new community in the dead of a frigid winter. It was a little intimidating at first, but we developed some great friendships with the couples who were living around us in the married housing/apartment complex on the base. There were four or five couples around us who became like extended family members. We were the only couple to have a baby at that point, so Marti was often pampered and Sonja never really felt like she was all alone even though we were so far away from our family and the warmth of Texas. We still exchange Christmas cards with some of those couples we bonded with in Indianapolis, and I am forever grateful for the support they provided Sonja.

I had a two-year active duty commitment in 1971-72, which was still in the midst of America's military involvement in Vietnam. When I graduated from A&M in '68, most of my classmates were commissioned and were stateside for one year and in Vietnam for a year. My expectation was that I would also eventually end up in Vietnam. Fortunately, that was never the case. From Indianapolis, I was assigned to Fort Jackson in Columbia, South Carolina, which was a college town (home to the University of South Carolina) and was a terrific place to be for my girls and me. The only down side was that I was assigned to a lieutenant colonel who was quite short and was also short on patience. In fact, the chip on his shoulder was taller than him because he had been passed over for so many promotions.

During my first week, I managed to anger the lieutenant colonel, who was my direct boss, even though I had done nothing wrong. Once a month the commanding general held a meeting with all the officers, and the new guys introduced themselves and mentioned something about their background. I stood up and said, "I'm First Lieutenant Neal Adams from Tyler, Texas, and I graduated from Texas A&M University." The commanding general stood up in this room packed with officers, walks up to me and says his name and class year to me. He asked me what I did at A&M, and I told him that, among other things, I was the head yell leader the year we beat Alabama in the Cotton Bowl. He spent the next five minutes talking about that game, and thanks to the A&M connection, we immediately bonded…which pissed off my lieutenant colonel more than I could have imagined. He rode my butt so hard I eventually said something to him. He was so livid that he gave me the worst job in the U.S. Army, and I became the "Postal Officer" for Fort Jackson, where I tried to manage 75 women from the civil service. It was more awful than I ever anticipated, and I began looking for anything else to do. Through the grapevine, I heard that the Judge Advocate General's Corps of the Army—the JAG—was in need of a couple of lawyers. I inquired about the opportunity, and I was told that they would love to have me as a prosecutor.

That was truly one of God's great blessings. I was reassigned to Headquarters Command Center at Fort Jackson, and for the next 18 months, I was one of the lead trial councils and had three full-time investigators. Not only was that terrific training for my future as a lawyer, but it also kept me out of Vietnam, where more than 58,000 Americans were killed between 1955-75. I even managed to have some fun with the military judge, who was a University of Texas graduate and gave me plenty of grief if something didn't go right in one of my trials. Overall, South Carolina was an incredible blessing, especially considering that the alternative could have been South Vietnam.

As my military commitment drew to a close, I began checking with some of my classmates from Baylor Law about opportunities in the Lone Star State. Sonja and I both wanted to live in Fort Worth, and one of my classmates was with a law firm in Fort Worth. After a little networking, I was hired by that firm in 1972, where I stayed for a year and gained a little experience in the civilian world. But I didn't enter the law field to work in someone else's firm. My father had been his own boss as an automobile salesman, and I had always wanted to be a business owner or entrepreneur at some level.

The opportunity presented itself right away, and three of us broke off from the first firm where I worked to form Adams, Keith and Meier in the fall of '73. My name was first only because it would allow our firm to appear in front of most others in the Yellow Pages, which was a big deal back then. But our three-person partnership didn't stand the test of time because the "Meier" in our firm was Bill Meier, who represented Tarrant County as a Texas State Senator from 1973 through 1983. The time demands of that role were too much for him to continue in our firm, so Darrell Keith and I formed the Adams and Keith Law Firm in 1975. We did well for a few years, as I built up a real estate practice. But we eventually parted ways when Keith began suing a number of doctors in medical malpractice suits. He moved to downtown Fort Worth, specifically to be closer to the Medical District, home to Tarrant County's five major hospitals as well as dozens of independent medical clinics.

With a couple of small kids (our second daughter, Paige, was born in 1974), Sonja and I had no interest in settling in downtown. We did our research, and we settled in Euless in Northeast Tarrant County so that our daughters could attend the outstanding public schools within the Hurst-Euless-Bedford Independent School District.

Obviously, education was extremely important to Sonja and me. Her mother had been a teacher, and Sonja had followed in her mom's footsteps by becoming a teacher…and being the primary breadwinner in our early days of marriage. I had been blessed with a number of great teachers while growing up in Tyler, and I believed that great schools were key components to keeping our country great, from one community to the next. After Darrell Keith and I went our separate ways, I spent about a year and a half on my own and then a few other lawyers joined me. I was also active as a volunteer in the community (I've always been a go-getter who was not afraid to stack activities on my to-do list), serving as president of the Rotary Club of Hurst-Euless-Bedford and the HEB Chamber of Commerce. Then in 1979, one of the lawyers I knew who had served on the HEB School Board mentioned he was leaving the board, and they were interested in appointing me. Because I was taking his position, I was scheduled to rotate off the board at the end of the year, which was four months later.

If I had asked Sonja, she probably would have suggested that I decline the opportunity. But one of the things that drives her insane about me is that I often tackle far more than the average person would ever attempt. In fact, I often have so many things on my plate that it is the equivalent of attempting to tackle Walter Payton, Jim Brown and Emmitt Smith at the same time. For whatever reason, I have always been able to accomplish the most when I have had numerous responsibilities. In other words, I not only accepted the spot on the school board; I also campaigned for reelection and won. I went on the school board in '79 and stayed on until 1986, winning my first two re-election bids. I lost the third one in 1986 by 55 votes, because I had ruffled too many feathers by doing the right thing. Within my first nine days on the school board in 1979, the superintendent took me to lunch and voiced concern about a contract the previous school board had approved with a union in the Midwest. It provided some incentives and advantages for local teachers, as well as some exclusive negotiating rights. But it was illegal. Consequently, I fought to end the contract and any association the HEB School Board had with the union. That angered some of the teachers, who were members of a union, and they fought like hell to make sure I was defeated in my re-election bids. They finally won in 1986 because of my strong support of a good superintendent, but by that time I had developed a niche in the field of education, which would open more doors in the ensuing decades than I could have ever imagined.

ADAMS' MOST DIFFICULT CHALLENGE

Neal Adams

When I was defeated in the school board elections in the spring of '86, it was a temporary blow to my ego. But it certainly worked out for the best. Sometimes you learn so much more from losing than winning, and it is most definitely the case that when God closes one door He usually opens another one. That was the case for me, and stepping back from the school board also made me aware of just how much time I had been spending in school-related issues. I had become the co-chair of the Legislation Committee for the Texas Association of School Boards representing the 1,100 independent school districts in Texas. It became an enormous responsibility and a major time commitment. But my father always used to say that if you are going to do something, do it right. I adopted the same attitude and applied it to everything I tackled, regardless of whether it involved career commitments, family activities or volunteer opportunities. Stepping back from the school board, however, did open my eyes in terms of time management, and it opened a door at the Texas Association of School Administrators (TASA) with its members consisting of the 1,100 independent school district superintendents and many other administrators. I was quite familiar with the Texas Association of School Boards when TASA approached me about becoming the lawyer who represented school administrators and superintendents. That was truly a Godly blessing, and I have spent three decades representing some great men and women who have often been falsely accused. So losing that school board election was a tremendous life-changing experience.

In hindsight, something else that happened in 1986 was also a tremendous benefit, although I most certainly couldn't see it at the time. By 1986, I had about 60 people working for me, including three associate attorneys. My law firm was on solid ground, and it was growing steadily through my education initiatives and real estate practice. When I had entered the law field, my goal was never to "get rich." I wanted to be my own boss; I wanted to make a positive difference; I wanted to help people and to fight for justice within the legal system; and I wanted to do things the right way to honor Jesus Christ, my family and Texas A&M.

Unfortunately, I temporarily lost my sense of direction. As I learned the hard way, it is quite easy to lose focus on what matters most when you take your eyes off of God. At some point in the mid-1980s, I decided that being rich and growing the firm as large as possible might be attainable and positive goals. Or to put it more bluntly, I may have become a little greedy, especially in terms of the real estate investments I was making. That came back to bite me when my favorite U.S. President of all time, Ronald Reagan, signed the Tax Reform Act of 1986 (TRA86), which decreased individual income tax rates, eliminating $30 billion annually in loopholes, while increasing corporate taxes, capital gains taxes and miscellaneous excises. The act raised overall revenue by $54.9 billion in the first fiscal year after enactment and also increased incentives favoring investment in owner-occupied housing relative to rental housing by increasing the Home Mortgage Interest Deduction. But the major impact it had on me at that time was removing many tax shelters, especially for real estate investments. TRA86 significantly decreased the value of many such investments, which had been held more for their tax-advantaged status than for their inherent profitability. In my opinion, TRA86 contributed to the end of the real estate boom of the early-to-mid 1980s.

Prior to 1986, a significant amount of real estate investments in the U.S. were being done by passive investors. It was common for syndicates of investors to pool their resources in order to invest in property, whether it was commercial or residential. They would then hire management companies to run the operation. TRA86 reduced the value of these investments by limiting the extent to which losses associated with them could be deducted from the investor's gross income. Consequently, it encouraged the holders of loss-generating properties to try and unload them, which contributed further to the problem of sinking real estate values.

When TRA86 was enacted, I had three title operations and a practice that was focused heavily on real estate practice. I was involved in 10 or 11 commercial projects—bank buildings, strip shopping centers, etc.—and I had violated a basic biblical principle in partnerships. Many times in church when you hear the term "equally yoked" it is in relation to marriage and making sure that your spouse shares the same fundamental Christian values as you. But it also applies to business relationships. I was not on equal financial footing with some of the partners I did business with in real estate, and there were trust issues, as well. The bottom line is that it was not a wise decision for me to be involved in projects totaling $35 million in debt. When President Reagan signed TRA86, I was in big trouble. In fact, I was teetering on the edge of financial ruin. I had been told that I needed to go file for bankruptcy. But I wouldn't. My father taught me at a young age that if I incurred a debt, it was my responsibility to pay it off.

I spent from 1986 to late in '89 doing everything in my power to save the real estate ventures. One of my former law partners in the real estate ventures, who had been the Republican nominee for Texas attorney general in the early 1980s, and I spent many hours together discussing possible solutions. I wrote a detailed plan and then gathered 18 bankers and their lawyers in a big board room and laid out a plan to settle the debts. I had worked for three years to reduce the debt to about $16 to $18 million, and if every banker would sign off on our plan, we could pay off the rest over a certain amount of time.

Seventeen of the bankers bought into our plan; one did not. In hindsight, the one banker who did not did me a favor, although I certainly couldn't see it at the time. I had to declare personal bankruptcy in 1989, which was a huge blow to my ego. But I learned so many lessons, especially ones about loyalty, in the aftermath of that bankruptcy. When I was a yell leader in college, I used to brag to my grandfather, who had a seventh grade education but was one of the smartest men I have ever known, about my hundreds of friends. He'd say, "Someday there is going to be a circumstance in your life where God is going to show you that all of those friends you have are only acquaintances. If you can count your real friends on one hand, those guys and gals will be stars in your crown in Heaven. If you can do that on your other hand, you will be blessed beyond compare." I thought about that many times following the bankruptcy. The two young partners who joined my firm in 1987 could have easily bailed on me, and I would have understood if they did. But they stayed right by my side—even when all the partners were taking home half as much as we were making previously to make sure our staff members were paid in full. Two or three bankers stuck with me, as did my CPA and one of my best friends, who was in real estate and helped me to restructure some investments.

Then there was Sonja, who never doubted me and never stopped encouraging me. Money was really tight in the midst of the bankruptcy, and it was time for our oldest daughter, Marti, to go to Texas A&M. We couldn't borrow any money, so Sonja went back to work as an elementary school teacher. I really had to swallow my pride, which is the lesson I really believe God wanted me to learn right from the start. My firm had been enjoying so much success prior to '86, and I had probably been focusing way too much on me and not enough on God. The bankruptcy was just the wake-up call I needed to regain humility and an eternal focus.

The lessons I learned during those difficult times made me a much better lawyer, partner and person. It made me less prideful and more compassionate. The difficulties in real estate also allowed me to focus more on education. I continued to do more and more work with TASA, and what we do at the top with superintendents and administrators positively affects the school districts at all levels. I have been so involved in education that I went on the Higher Education Coordinating Board in 2001, and I spent a considerable amount of time in the legislature. On so many levels, I believe God has enabled me to make positive differences in education, from the public schools to the public universities. I feel like I am making a difference in the lives of young people, which is so much more important than merely making more money. If not for the bankruptcy in the 1980s, I am not sure if that would have been my perspective or if people would have been my top priority.

We still do a great deal real estate work, and we represent a number of interests in the Dallas/Fort Worth area, including residential and commercial developers. Everything we do in our law firm now is focused on people, whether it's working with superintendents, hospital districts, banks or the DayStar Television Network, one of the premier Christian TV networks. I also continue to do a considerable amount of volunteer work with my church, the schools systems and, of course, Texas A&M. Bill Youngkin, who is based in College Station, and I have long been known as the lawyers for the Quad. For many years, if any member of the Corps of Cadets wound up in legal trouble for hazing or anything else, one of us would handle it. After all the legal issues were cleared, Bill or I would call the young person and his/her parents into one of our offices. We would talk about the experience and then mom or dad would typically pull out the checkbook to pay us.

We still don't accept any payment. Instead, we remind them to pay it forward. I tell the young person that one day he/she will have the opportunity to help an Aggie in a time of need or trouble. I want you to take care of that Aggie like I'm going to take care of you. I have done that, and Bill does the same thing. What I have discovered through good times and bad is that if you focus on honoring God and helping people, everything else will take care of itself. As Ronald Reagan so eloquently said many years ago, "Live simply, love generously, care deeply, speak kindly, and leave the rest to God."

ADAMS' ADVICE TO YOUNG ENTREPRENEURS

Neal and Sonja Adams with former A&M athletics director Bill Byrne and wife Marilyn

People. Period. Exclamation point, too! If you want to be successful in business or in any other area of life, develop your people skills and focus on building meaningful relationships with people. I am thoroughly convinced that business is 99 percent about people, and people are all looking for genuine and meaningful relationships. To quote the great Ronald Reagan again, "Surround yourself with great people; delegate authority; get out of the way."

I understand that some people are looking for the cheapest hotel, the best bargain on the used car lot and the most inexpensive attorney they can hire. But the majority of people you encounter walking across the Texas A&M campus or walking the downtown Fort Worth streets during lunchtime in expensive suits want to associate with people they trust and admire.

That's why my fundamental piece of advice is to treat all people—not just perspective clients or customers—with tremendous respect, sincere genuineness and a "Golden Rule" approach. To clarify, the Golden Rule is the concept that people should treat others in the same way they themselves would like to be treated. It is often expressed as "Do unto others as you would have them do unto you," which is one translation of a Biblical verse, Luke 6:31. If everyone would operate his/her business by this simple principle, the world would be a much better place. You can't build a business based on trust by tricking customers and tweaking prices. You must be genuine and you must be a person of integrity.

Former Texas A&M University President and former U.S. Defense Secretary Robert M. Gates, while speaking at a commencement ceremony at West Point, stressed the importance of integrity, especially in an era where it often seems to be lost. "A fundamental quality of leadership is doing the right thing when it is the hard thing—in other words, integrity," Gates said. "Too often we read about examples in business and government of leaders who start out with the best of intentions and somehow go astray. I've found that more often than not, what gets people into trouble is not the obvious case of malfeasance—taking the big bribe or cheating on an exam. Often it is the less direct, but no less damaging, temptation to look away or pretend something didn't happen, or that certain things must be OK because other people are doing them; when deep down, if you look hard enough, you know that's not true. To take that stand—to do the hard right, over the easier, more convenient, or more popular wrong—requires courage."

One of the best business books I have ever read—and one that I would highly recommend—is titled, "*American Turnaround: Reinventing AT&T and GM and the Way We Do Business in the USA.*" It was written by Ed Whitacre, the former Chairman and CEO of General Motors and former chairman of the board and CEO of AT&T Inc. He also served as national president of the Boy Scouts of America from 1998 to 2000. Whitacre, who began his career with Southwestern Bell in 1963 as a facility engineer, was born in Ennis, Texas and graduated from Texas Tech. I had long admired Whitacre's leadership style and effectiveness from afar until I read his book. From that point forward, I was basically mesmerized by his leadership genius. Again, I highly recommend the book because it is so memorable in so many ways. But I believe the best lessons that he teaches involve people.

"People are the No. 1 asset of any business," Whitacre wrote. "The No. 1 asset; and if you only get one takeaway from this book, I hope that is it. Because if you don't get that aspect right—the people part—you will fail." I wholeheartedly agree. He also added this gem: "People aren't a commodity—they're a treasure to be cared for and looked after. If people are with you, and they're feeling motivated and inspired, you can accomplish just about anything."

In other words, it's not just about treating potential customers with respect, dignity, appreciation and so forth. If you also treat your employees—no matter if he is your partner or your janitor—with the same level of respect, you will create a tremendous sense of loyalty that will stand the test of time…and even bankruptcy. I will never forget how so many of my employees and partners stood by me in times of trouble simply because they trusted me and appreciated the way I had treated them.

I can often tell whether a young lawyer is going to make it or not with my law firm after just a few months. It's not about his knowledge of the law or her presence in front of the jury. I can tell whether he or she is a keeper by how the person treats the receptionist in my office. The receptionist is the most important person in our office because she is the first person our clients meet. If she doesn't have a smile on her face or greet them the right way, she sets the tone for the office in a negative way. Every phone that rings in the office comes through her. If she projects a smile through her voice, it will impact us. Some of the younger people who I hired just did not get it.

I had a young lawyer once who was obviously born with a silver spoon in his mouth. After a month on the job, my receptionist entered his office and said, "I have some boxes to move, and Mr. Adams asked if you would help me take them to storage." He told her that he did not go to law school to move boxes. She said, "Do you really want me to go tell Mr. Adams that?" He said he did, and I soon explained to him that my receptionist was a helluva lot more valuable than him and his haughty attitude. I didn't fire him on the spot, but I certainly threatened as much. I told him, "If you are going to have that attitude then you don't need to be at my law firm. I would suggest you start looking elsewhere because you don't fit where we are because we are a family and we work together. I respect what she does for me. I want to respect what you do for me, but you are not starting on the right foot."

He didn't practice law at my firm very long. He continued to have the same problem, and he refused to treat everyone in the office with the same level of respect. Perhaps he would have if he had spent some time with my grandfather working with the "hands" in those fields in East Texas. Unfortunately, it's harder and harder to find young people with humility, and it is equally as difficult to find young people who can really communicate. You may "connect" with colleagues on LinkedIn; "friend" fellow acquaintances on Facebook; and "follow" familiar names on Twitter. But I want to hire people who can really communicate without a smart phone in their hand. Technology has changed so many things in my world.

When I started in the legal profession more than four decades ago, there were no computers, no Internet websites, no "cloud" storage options, no copy machines, no scans, no texts, etc. The largest expense in my law firm was books and keeping those books up to date. Today, there is no need for keeping books up to date…or for even keeping books. Every trial lawyer utilizes PowerPoint or some other electronic form of communications/documentation with a smart phone or smart tabloid. Some of the changes are good—and certainly things are more accurate and instantaneous—but we are in danger of losing interpersonal skills and a personal touch.

The world changes, and if you don't change along with it, you are going to have trouble. On the other hand, if you can maintain a personal touch and a human connection in an impersonal world, you will set yourself apart and distinguish yourself in the brightest light with just a little effort: a handwritten note instead of an email; a phone call instead of a text; and a hand-delivered document instead of a scanned document. Don't be afraid to get involved with people and organizations and to develop a meaningful relationship. If you commit to making one real new connection or friendship each week—as opposed to hundreds of social media connections—I believe you will be remarkably successful. It's not about numbers; it's about relationships with people. Period.

Finally, I go back to the simple, but eloquent words of Ed Whitacre. Regarding his Texas upbringing, he wrote: "The lessons of life that got handed my way when I was growing up were pretty straightforward: Use common sense. Treat people like you'd want to be treated. Never think you're better than anybody else—because you're not. Be courteous. Be on time. Don't be the kind of guy who's all hat and no cattle. (A phony, in other words). Don't give up—hang in there. Be who you are. Be thankful. ... Fearlessness has always defined Texas. People in Texas are just a little different. Texans, at their core, are fundamentally optimistic about the possibilities in life. As a result, they tend to think big and aren't afraid to give things that matter to them a real shot. They will hang in there until they accomplish what they are trying to do. Hanging in there is the true measure in Texas. The thing most people truly respect isn't whether you were successful or not—it's that you gave it all you had."

While that certainly applies to most Texans, it definitely applies to most Aggies. From the bottom of my heart and the center of my soul, I really believe there is something special about Aggies like you and me. We could have chosen an easier path and a much easier school. But from the beginning of the Agriculture and Mechanical College to now, I believe Aggieland attracts competitors and courageous individuals. There was a reason why so many military heroes chose A&M before defending our country in various war efforts. And even today there is a reason why courageous and ambitious young people choose to hone their skills at Texas A&M. Aggies are generally daring, brave and bold enough to sail unchartered waters and to embrace the challenges of entrepreneurship. Obviously, you have what it takes to follow and achieve your dreams.

My last piece of advice is to remember that as you travel down life's highways, you will experience mountaintop moments where everything goes your way in business and personal endeavors. Be thankful for those times because you will also inevitably experience valleys of hardships and trials where everything seems to be going against you. My advice is to be grateful for those times, as well. I've discovered throughout my life that you learn more and grow as a person during the valleys. In other words, always be thankful for the blessings that come your way, regardless whether they take you to the top or the bottom.

9.
Michelle Lilie
CPI Wirecloth & Screens, Inc.
Texas A&M Class of 1991

LILIE'S PATH TO TEXAS A&M

A family of Houston Cougars and one die-hard Aggie

No one who knew me during my youthful days in Houston and Pearland would have ever predicted I would one day become such a dyed-in-the-wool, maroon-blooded, tradition-touting, 12th Man towel-waving Aggie. After all, long before I ever fell in love with Texas A&M, I was raised on red… University of Houston Cougar red. Both of my parents attended UH. My mother delayed college until later when in 1968, my father, who had played baseball at Houston, first opened his business. My uncle, Ken Lilie, was nine years older than my dad and had been one of the star players for the 1953 Cougars' baseball team, which was the first squad in school history to make it to Omaha for the College World Series.

As a result of conference realignment in the mid-1990s and again from 2010-2012, Houston is no longer one of the most consistently prominent athletic programs in the Lone Star State. But back when I was growing up in the 1970s and early '80s, the Cougars often ruled the roost in the Southwest Conference in the most high-profile sports: football and men's basketball.

My parents were avid supporters of the Cougars in good times and bad. My formative years just so happened to be really, really good times for the Coogs. Houston joined the SWC in 1976 and promptly won the league title in football and earned a trip to the Cotton Bowl in its first season. The Cougars also won the football title in the SWC in 1978 and '79, and my dad attended every one of those Cotton Bowls. The entire family—my dad, mom, younger sister and me—went to one of those Cotton Bowls together, but it was so unbelievably, teeth-chattering frigid that my mother ended that family New Year's Day trip. After nearly freezing on that first journey to Fair Park in Dallas, my mother required that my dad drop off his girls at my grandparents' house before he continued to follow his beloved Cougars. My sister and I were more than happy to watch the game on television by the warmth of my grandparents' fireplace.

I remember attending many UH football games with my parents, but what I most vividly recall were the basketball games and those terrific teams coached by Guy V. Lewis. From 1982-84, the Cougars, who became known nationally as "Phi Slamma Jamma," made it to three consecutive Final Four appearances behind legendary players like Akeem Olajuwon (he had yet to become "Hakeem"), Clyde Drexler, Michael Young, Rob Williams and Greg Anderson. "Texas' tallest fraternity" won plenty of fans because of the team's athletic, fast-paced, rim-rattling style of play. Unfortunately, the Cougars could never shoot free throws well enough to win the national title, but they were certainly fun to watch. And it was awesome for a kid like me to get to know many of the players because my family attended so many of the games. I was blessed in that regard and in so many other ways, as well.

My family had moved to Pearland when I was six years old and we lived on a golf course in a neighborhood where everybody knew each other, everybody looked out for each other and many of us traveled together. Families in the neighborhood went on spring break ski trips together; we rented house boats on Lake Travis together during the summer; and we often went on Christmas break ski trips together. To this day, I still stay in touch with the girls from my neighborhood and our mothers still have dinner together once a month even though most of them do not live in the same neighborhood. The sense of community was so strong, and I look back on my entire childhood with many positive memories.

Our parents did so much for us, from driving us across the country for vacations (we never flew anywhere because my dad loved his motor home) to providing us with a great foundation for future success. My sister, K.K., who is four years younger than me, and I both inherited many qualities from our parents, and I definitely was blessed with my father's gift for gab. My dad never met a stranger and never had a problem striking up a conversation with anyone at any time. That helped him in business, and it has come in quite handy for me, as well.

All of those trips we made following the Houston Cougars also made me a passionate sports fan, especially college sports. I loved to play sports, as well. My mother's father taught me how to ride a horse, while my dad's father gave me a great love for baseball/softball. We'd regularly play catch together in the backyard, which led me to becoming a pretty good second baseman. I still remember one of the worst punishments my mother ever gave me was not allowing me to go to softball practice. I was usually well-behaved at school, but I was tired one day in fifth grade and snapped at a beloved teacher, who then called my mother. I was shocked when my mother told me that I had to sit out of practice all week for being disrespectful. I was very disappointed, but I learned my lesson. I loved softball and played through my freshman year in high school. I would have continued playing, but I had to make a difficult choice: softball or cheerleading. I chose to cheer, and my parents supported that decision.

My parents supported us in many ways, allowing us to make our own decisions without ever pressuring us. Essentially, that's how I wound up at Texas A&M, even though I didn't have any family ties to Aggieland. While my sister followed our parents' footsteps and earned her undergraduate, master's and PhD from the University of Houston, I began expressing some interest in A&M during my sophomore year at Pearland High. My best friend's name was Brooklyn, and her older sister came to A&M, where she lived in one of the new dorms. Brooklyn and I made the trip to visit her sister in the dorm room, and I believed Aggieland was like a slice of heaven. I told my parents how much I enjoyed A&M, and my mother later shocked me when she purchased tickets to an A&M-Texas football game at Kyle Field in the mid-1980s. My mother had never been to an A&M-Texas game, but because I had expressed an interest in being an Aggie, she and my father supported it and arranged for me to experience some of the greatest traditions in all of college athletics.

Not only did my mother secure four tickets for us on the Kyle Field old track (my uncle and cousin accompanied my mother and me), but she also arranged for us to attend Aggie Bonfire. I was probably 14 or 15 when we attended the Bonfire and the game, and I was thoroughly impressed with everything. The camaraderie and warmth of Bonfire—not just the actual heat from the fire, but the brotherhood—along with the remarkable atmosphere of the game made a lasting impression on me. In fact, I enjoyed it so much that it became somewhat of a family tradition. One of my friends had enrolled the following year as a freshman at the University of Texas, and my entire family drove to Austin with her family to go to the game and celebrate Thanksgiving together. As I look back on those times now, I can't thank my parents enough for being willing to allow their daughter to experience something that forever shaped my life. After those two trips to the A&M-Texas games in College Station and Austin, I felt myself becoming quite protective of Texas A&M.

I knew I wanted to apply to Texas A&M, but I was raised to never place all your eggs into one basket. Consequently, I also applied to Baylor, TCU, SMU, Texas, LSU, Southwestern and, of course, the University of Houston. I loved UH because of my parents, but I never seriously considered it because I wanted to live away from home. As I began to visit some of those schools, I quickly nixed most of them for one reason or another. Eventually, I visited Baylor and I loved it, primarily because I stayed with a family friend who drove a convertible Corvette, dated the quarterback of the football team and was a member of a great sorority. What 17-year-old wouldn't be impressed by that? I had a great time and thought Baylor might be right for me, but then I questioned myself when my parents picked me up and began driving back to Houston.

I was literally crying in the Suburban as my father drove home because I was so confused. I still loved A&M, even though I had just fallen for Baylor. As the tears flowed, my parents encouraged me to write down the pros and cons of each school, and then my father made what I thought was a monumental sacrifice. He asked me if I wanted to swing by the A&M campus for one more look. I had no idea that the A&M campus was actually on our way home from Waco to Pearland; I just was impressed my father was willing to go out of his way for me.

Michelle Lilie (far left) with her father, Glenn, and sister, K.K.

I am so glad we made that visit, and I am also so happy that it was an absolutely miserable, gray day in Aggieland. My father pulled the Suburban up to the Memorial Student Center, and I remember being rather irritated that my mother was making me get out of the vehicle in a driving rain storm. Out of nowhere, this college student runs up to the vehicle carrying an umbrella and says, "Howdy! Are you folks here for a visit?" My mother proceeded to embarrass me by telling the young man my entire life story, but he escorted my mother and me into the MSC and walked us through the facility. By the end of that tour, the young man who had met us with the umbrella and taken the time to show us around had convinced me that Texas A&M was the place to me. He was just one guy, and I don't even recall his name, but he seemed to embody the friendliness and warmth of the entire student body at Texas A&M.

As we left A&M that day, I told my parents I had decided to be an Aggie. I never wavered again. The final visit and that one remarkably friendly young man sealed the deal for me. It's a decision I have never regretted. Several other classmates from Pearland also joined me at A&M, but I took a blind chance on my first roommate, which worked out fine, and I went through rush to find a sorority. Keep in mind that sororities were essentially in their infancy in the 1980s at Texas A&M, and many "old Ags" frowned upon the Greek system ever planting roots in Aggieland. But Chi Omega was great for me, and I met some of the closest friends I could have possibly imagined.

For the most part, I also did well at A&M with my grades and classes, primarily because I avoided math classes as if they were carrying an incurable disease. While I inherited my father's interpersonal skills, I certainly didn't receive his mastery of math. Growing up, I always loved spending time with my dad...unless he was helping me with some homework assignment that involved numbers or equations. I struggled with numbers in high school to the point that my mother finally allowed me to hire a tutor, who was younger than me and happened to be the son of two NASA engineers. Quite literally, he was the son of rocket scientists, and while he wasn't much of a conversationalist, he did help me survive my math requirements. But once I arrived at A&M, I chose a degree plan (communications and marketing) with as little math as possible.

I graduated in December of 1991, although I probably could have walked the stage in May of '91 if I had paid a little closer attention to all the specific requirements I needed to complete my degree. As I entered what could have been the last semester of my senior year, I discovered one class I had to take to graduate was not offered in the spring of '91. I was initially extremely disappointed, but my disenchantment disappeared when my mother noted that my clerical mistake would enable me to stay on campus for one more football season. It was a fun fall as the Aggies went 8-0 in the Southwest Conference, won the league title and earned a trip to the Cotton Bowl. I soaked it all in and savored every moment.

LILIE'S PATH TO ENTREPRENEURIAL SUCCESS

I never planned on going into business with my father. But his success as a business owner did take the pressure off of me after I graduated. I could take some time deciding what to do with the rest of my life. My dad had once sold shoes to earn money in college and later worked for a steel wire company that specialized in providing key products for the oilfield industry. In a nutshell, a "shale shaker" is one of the most important devices on a drilling rig for removing drilled solids from the mud. A wire-cloth screen vibrates while the drilling fluid flows on top of it. The liquid phase of the mud and solids smaller than the wire mesh pass through the screen, while larger solids are retained on the screen and eventually fall off the back of the device and are discarded. In the old days, it was once common for drilling rigs to have only one or two shale shakers, but today, high-efficiency rigs are often fitted with four or more shakers, thus giving more area of wire cloth to use. Depending on various circumstances, the wire-cloth screens are manufactured in numerous sizes to control the flow rate per unit. Bottom-line: the wire-cloth screens are vital filtering products in the oilfield. Screens have been around for many decades, and my father was sharp enough to realize in the late 1960s that the demand for wire-cloth screens was strong enough that he could go into business for himself.

He and my mother did just that in 1968, opening CPI Wirecloth & Screens, Inc. The funny thing is that in order to initially qualify for some funding and accreditation, my father had to document the size of his warehouse. He listed the size of their home garage...in inches, not feet, but he never clarified that his warehouse was not actually a warehouse at all. He knew he could make it in the short run without a true warehouse, and my mother, my father and his friend started the business with a little knowledge about wire-cloth screens and some big dreams. He started the business before I was born, but it was a huge part of my childhood. I went to work often with my father when I was young, and as I matured, he put me to work.

Starting in junior high, I worked all summer and during Christmas breaks at the company. I filed orders; I ran things from the executive offices to the warehouse; I typed letters; and I did just about anything else I was capable of doing. Many of the people who worked for us back then still work for us today, an amazing testament to my father's people skills. Another sensational example of my father's leadership ability as an entrepreneur was how he adapted to difficult circumstances in the marketplace. When the oil and gas business was thriving, my father's business also flourished. The demand was constant, the orders were consistent and the profits were continuous. It's never "easy" to run a business, but there are times when the economy or a trend in a particular industry allow smooth sailing.

That was the case for my father's business during much of my early childhood, but things changed with the oil glut of the 1980s. I didn't understand it at the time, but the world price of oil, which had peaked in 1980 at $35 per barrel, began to decline in the early '80s as a result of slowed economic activities in industrial countries following the 1970s energy crisis. And by 1986, the price had fallen from $27 per barrel to below $10. What that meant to me was that my dad was a little more stressed and a lot less busy at work. The wire-cloth screen business was what he knew, but the demand from oilfield companies was diminishing.

Instead of panicking, however, my father began improvising and diversifying. While the oilfield orders were trickling in, my father noticed that we were filling quite a few orders for a housing authority in Mississippi. A significant amount of raw material had been purchased, and my father sent someone to figure out why the housing authority was so interested in wire-cloth. Upon further investigation, my father learned that many of the residents of the housing authority were ripping off the existing screens so that they could open the windows to allow fresh air inside the particular apartments/units. But that created a number of other problems for the operators of the housing unit, increasing the probability of weather damage to the windows and decreasing protection from intruders—both humans and insects. The housing authority was using the wire-cloth screens to repair or replace the screens that had been removed, which gave my parents an ingenious idea: develop a patent to manufacture and produce window and door screens. In his typical go-getter style, my father created screens that could cover windows and doors, which could be unlatched from the inside, but could not be removed from the outside. And the most impressive selling points were that the screens could not be cut—not even with an industrial-strength blade—and they could withstand winds of up to 140 mph.

Instantaneously, my father had opened up an entirely new—and quite profitable—stream of income. One of the first big breaks was when hurricane testing passed in Miami-Dade County. The screens provided outstanding hurricane protection for all levels of housing, and then school districts began realizing that our screens could save thousands upon thousands of dollars each year by preventing break-ins and vandalism. We didn't initially realize it, but we quickly discovered that public school districts across the country spend millions each year in repairing broken glass.

Michelle Lilie with Cybil Armbruster, Kristen Glymph and Claire Glymph at a basketball tailgate

Thanks to housing authorities, school districts and the threat of hurricanes along the coastlines, the window and door screen business took off in a big way during my college days at Texas A&M in the late-1980s. Many of my college friends joined me in the summers in working for my father's company, and we sold and marketed screens to universities like A&M and LSU. We struck deals with housing authorities and school districts across the country and around the state. Typically, our customers were not just satisfied…they were ecstatic with the results of the screens. Our clients were our best promoters…even when one client removed the screens from the schools in Galveston. We had sold the screens to one superintendent in Galveston, who decided to paint them all purple—the school color of Galveston Ball High School and a prime Mardi Gras color, as well. The next superintendent didn't like the way the painted screens looked, so she had them removed. During the first weekend without the screens, 11 schools within the district were burglarized or vandalized. Obviously, the screens were re-installed.

The screens were an ingenious idea on the part of my father, but the only problem with that side of the business was that once the screens had been sold and installed, there was no reason for those businesses to continue being our partner. It wasn't like the oilfield business, where if we made a great product and provided great service that our clients would return to us over and over again. The window and door screens were so effective and were made so well that there was often no reason for one of our customers to ever call us back after the initial purchase and installation. That bothered my father, who had often spent so much time developing a relationship with the key decision makers at housing authorities, school districts and so forth.

Once again, he conceptualized a golden idea that proved to be my initial entry point into the company on a full-time basis. As I previously stated, I never planned on going into business with my father. But as I planned for my graduation from Texas A&M and examined potential career opportunities, I kept coming back to the fact that my father had built a tremendously successful business with his people skills, creativity and ability to adapt to changing economic environments. Being like my father in so many ways, I believed I could hit the ground running at full speed with CPI Wirecloth & Screens, Inc., especially if there was a niche area for me to prove myself. The niche turned out to be my father's golden idea to continue the relationships he had built with so many housing authorities.

My father's concept was called "GISCO," which stood for Government and Institution Supply Company. Back in the early 1990s, there wasn't a Walmart on every corner in practically every community, especially the smaller towns where so many of the housing authorities were located. My father's vision was to stock the housing authorities with all the supplies they needed to run the business maintenance on a day-to-day basis, which would save the individual agencies plenty of time and at least some money. Instead of sending the maintenance man into town to purchase tools and supplies from a retail outlet on a regular basis, my dad believed he could benefit from the existing relationships he had fostered and could stock the various agencies across the state. He began transforming some of our warehouse space in Pearland into a multifaceted storage location for all types of products and supplies.

He explained the concept to me, and I went to work on an intern basis during my senior year in college, joining my father's full-time GISCO representative, Bob Wetzel, who was a gem of a man. I hit the ground rolling, crisscrossing the state and hitting practically every small town you have and probably haven't heard of in the Lone Star State. Remember, this was long before cell phones and GPS navigation systems, so I had to figure out where to go on my own. My best friend—aside from Bob Wetzel—was inevitably the manager or the customers at Dairy Queen. Practically every small town in Texas has a Dairy Queen, and it's the focal point of small town directions. As Dad pointed out to me, if you can find the Dairy Queen, you are never completely lost. I'd find the Dairy Queen and then find my housing authority, where I would meet with someone and take their order for tools, cleaning supplies, rags, paper towels or practically anything else that it took to run and maintain the upkeep of the properties. Our prices weren't any better than what anyone could find at Walmart, but we were providing these agencies a tremendous service that was certainly saving them time and the hassle of traveling into bigger communities to purchase goods.

I enjoyed my time as an intern so much that I approached my father about full-time employment. He approved and then helped to conceptualize the use of consignment cages. Utilizing the same virtually indestructible materials that we used to cover windows and doors, my father designed little cages where goods could be stocked and stored to provide even more convenience and immediacy to the housing authorities that were utilizing GISCO. With storage facilities on location, we could stock five paint brushes, three shovels, 20 rolls of garbage bags, 15 different types of light bulbs and so forth so that the housing authority could immediately access the products they needed. I would then make my visits on a regular basis and document the inventory, ordering more if necessary and billing the agency for the amount of product that had been used. It wasn't a sophisticated system by any stretch of the imagination. Although computers did exist, I operated almost entirely with a clipboard and paper.

I learned quite a bit about inventory, business practices (good and bad) and the state of Texas roadway system during the next five years as I traveled on a daily basis. Primarily, I developed and enhanced my interpersonal skills. I was young and blonde, so I knew I had to prove myself with every customer. Being with Bob Wetzel, a chain-smoking, seasoned salesman with at least 40 years of experience, certainly helped my credibility early in my career. But eventually, it was vital that I became the trusted contact and face of the GISCO operation. During the mid-1990s, I saw an opportunity to buy the GISCO operations from my father because of the creation and evolution of the Women's Business Enterprise Alliance, which was established in 1995. Then and now, the Women's Business Enterprise Alliance works to increase the opportunities and growth of female-owned businesses. The WBEA is the third-party certifying organization for women-owned businesses in 94 Texas counties.

Businesses that are at least 51 percent owned by a woman and meet specific criteria as outlined by the Women's Business Enterprise National Council standards and procedures are eligible for certification, a designation recognized and required by most major corporations and governmental agencies as a purchasing criterion. The bottom line was the creation of the Women's Business Enterprise Alliance generated enough incentives and advantages for female entrepreneurs that it was extremely beneficial for me to buy the GISCO operations from my father. Unfortunately, I couldn't afford to buy the business from my father, so my mother and I went into business together. My mom also possesses a great business mind, and she had gone back to school to finish her degree. Although my dad never officially graduated (he later received an honorary degree from the University of Houston), my mother walked the stage as a member of the Phi Beta Kappa Honors Society and accepted her diploma with a degree in psychology in 1994. With her education completed, she was ready for our new endeavor.

With the WBEA incentives and opportunities, I began expanding the GISCO concept, hiring inside salespeople and taking bids for much larger cities and housing authorities than we had ever previously attempted to service. Essentially, we tackled virtually any project that dealt with supplies. We began doing quite well, and I started handling some human resources projects for my father. I believed my own business was about to take off, and I needed to know the human resources end of the business to expand as much as possible.

There's no doubt in my mind that we could have been remarkably successful…if not for that little chain known as Walmart. Walmart went from being primarily a retailer in big communities to expanding into smaller towns and opening up new concepts such as the Neighborhood Walmart and the Walmart Supercenter and Six Flags Over Walmart.

OK, so the last one was a joke, but Walmart began an incredible expansion in the mid- and late-1990s that, according to the *Huffington Post* in October 2014, has resulted in the Walton family's combined wealth of $154.8 billion. To put that in perspective, that's enough to purchase all 241,450 homes in Seattle, which are worth a total of $111.5 billion or every single-family house, condo and townhouse in Dallas at $109.4 billion. Obviously, there was no way I could compete with Walmart's prices and accessibility as the retailer expanded. Furthermore, while the WBEA initially seemed like an incredible benefit, it quickly became a limiting ball and chain. Minority groups complained vehemently that women weren't a minority and shouldn't be treated as such by being given assistance, tax breaks and incentives from the government. Every time I turned around we were being interviewed or investigated to make sure that we really were a female-owned and operated company. Our offices were together with CPI Wirecloth & Screens, Inc., and it became quite a hassle to prove over and over again that my mother and I owned our company and were entitled to the WBEA benefits.

LILIE'S MOST DIFFICULT CHALLENGE

The rapid decline of the GISCO business that my mother and I originally believed to be such a golden opportunity was a serious blow to my ego. I didn't feel like a failure, but I definitely felt like I had failed to achieve my entrepreneurial goals and dreams. I wanted to be as successful as my father in building a business, and I also wanted to be as creative as he had been in developing a new income stream when the oil and gas industry took a turn for the worse. Unfortunately, I could have been as creative as Steven Spielberg and George Lucas combined in ways to stock and distribute supplies, but I still wasn't going to beat Sam Walton's retail tidal wave that was sweeping the nation. I didn't do anything wrong; I just picked the wrong business to tackle. Pride kept me from dissolving the GISCO business right away, but the handwriting was clearly on the wall.

Fortunately, I had been dabbling in human resources and purchasing, doing more and more with CPI at about the same time GISCO was unraveling. From a business standpoint and an overall maturity level, my

Michelle is a doting aunt to Madison, Jaxson and Sydney Jenkins

father had taken notice of my drive, dedication and willingness to tackle new challenges. One day I received a phone call from the dean of San Jacinto College-South Campus, who happened to be a wonderful teacher and longtime friend of my father's. When I answered the phone, she said, "Michelle, your father tells me that you want to enroll in an accounting class."

I was dumfounded. There's absolutely, positively no way I wanted to take an accounting class. As previously stated, I was uncomfortable with numbers and math of any kind. In fact, my first response was: "I beg your pardon? An accounting class?"

What I later realized was that my father was trying to expand my skills and stretch me as an entrepreneur. He was grooming me to lead a company with far more potential than GISCO, but first I had to step outside of my comfort zone. My father knew I couldn't oversee a major business without a firm understanding of numbers, finance and accounting. Reluctantly and begrudgingly, I took the accounting class, and benefitted from it tremendously. In fact, I gained so much from that class that I took another one. And instead of focusing only on marketing and human resources—the things I had always enjoyed—I started becoming more involved with the finance meetings, having intelligent conversations with our CPAs and understanding the purpose and results of audits.

I never thought I could—or even wanted to—grasp accounting, finance or anything of the sort. But once I stepped out of my comfort zone, I took off in a full sprint. I spent one summer working in the sultry, non-air conditioned warehouse. I didn't do any welding, but I sweated it out with the warehouse workers, learning every aspect of the entire CPI operation. I also learned a great deal about the personalities of the employees within each department. The workers in the warehouse possessed an entirely different mentality than those in the accounting department, and it was important for me to learn how everyone thought so I could understand how to best motivate, evaluate and educate the various departments.

I also began learning the purchasing side of the business, which intrigued me. It was like fitting a puzzle together to make certain that we had just enough supplies to make the screens without ordering too much. Purchasing supplies seems like such an easy thing to do…until you are charged with doing it. Rest assured, it is not as easy as it sounds. But over time, I learned the art of ordering, just as I had learned to understand and appreciate the numbers of business. As I matured and learned the business into my early 30s, I really believed I had it all figured out.

I was wrong, of course, which my father pointed out a couple of times. One time, in particular, I remember telling my father that we needed to pursue my marketing ideas. He hesitated, and I pointed out that, "Daddy, I have a degree in marketing and I'm telling you that this is the way it needs to happen." Very calmly, he looked straight at me and said, "Yes, I know. I paid for that degree. But that doesn't change the fact that I started this company in the 1960s before you were even born and your Texas A&M degree does not match my decades of business experience." I was momentarily insulted, but then I realized he wasn't putting me in my place or talking down to me. He was pointing out that there is no substitute for experience. Knowledge is indeed powerful, and reading about something can certainly awaken and enlighten you. But until you have actually been in the business trenches for a significant amount of time, pulling the trigger on a deal is still a theory, not a battlefield strategy.

My parents had poured their heart and soul, along with their time, money and energy, into building CPI and nurturing it through good times and bad. They weren't going to merely give me the keys to the business and step out of the way because I believed I was coming of age or because I had learned various aspects of the business. But somewhere around 2007, my father did begin turning over more and more responsibility to me, as well as to my brother-in-law, Jay. This is a family-owned, family-run business, and my brother-in-law and I take our leadership roles within the company very seriously. My father still maintains a significant presence within the company, and whenever he walks into the office, many of our longtime employees still hang on his every word. I love seeing the loyalty that so many of our employees still have for my father, and it serves as a constant reminder to me that, generally speaking, people don't care how much you know until they know how much you care.

Our staff members—we now have about 60 employees—truly understand that we view them as part of our extended family. That's one of the primary reasons we have resisted the numerous offers we have received to sell our operations. We've heard many times that we are the last of a dying breed: a family-owned, small manufacturing business in a world of behemoths.

We realize, of course, that we are unique in this day and age. But we are certainly not dying. On the contrary, we are thriving by being unique. Despite my father's reluctance, we have implemented some modern methodology and practices (emails, digital technology, electronic transfers, robotic welders, etc.) into our day-to-day operations. But what makes us so different—and typically so popular among our loyal clients—is that we maintain a personal touch and as much personal communication as possible. That's how my mother and father started the business in the 1960s, and that's how we will run it as long as our doors are open and our screens are being shipped.

I feel extremely blessed to be in one of the primary leadership roles of CPI, and when I look back in time, I realize that the greatest blessing in my life as a professional/entrepreneur was what I once viewed as my worst business nightmare. If circumstances had been so much different in the market place and the GISCO business would have survived, I would have never been in position to lead CPI. The end of the road for GISCO forced me to go in a different direction. I had to grow, learn, do uncomfortable things and stretch myself beyond where I had ever been in my life. In the process of doing those things, I was preparing myself to help lead a company with so much more potential than GISCO ever possessed.

Quite frankly, the angst I endured, the lessons learned, the pride swallowed and the challenges encountered after the decline of GISCO were some of the greatest blessings in my life as an entrepreneur. They prepared me for far more recent downturns in the price of oil and the downturn in drilling. The changing economy brought us to a conclusion that an overseas venture was viable. We are meeting the challenge by opening a manufacturing facility in Romania to serve the Middle East, North Sea and Russia. The price of oil didn't affect the drilling activities in those geographical locations. As a result, we seized an opportunity that may have otherwise not been considered.

LILIE'S ADVICE TO YOUNG ENTREPRENEURS

I vividly remember a conversation I had with a young man entering my freshman year at Texas A&M. He was conducting interviews of incoming students and was questioning me about why I thought I would excel within the National Agricultural Marketing Association (NAMA) Presentation Team, which had a strong reputation for doing some amazing things in the marketing world. I wasn't interested in agriculture,

Ready for the rodeo with K.K.'s crew

but I was interested in being part of a prestigious group that had traditionally been dominated in terms of membership by young men. I was sitting at a long table at Rudder Tower, and I began telling him all the things that I did in high school. I said I had been very involved in this organization and that one, which would make me perfect for NAMA. In mid-sentence, he stopped me.

He was not being disrespectful, but he was letting me know that I was now in a different world. He said every other person he was going to interview that day had also been a star in high school. "You are just a tree in a forest here," he said. I remember gasping, thinking, "Wow this is what A&M is all about. Everyone here has done all the things that I have done. They made the grades that I did and they are all trying to move forward in their college ways like I am. I'm almost starting over here." That moment my freshman year made me realize I was going to have to really decide what I wanted to do and fully dedicate myself to doing it. Merely going through the motions was not going to cut it. Simply taking the mandatory classes and fulfilling the degree requirements wasn't going to distinguish me. I had to work a little harder, stay a little longer and shine a little brighter just to get noticed, especially in a male-dominated world like NAMA.

Being a part of NAMA at A&M turned out to be the perfect training for me to enter the male-dominated oil and gas industry years later. I learned right away that if I wanted to be respected as a peer in NAMA—and later in the oil and gas industry—I needed to prove myself. I wanted to follow my father's entrepreneurial footsteps, and I wanted to be viewed as a business owner in the making. I also realized fairly quickly that I needed to present myself in a serious manner because some of the unwritten rules were a little different for females than they were for males.

I worked very hard at A&M, and I was blessed with some great professors like the late Dr. Howard Hesby, who arrived at A&M's Department of Animal Science in 1971 and positively influenced thousands upon thousands of Aggies, including me. He was very much a man's man, but he was encouraging to the girls involved with NAMA. He would teach you what you needed to do to prepare to be in the business world. You would go and interview professors. He had us all over the campus doing stuff. At the end of the semester, he would bring in the top agricultural companies, allowing us to participate in complete interviews. They were mock interviews, of course, but they were beneficial in preparing me for the future and dealing with corporate leaders. I encourage any ambitious students to be involved in as many of those types of organizations as possible. It's not enough to merely take the mandatory classes. To distinguish yourself and prepare yourself for greatness, you need to do even more than the average student.

I think that is especially true for young women. There are far more opportunities for women entering the business world today than there were when I was coming out of A&M in the early 1990s. But the rules are still different for women, and they probably always will be. You can fight that, or you can accept it and learn to play by different rules. I chose to accept it, which has allowed me to fit in and climb the corporate ladder more quickly than may have otherwise been possible.

There are no limits to what women can do in the workplace, but there are some things women need to realize they must control and conquer. Women are typically nurturers, which is great in dealing with children, but it can be viewed as being weak in the workplace. Women are also typically more emotional than men. One thing I would stress to any young woman reading this is to control your emotions and to realize that sensitivity is often looked upon as being weak. If you take it the other direction and attempt to take control in the boardroom, you may be viewed as a control freak. To be confident as a woman is much more important than it is to a man in a business setting, but it is also important not to be perceived as a know-it-all. You must be confident to hold a conversation and give answers, but don't take over a conversation. You must strike a balance, and you have to realize that men will often look for weaknesses in you until you prove that you can handle any circumstance.

I think another important thing to remember is not to try to be one of the guys. I love to talk sports, and I do so with virtually any man. I also love to play golf, and I would highly advise a young woman to learn to play golf. You can make so many deals on the golf course, and if you prove to be a decent player, you can earn instant respect, especially among your male counterparts. But there's definitely a line to draw in terms of being one of the guys. You just can't do it. You can't tell the same jokes or swap the same stories. I don't try to be something I am not in a bar or in a setting that is dominated by men, and I have been in plenty of them. I think it is important to be perceived by male peers as a strong woman. I think you should be as attractive as possible in a professional manner, but you never want to dress in the work place or the work setting (a business retreat, for example) in a manner that could be deemed as "provocative." Again, there are different rules for women. You don't have to like it, but you can waste an immeasurable amount of time and energy in attempting to fight it.

Finally, I think it is extremely important to learn to be comfortable in virtually any setting. That's not always easy, especially when you are surrounded by successful people who may seem out of your league in terms of their overall success. I've been heavily involved with the Houston Livestock Show and Rodeo through the years, and I have also served on numerous committees with the 12th Man Foundation, the fundraising organization for Texas A&M athletics. In both volunteer roles—but especially with the 12th Man Foundation—I have often been the only woman and the youngest person on a committee comprised of multi-millionaires and absolutely incredible success stories from all business fields. It can be extremely intimidating to even sit at the same table with some of the remarkable businessmen I have worked with through the years.

I can vividly remember the very first meeting I attended while serving on one of the key committees at the 12th Man Foundation. I was a nervous wreck. I knew everyone, but I didn't know them very well, and I was the only female in the entire room. I was the youngest, by far, and I was the only person in the room who did not have a building on the Texas A&M campus named after me. I remember thinking, "How do I sit? Do I sit up right? Do I lean back? Do I cross my legs? I am typically a very confident person. But in that setting, sitting at a long boardroom table that was surrounded by successful people, I was intimidated. To be honest, it was the first time I can remember feeling that way since my freshman year when that guy said you are nothing but a tree in a massive forest. I got a nervous feeling as I sat in the boardroom, and I had to tell myself to not show any emotion. It shocked me.

But I reminded myself that people believed I belonged on that committee. And after being quiet and listening for some time, several men called on me to ask me my opinion. I spoke confidently, even though I practically felt like I was going to be sick. After the meeting, I hopped in the car. I hadn't even left yet, but I called my father and admitted to him how uncomfortable I had been in that setting. In fact, I said that it was the most intimidated I had ever been in my entire life. I will never forget his response.

"Good," he said. "We all need to be challenged. We all need to face our fears. We all need to step outside of our comfort zone."

Indeed, that has been the key to my success at every step in my journey. Whenever I have been willing to step outside of my comfort zone, it has been the first step to an amazing new place in my entrepreneurial career. Remember that if you are ever nervous or frightened about taking the next step.

10.

Larry Hodges
President/Founder of Copy Corner
Owner/General Partner of DoubleDave's Brazos Valley
Texas A&M Class of 1988

HODGES' PATH TO TEXAS A&M

Larry Hodges with his children, Lauren and Hank

Prior to the recent acceleration of the entrepreneurial/startup community in Bryan-College Station, whenever I spoke to a class at Texas A&M, the students were always intrigued by the fact that my business career began while still a student at A&M. It's not so uncommon anymore for a student to start a business while in school, and I love that! Personally, it was certainly not my plan to start a business entering school, but when my buddy, Nick Bregenzer, noticed an opportunity to fill a niche in the marketplace, I didn't wait to earn my undergraduate degree in finance or bide my time in someone else's office before beginning the pursuit of my entrepreneurial dreams.

It's not that I'm impatient, but I've always believed that the best time to act on an idea or begin pursuing a dream is now. Not when the financing is just right, not when everything is perfectly in place and not when all the obstacles have been removed from the path leading toward your dreams. As Zig Ziglar once said, "You don't have to be great to start, but you have to start to be great."

My entrepreneurial path can be traced back to my junior high school days in the late 1970s. Each day in the spring, my friend, Stephen Matthews, and I would race out of school following the final bell and ride our bikes from Johnston Junior High in southwest Houston to the Westbury American Little League baseball fields. We landed a job chalking the batter's boxes and foul lines on each of the fields prior to the first games of the evening, which would begin at 5:30. We didn't make much money, but it felt great to make our own, and it certainly gave me a sense of satisfaction. Westbury won the 1966 Little League World Series, and the community took great pride in not only the quality of play, but also the quality of the facilities. We loved our work, and it was a big responsibility for a couple of young teens. If I had a game later that evening, my mom or dad would bring my uniform to the ballpark, we'd eat dinner from the concession stands, and I would change in the restroom.

Westbury was a great place for Little League baseball and a terrific place to grow up. My mom and dad, Patti and Buz Hodges, are both from Virginia, where I was born in 1965. My dad, who'd attended the University of North Carolina to play football, was in the mortgage business. His career took us to Atlanta when I was a toddler, before landing in Houston in 1969, as Texas' population began to explode. I had no previous ties to the Lone Star State, but it's really the only home I've known.

I didn't initially have any allegiance for Texas A&M. In fact, I remember liking Nebraska in kindergarten because my teacher was a Cornhusker, and who doesn't love their kindergarten teacher? As a young, avid sports fan in the mid- and late-1970s, I had a great appreciation for the University of Texas because the school produced my favorite player, the great Earl Campbell. The 1977 Heisman Trophy winner, Campbell was the first pick of my hometown Houston Oilers in '78. He led the Oilers to the brink of the Super Bowl at the end of the '78 and '79 seasons. I loved Campbell, the Oilers and the whole "Luv ya Blue" phenomenon that swept across Houston. I guess since we lived in Houston, I also followed the University of Houston. The Cougars won three Southwest Conference football championships—1976, 1978 and 1979—in a span of four years, and then Phi Slamma Jama came along in the early 1980s, capturing the imagination of basketball fans everywhere.

I loved sports, and my dad cultivated my appetite for competition by coaching many of the teams my brother, Doug, and I played on prior to high school. My father had a successful career in the mortgage business, but he always found time for coaching and teaching. Dad worked hard, and I probably inherited my work ethic, determination to succeed and love for competition from him. Dad had opportunities to climb the corporate ladder even higher, but while his career was extremely important to him, family was his top priority. His decisions kept us in Houston, allowing Doug and me to stay where we loved and permitting my parents to stay involved. Dad relished every minute working with his sons and our friends. He'd often pick up teammates and take them to and from practices and games. He was tough on everyone when stressing fundamentals, but he'd always find something positive to say after games. And if he wasn't building us up, my mother was taking the lead in that regard. She was a hall of fame team mom. To this day, our friends still recall the fond memories of my parents' involvement.

Dad taught me so much about baseball, football and life by coaching my youth teams, and he also taught me the value of a hard day's work. My time at the Little League fields did not lead me to fame, fortune or early retirement. So once I reached the driving age, I started earning the really big bucks with my childhood friend, Dave Coolidge. I learned to mow the lawn at an early age, and I utilized that skill to go into business with Coolidge, who was one year ahead of me in school. During the summer following my sophomore year in high school—Coolidge's junior year—we began what was essentially a hand-me-down lawn service.

Dave's older brother closest to us in age, Andy (A&M Class of '86), had acquired an expansive list of customers. As Andy's clientele grew, he allowed Dave and me to service some of the customers' lawns he didn't want. In other words, we received the hard-to-please customers whose homes were located the furthest away from our neighborhood. One yard required us to travel up South Post Oak to Loop-610 past Bellaire and to merge on to US-59 past what used to be The Summit (now Lakewood Church). It was worth it because we made a whopping $8 ($4 apiece).

Dave's father, John '52, allowed us to use his station wagon and lawn mower. My dad loaned us his edger, and we had two brooms! We did enough yards each week to make $30 to $40 each. That was enough money to pay for an occasional pizza buffet and then to allow us to ask a couple girls out on a date from time to time. Primarily, the flexibility of the yard business allowed us to work out as much as possible in preparation for football season. Life was good!

We were blessed to play for some great coaches. In 2014, former Westbury head coach T.J. Mills was inducted into the Texas High School Coaches Association Hall of Honor. Mills had been successful at Luling before arriving at Westbury, and it was obvious to most of us that he had a tremendous gift for coaching and leading. Mills later made history as the head coach at Sealy, compiling a 63-1 record during a four-year stretch (1994-97) in which he won four state titles. Amazingly, Mills' teams at Sealy won 24 consecutive playoff games.

Coach Mills, who died unexpectedly in the summer of 2015, was sharp enough to surround himself with great people. Our defensive backs coach, for example, was Willie Amendola, who eventually guided Spring Dekany to a Class 5A state championship in 2011. Amendola's youngest son, Danny, became a star receiver at Texas Tech and in the NFL. Both men were great at identifying leaders and building cohesive teams around trust, shared values and goals. They were great communicators and motivators, and they knew their audience was 17- and 18-year-old young men, as they tailored their messages toward us. I learned plenty from them about leadership and teamwork, lessons I carry over into business and life.

Another one of my childhood friends, Jim Robertson (Class of '86), was a diehard Aggie, although most of his family members were Longhorns fans. His mother and father gave him a pair of tickets to the 1982 Texas A&M-Texas game in Austin, and he invited me to attend. We drove in the rain from Houston to Austin on game day and watched the No. 14-ranked Longhorns destroy the Aggies, 53-16. The following year I attended the 1983 A&M-Texas game in College Station. The game started well, as A&M jumped to a 13-0 lead. The No. 2 Horns weren't fazed, however, and rallied for 45 unanswered points and a 45-13 win.

Fortunately, I did not make my college choice based on the outcome of two football games. Though I thought about Texas or even playing football at a smaller school, when it was time to make the decision, I knew I was ready to move on to the next phase of my life. And I knew Texas A&M was where I was supposed to be. I felt comfortable in Aggieland and several of my best friends who were a year or two older than me were already there. Deep down, I felt called to be an Aggie. Looking back, I can't imagine how different my life might have been I had chosen another path.

HODGES' PATH TO ENTREPRENEURIAL SUCCESS

During the summer prior to my senior year in high school, Dave Coolidge and I gave up our "lucrative" lawn service—hard to believe we'd forgo splitting $8 a yard, right? Dave worked construction downtown, while I went to work for attorney David DuBose, a longtime family friend. Mr. DuBose was an entrepreneurial, transactional lawyer who cranked out legal documents—primarily for mortgage companies. Back then, it was necessary to physically deliver legal documents. Remember, this was long before emails and the Internet. It was my job to deliver the papers from his office to the courthouse or wherever else the paper trail took me.

Mr. DuBose was essentially a one-man shop with a great support staff. We would talk daily, whether it was over lunch or at the end of the day. Among other things, we discussed my future career path. DuBose earned an undergraduate degree in accounting from the University of Houston, working his way through college and then law school at the University of Texas. He was what I respectfully refer to as a "grinder." He was focused and could flat-out work, and I had a great deal of respect for him. I also paid close attention when he shared his entrepreneurial perspective or advice.

He encouraged me to think about majoring in accounting, which would give me a foundation for practically any business endeavor. Practicing accounting for a while after school would allow me to gain a perspective about many different types of businesses, as we both knew one day I would be working for myself. I seriously considered it, especially the following summer when I worked in his office again, before my freshman year in 1984. When I arrived in Aggieland, I was fairly sure I was going to be an accountant and I enrolled in the business school, which had not yet received the "Mays Business School" name. My first two accounting classes were fine, but my first intermediate accounting class made me realize accounting might not be for me.

It's not that I didn't like numbers; I loved numbers. I especially loved statistics. I grew up reading the *Houston Chronicle*, and I would check the Astros' box score each day and compile my own statistics. Back then, the box scores didn't have the season batting and earned-run averages for different players, so I would keep statistics on my own and see how accurate I was by listening to the game on the radio later that evening. I did the same with the Oilers, keeping a running tab on Earl Campbell's rushing totals, Dan Pastorini's passing efficiency and so forth. Not exactly debits and credits.

I was waiting tables and bartending at a J.T. McCord's restaurant in College Station, and I began observing my customers and asking them about their occupations. I learned a little about occupations and a lot about people. The more I listened and learned, the more interested I was in possibly pursuing my own business. With that in mind, I decided to major in finance, which proved to be a good decision for me.

Another wise decision I made regarding my future was to join the Kappa Alpha Order fraternity during my sophomore year in 1985. That may sound like a contradictory statement to some people who view fraternities as party houses equipped with beer-drinking buddies. While I won't deny that we did consume plenty of beer, being a member of the fraternity also introduced me to some outstanding, intelligent, talented and ambitious men, some of my best friends still today. My experience as a member of Kappa Alpha made a lasting impression on me. It expounded on things I had learned growing up in the areas of leadership, service and hard work. We had an outstanding group of men. Many were second- and third-generation Aggies from families like the Cauthorns, Jaynes, Milsteads, Paynes and Whisenbakers. We were Aggies first, but we loved what Kappa Alpha represented. In fact, the core values of A&M and KA are very similar.

The economy in the mid-1980s wasn't great, and I probably paid attention to the economy more than most college students. I remember thinking to myself: Why in the world are so many of these guys in the dorm (Aston) majoring in petroleum engineering? Growing up in Houston, I remembered the roller coaster, energy-dependent local economy, and I couldn't understand why so many intelligent people would study so hard and enter such an unstable industry. Those people were practically studying around the clock, while I was enjoying all the "other" educational opportunities in Aggieland. I definitely had more fun than most of those guys did. Of course, I laugh at myself for my short-sightedness. I understand now why they would be willing to study so hard!

Buz and Patti Hodges (back row, center) always encouraged their boys' competitive desires

My roommate, Todd Harris '88, talked me into taking a management 489 class called special topics in entrepreneurship. Enrollment was extremely limited, primarily because it was co-taught by the legendary Clayton Williams. It was a three-hour, Thursday night class in which we read some good books, interviewed local entrepreneurs and made a business plan. I still remember my interview with local entrepreneur John

Raney '69, who became our state representative and a very dear friend. Every other week, "Claytie" would fly in from Midland and provide a real-life perspective on entrepreneurship that was as entertaining as it was enlightening. Williams referred to the class as "Bullshit 101," and he was awesome. About halfway into the class, he would often ask, "Who's hungry?" We'd head to Chicken Oil Company for beers and burgers…on him! We patiently waited for our turn sitting next to or across from him, and the beer seemed so much colder sitting in those seats.

I related to Williams' charismatic personality. Back in the mid- and late-1980s, I didn't study as much as I should have. I was far more interested in meeting people, networking and making the absolute most of my college experiences. In assessing the things I wanted to accomplish before I graduated, near the top of my list was serving as the president of Kappa Alpha Order. I wanted to give to the younger guys what KA had given to me. To do that and to serve a full term, however, I needed support from my parents to delay my graduation until December '88. It's not like I was just zipping through it, but if I had continued as planned I would have graduated in August '88. Waiting until December would allow me to spread it out and serve a full term as president. As things turned out, the extra semester changed my life forever.

With graduation inching closer, I was prepared to begin the newspaper-examining, résumé-mailing, job-searching process. That is until my friend, Nick Bregenzer, returned from a summer internship he'd done with R.H. "Steve" Stevens, an Aggie who at the time was a partner at Arthur Andersen in Houston. Nick and I were sitting outside the fraternity house one August evening, most likely with a bag of Red Man chewing tobacco and a cold beer, and he said he believed there was a good opportunity to open a copying and printing store on the south side of the A&M campus. While I had been working at a restaurant during college, Nick had been working at Kinko's (now FedEx Office), which was then located in College Station's Northgate District. The only other copying shop in the area, "On the Double," was also located in Northgate. Even at 22, we could both see that College Station could only grow toward the south.

I had not come to Texas A&M to get into the printing business. On the other hand, with the economy still wobbling from the '87 market crash, Nick's idea was intriguing. College Station and Texas A&M were growing rapidly, and there appeared to be no slowing down for the foreseeable future. Kinko's Graphics Corporation was the behemoth of the full-service document copying industry in the late 1980s. In 1989, for example, Kinko's had more than 200 locations nationwide. Kinko's also produced résumés, brochures, graphics and so forth for their customers, which was a major part of its business because the lack of technology at the time. Not only were personal computers rare, but quality home printers were practically non-existent. If you wanted to make a flyer, a brochure, a poster or a really nice résumé, it was a necessity to go to Kinko's…or a similar shop.

Kinko's possessed a national name, and the College Station location was a top performer. But there was an opportunity to carve a niche in the marketplace by providing a better service. We believed we could do it better and beat them at what they did, but we also knew we needed time. The niche product/service that could buy us time was coursepacks. Essentially, we believed our College Station start-up could immediately go toe-to-toe with Kinko's or any other competitor because of our connections with the students and faculty at Texas A&M (known as the Aggie network).

Coursepacks were basically supplements that professors were preparing and using to tailor and teach their courses. It didn't necessarily replace a book, but the coursepacks could be copied, bound and updated each semester with the latest findings, studies, statistics, articles, notes and so forth. The coursepacks could also include tests from previous semesters, essays from former students, illustrations, slides and whatever else the professor viewed as helpful in making points and teaching the class.

We discussed the idea with other friends for a few weeks and then sat down with one of Nick's entrepreneurial friends, Dennis Averitt. (Both Nick and Dennis have enjoyed multiple entrepreneurial successes in their post-A&M careers). Though Nick and I thought we knew a little something about business and selling, we really knew nothing about the copying/printing business. Nick had already been selling the coursepacks at Kinko's, and we considered Dennis our resident expert in the industry because his dad had been in the printing business. That was good enough for us.

Nick and I began crunching numbers, looking for locations…and dreaming. At some point, we figured out that this really had potential if we found the right location. We'd been well-versed in the theory of the top three components to success—especially in retail and restaurants—location, location and location. Fortunately, we found an ideal spot on the corner of what is now George Bush Drive and Texas Avenue. As far back as I can recall, the main College Station Post Office was located in the strip center at the corner of Jersey Street (now George Bush Drive) and Texas Avenue. In the late-1980s, it moved to its current location in south College Station along FM 2818 (Harvey Mitchell Parkway), and the timing of that move was outstanding for three young entrepreneurs seeking an opportunity to lease a prime, but aged piece of real estate.

We began inquiring about what it would take to lease the 2,800-square-foot location, which was situated at that time in the same strip center as Academy, Brown's Shoe Fit and Stacy's Furniture, among others. We called the local postmaster and discovered it was a relatively simple process in which we could lease the property from U.S. government. All we needed was the up-front capital to turn our vision into a reality. We, of course, had no money, so we came up with a business plan and a proposal and then presented our pitch to my dad. After careful consideration, my father loaned us the money. Mr. DuBose drew up the loan document, and in November 1988, Copy Corner opened for business. When we opened, we had one Apple Macintosh Computer, which cost $3,500…and it didn't even feature a hard drive. We rented some used copiers from a couple of guys about our age, Steve Vaughan and Boyd Sheffield, at a place called Texas Copy. They both became great friends and we still do business together today. We also bought one laser printer, which was top-of-the-line technology at the time. It produced four pages per minute, only black and white, of course.

We didn't do much business in November and December of '88, but we were open and our primary focus early on was speaking to every professor who would listen about producing the coursepacks for the spring of '89. We made flyers advertising our coursepacks and inserted them into campus boxes everywhere.

Our first big break was when Dr. Lawrence Wolken within the Department of Finance bought into the vision being sold by a couple of 22-year-olds. Dr. Wolken's Finance 341 course was a requirement for every business major, and that meant every one of those students—probably 1,000 or more—would need to come to Copy Corner and purchase a coursepack. This was a huge job for us, as we didn't have any high-volume, production equipment. He delivered the material to us early, thank goodness. In order to complete the order and still get ready for more, Dennis kept one machine running for what seemed like forever and we finished the job. Each coursepack could be sold for about $10, so that job alone provided us with plenty of inspiration and enthusiasm. Once we had a respected professor like Dr. Wolken on board, it became a little easier to convince other professors to give us a shot.

After we began generating some serious momentum with our coursepacks, Kinko's dropped the prices of their coursepacks by nearly half in an attempt to slow us down. That was a serious concern because we couldn't afford to match the Kinko's price cuts and still make enough to cover our costs. But just when we needed it most, Xerox showed up at our store offering a big production machine for free for three months. In return, we paid a small fee for the copies we made. If we wanted to keep the machine after three months, we could either lease or buy it. We kept it, of course. When we had first started, Xerox wouldn't even return our calls, but the timing of the offer was, without a doubt, an early game-changer. We were shaking things up, and they wanted in, which was a huge confidence boost for us. Just as important, the new machine allowed us to produce more coursepacks for less money. This let us counter Kinko's in the price war. It was the beginning of some butt kicking…or so we thought.

We worked hard, and we quickly began building a list of professors who ordered their coursepacks from us. Just as we were beginning to feel quite confident about our success, our ability to pay the bills and to compete, we were blindsided by a dose of reality. Kinko's, with all its corporate clout, went beyond cutting prices and served us with a temporary restraining order from selling the coursepacks. According to the Kinko's claim, the process of soliciting, compiling and selling coursepacks was a "trade secret." In reality, the claim didn't have any real merit, but it had real money behind it. Kinko's was trying to intimidate us…and it worked. We were scared to death. We didn't have much money, and we certainly didn't have any to spare. With the start of the 1989 spring semester right around the corner, we desperately needed to be selling coursepacks and doing as much business as possible.

We hired Jon Miller, a local attorney, and he advised us to temporarily stop soliciting professors, but to continue producing the coursepacks we had already contracted. We had a court date set for Thursday, the first week of school. We were under the gun on many fronts. In fact, my mom and Nick's mom, Fran Bregenzer, showed up that week to help, and they did what moms do. They worked! On Thursday morning, we woke early and went to court, each of us wearing the only suit we owned (our interview suits). John Delaney, Judge of the 272nd District Court in Brazos County, ruled in our favor and dismissed the restraining order. We celebrated briefly…and then worked through the night. A few months later, just when we thought we could let our guard down and move on, Kinko's filed a civil suit.

It went on for nearly a year and a half, and it was terribly frustrating and exhausting. We were gaining momentum at the store, but were essentially working to pay for our defense. But in one of my favorite personal examples of "turnabout is fair play," Basic Books, Inc., a collection of eight book publishers, sued Kinko's Graphics Corp. in federal court for copyright infringement, alleging that in photocopying copyright-protected materials that appeared in published books to create university coursepacks, Kinko's infringed on the publishers' copyrights. The case arose in a high-profile Kinko's in New York. To make a long story short, the court ultimately found that Kinko's was guilty of copyright infringement. It ordered the company to pay $500,000 in damages to the publishers and issued an order forbidding it to prepare anthologies without securing permission from and prepaying fees to the appropriate publishers. All told, Kinko's paid almost $2 million in damages, fees and other costs.

This became a headline-grabbing, far-reaching copyright infringement case that gained national attention. In the midst of defending itself in this particular high-profile case, Kinko's may have lost some of the venom it possessed for a start-up competitor in College Station. With the civil suit against Copy Corner still pending into our second year of operations, Kinko's eventually offered us the opportunity to settle out of court as long as we sold the business. We considered it. We began preliminary discussions with Ginny's, a printing company in Austin.

We didn't have a tremendous amount of money invested in equipment; Nick had already moved to Houston to pursue his work at Arthur Anderson; Dennis was teaching; we had an opportunity to repay our loan, pocket some cash and move on to something else; and it certainly would have been a quick, easy solution to what had become a long, messy situation. At this point, I knew we had something and the competitor in me was not content to throw in the towel. With only a bit of hesitation, we turned down the offer and prepared to stand our ground. Kinko's took the hardball stance, threatening to continue the lawsuit. After several more months in which I continued to live off of $800 a month, Kinko's returned again offering a deal that required us to pay an astronomical settlement figure. We countered and they eventually accepted a far more reasonable number. I breathed a huge sigh of relief and then considered my next move. About six months after settling the lawsuit, business was going well. While we could still live off of Jack In The Box's "three tacos for 99 cents" deal and fountain drinks from the Zip'N convenience store, we paid my dad back, too. My mom and dad had always encouraged and supported my decisions, and they still do. The day we drove down to Houston with that last check was quite gratifying.

Whatever happened to Kinko's? Well, by 2003, they were 1,200 stores strong when the company was sold. Still today, I can't help but to think it was the beat down we put on them here in Aggieland that made those poor guys sell their little business to FedEx for $2.4 billion…cash!

Meanwhile, we began looking to expand, and the first option was to open a Copy Corner in Houston, where Nick's wife, Shannon, could oversee day-to-day operations. She was fabulous, and I even signed a letter of intent on a location in Sugarland. But before I jumped in with both feet, I considered all other options. Just before we needed to make a decision, Louis Newman of Bryan-based Newman

The first Copy Corner location on the corner of Texas Avenue and George Bush Drive

Printing Company, contacted me about buying the On the Double copy shop in Northgate. The owner had reached out to Louis and let him know that she was interested in selling. It was a great opportunity for us to expand locally and to eliminate one of our two biggest competitors. This time we had a little credit and a strong enough reputation and balance sheet to acquire a bank loan—and we expanded into Northgate. As technology evolved and we moved into digital printing, I realized I didn't need the Northgate location and we soon merged the two locations into one bigger store.

We certainly were not on working on "Easy Street" those first few years, as we made most of our money at the start of the fall and spring semesters, often working around-the-clock. My brother, Doug, was working with me while he finished school in 1990-91, and at the beginning of each semester, he'd make sure the machines stayed running while I'd grab a solid three- or four-hour nap. We were working 24 hours a day, seven days a week.

The hard work paid off, though. By the mid-1990s we were able to expand from our original 2,800-square-foot location on the corner of Texas Avenue and George Bush Drive into an 11,000-square-foot facility in the same center. With each year, our reputation grew a little stronger in the community, our profits slowly increased and our team gradually expanded. Nevertheless, until we moved into our current location and started selling the coursepacks at the bookstore, I still worked a ridiculous amount of hours at the start of each semester. From the time I was 22 until the time I was 38, I typically was in the store from 8 a.m. to after midnight during the first week or so of school. Before credit cards became the preferred payment method for just about everything, I remember going home in the wee hours of the morning with $30,000 to $40,000 in cash and checks so that I could go to the bank the following morning to make the deposit. Though I said earlier that I never obsessed about money, there were many nights as I drove home, I did obsess a little as I wondered what I would do if someone had tried to take the money. At the time, each day's deposit from selling those coursepacks represented about a week's worth of production work. We were lucky and blessed that it was never more than a thought.

In the mid-1990s, we ventured into the tutoring business and also tried our hand at the bar business. Both could have been quite good but I learned some life lessons and discovered that my hands-on approach made owning and operating multiple businesses rather difficult for me. As I matured a little and got a better grip on life, I was determined to fix that problem. I decided to fire another entrepreneurial bullet in 1998, returning to my restaurant roots. Owning a restaurant had always been in the back of my mind when one day an opportunity landed in my lap. I met a guy named Hutch Harper, who had just moved from Austin. He was a commercial real estate broker, lived in the neighborhood and had a young daughter who was close to my daughter's age. Hutch and I quickly became friends, and he knew I had the entrepreneurial bug. He called me one day in 1998 and asked if I would be interested in expanding my business horizons.

With my curiosity fully piqued, he told me that he had been contacted by David Miller, who let him know that he was interested in selling his DoubleDave's Pizzaworks locations in Bryan and College Station. Like practically everyone else in the community, I enjoyed DoubleDave's and I loved the Peproni Rolls™. Miller was a traveling man and serial entrepreneur who'd previously lived in a number of places across the country. He discovered the pizza roll in Pennsylvania, I think. He eventually landed in College Station, and in 1984 opened the first of four locations in the Brazos Valley. That also happened to be the same year I arrived as a freshman at Texas A&M. I had eaten at DoubleDave's regularly as a college student, and the idea of being involved in another business venture appealed to me. The timing seemed right, and the restaurant business would provide us with a hedge against changing technology, although I think there was more talk about paperless offices in 1998 than there is even today. We were about to welcome our second child into the world, and in my strange way of thinking, I figured that if we were adding a son to the family, we might as well add a business, too. Looking back, it was a crazy year, but quite fulfilling, as well.

I began discussing the opportunity with potential partners, and I also examined the four existing DoubleDave's locations (George Bush, Harvey Road, Northgate and 29th Street next to Blinn). I took a long look at the way the businesses were run, and I talked to the managers at each of the existing locations. I decided to go for it, and we also purchased the rights to DoubleDave's in Conroe, The Woodlands and North Houston. I produced a plan and a strategy to expand the business. I offered each of the managers in Bryan-College Station 2.5 percent of the partnership if they could come up the money to buy another 2.5 percent. All four of the guys were in their early 20s at the time, and they leapt at the opportunity to buy into the business. Each of them borrowed the money from their family, and they were energized to make it work. I was energized, too, because I believed some new strategies could produce some positive results.

I was right. For the most part, the existing facilities were old and in desperate need of a facelift. We cleaned them up, started marketing and increased sales by 20 percent almost overnight. Then we started refining and executing our plan. When Miller was running DoubleDave's, the restaurants were known as much for their Global Beer Tour as the Peproni Rolls™. In the mid-1980s, you couldn't buy imported beers at most grocery stores, so Miller placed a major emphasis on stocking and selling beers from around the globe. It worked beautifully for the time and place, but I decided to switch gears. We kept the beer and the old pizza parlor feel but we placed a much greater emphasis on creating a family-friendly environment. We wanted DoubleDave's to be the place to eat pizza and Peproni Rolls™, and we knew there was a generation of Aggies all over the state who had eaten their weight in Peproni Rolls™ and were now raising future Aggies. That move paid major dividends, and the next one took us to another level.

We took a long look at the locations of the restaurants and decided we had to move things around to bring more people into the restaurants and to be more efficient in our deliveries. We shut down the restaurant on George Bush Drive and moved to South College Station in the Kroger Center on Rock Prairie. Instantly, that store became the No. 1 DoubleDave's in the state. Over time, we also closed the Northgate location (families didn't want to fight for parking spots), the store near Blinn College and the Harvey Road location. We then opened a location on Texas Avenue in College Station (in the same remodeled strip center as the original Copy Corner) and one in Bryan in the Kroger Center off Boonville Road. We went from four stores to three in Bryan-College Station, but we did 50 percent more business and were more strategically located to better serve the community's growth with delivery services. Through the years, three of the four original managers moved on to other successful ventures while one, Mike Deo, is still my partner. We've opened restaurants in The Woodlands, Spring and Conroe, and though we haven't always been rolling in the dough, it's been fun and it's been a solid investment for my partners.

HODGES' MOST DIFFICULT CHALLENGE

Looking back on the hours I've worked through the years and the amount of sleep I've missed in order to keep a copy machine humming or to formulate a new deal, it's been gratifying because of where we are today. I'm proud of so many things we've accomplished through the years, from the customers we have served to the remarkably talented people I've had the privilege of working with at Copy Corner and DoubleDave's. When Copy Corner first opened in the mothballed post office building, we basically had three team members who were also college students. With the help of some great friends, we remodeled the building ourselves, with the exception of wiring the electricity.

When we first opened, we used to carry postage stamps because so many walk-in patrons—especially older people—would enter our building thinking it was still the post office. I vividly recall the looks on their faces when we told them this was no longer the post office. But in an attempt to serve and win favor in the community, we gladly took their letters, either putting them in our outbox or if it was too late, we'd put a stamp on them and drop them off at the actual post office at the end of the day. We did anything we could to build goodwill and our business. In the early 1990s, I remember Bucky Richardson wearing a Copy Corner T-shirt to the football press conference. He appeared on local television and in the newspapers wearing the shirt. That was social media in those days!

From those humble beginnings at Copy Corner, we now employ roughly 60 people. We have a satellite location in the Memorial Student Center on the Texas A&M campus, while the main store occupies the majority of the building we built in the middle of three acres on Texas Avenue. After topping out at nine DoubleDave's in 2008, I had to re-assess my goals for my team and the restaurant business. After several years of winding down, we now operate the three stores in Bryan and College Station. One of the fun things for our team and the entire DoubleDave's System across the state is that we're now the "Official Pizza of Texas A&M Athletics," and we're serving pizza and Peproni Rolls™ in Kyle Field.

In August 2013, we celebrated our 25th anniversary at Copy Corner, and so many of the exceptionally talented young people we've employed through the years returned. We've had numerous people at Copy Corner who met at work and later married. We employed a couple of kids whose parents worked with us when they were in school. We've always worked hard, but we've had lots of fun, too. I often joke about us being one, big, happy, dysfunctional family.

If I have one regret, however, it's that I may have been too focused on building the business that I did not always fully enjoy the journey or take enough time for my family and myself. I was reminded to never take my health, my time or even the next day for granted on Martin Luther King Jr. Day in 2011.

On the morning of January 17, 2011, I wore my sweats to work and had my gym bag packed for a lunchtime workout. Unfortunately, that workout never happened. Classes for the spring semester at A&M began the next day, so it had been a busy time as we prepared the coursepacks and other orders for the first day of school. I was at a stopping point, and I was about to take a break and head to the gym when I suddenly felt lightheaded. I told myself I was OK, that it was no big deal. But as I was trying to convince myself of that, I felt the numbness in my left leg.

From left, Doug Hodges, David DuBose, Larry and Buz Hodges

I knew something was wrong, and I had pretty good idea I was suffering a stroke. Years earlier, my friend, Jim Moffitt, had me make 20 copies of a flyer identifying the signs of a stroke. For some reason, I had this clear picture in my mind of that flyer as now the entire left side of my body went numb. From the upstairs break room, I called downstairs to my dear friend and office manager of nearly two decades at the time, Vicki Ward. She calmly drove me to the College Station Medical Center, and I called my neighbor, Dr. Ron Nelson, while en route. He called ahead and they were waiting for me. Vicki also reached out to my personal physician, Dr. Philip Alexander. Dr. Alexander was waiting for me at the ER, and I recall having a seizure. But I don't recall much more during the next 48 hours.

An MRI confirmed I had suffered an ischemic stroke, which is caused by a blockage in an artery to the brain. The MRI also indicated it was probably not the first stroke I'd suffered, just the most severe. Because

I was in good shape and didn't have any of the warning signs of the typical stroke victim, my buddy and cardiologist, Dr. Ricardo Gutierrez, also tested me for what is called a Patent Foramen Ovale (PFO). By inserting a tiny camera in my throat, down my esophagus he looked for a tiny hole in the wall that separates the two upper chambers of the heart. In the womb, the foramen ovale allows blood from the mother to circulate from the umbilical cord to the fetus. The hole naturally closes at birth in more than 75 percent of all babies, but I was one of the 20 to 25 percent of the population that still had the tiny hole as an adult. Having a PFO does not automatically mean you will ever have a serious issue, like a stroke. In fact, for a healthy person like myself, the risks associated with fixing the problem are generally considered greater than the problem itself

So, facing a life on blood-thinning medication, I then began seriously considering another option Dr. Gutierrez had mentioned in which a tiny wire mesh disc was inserted into the hole in my heart to close it. I studied the procedure and was referred to cardiologist Dr. David Fish at St. Luke's, Houston Heart Institute, where he is one of the world's leading surgeons for these types of procedures. I discussed the surgery with Dr. Fish and he said that he'd choose surgery for himself—and even more convincing—for his son, too. I prayed about it; I mulled over the options; I discussed the pros and cons with my family; and I finally decided that at 45, the surgery—even with the risks—was a better option than the blood thinners or the likely occurrence of another stroke.

I felt at peace immediately prior to the surgery, and when I learned that another one of the heart surgeries scheduled for that day was on an 18-year-old football player who'd suffered a stroke after practice, I also realized I was lucky. I could have suffered a stroke many years earlier, on a football field, driving a car, etc. and it could have been much worse…even fatal. My only major worry as they wheeled me into the operating room was for my kids. I truly was at peace with my eternity, but I couldn't quite stretch my faith that morning to think about my kids, only 12 and 15 at the time, growing up without their dad. Like He always has in trying times, God calmed me that morning and I knew it was all right.

Fortunately, the surgery went well. I don't feel the same as I did before the stroke, but I'm happy and healthy. The left side of my body is still numb—it might always be—and I simply can't push myself physically at work or in the gym like I once did in my 20s, 30s and even my mid-40s. When I don't sleep enough or don't eat well, the side of my face feels like I have been in a boxing match. It's kind of a weird sensation, and I wouldn't wish it on anyone. But for me, it's a reminder of sorts to slow down from time to time and to remember each day is a gift. Entrepreneurism is an important part of my life and I truly believe I've made a difference to some, because of my chosen path. On the other hand, the stroke was also a humbling reminder that I am not in control and that faith, family and friends are more important than opening the next business or making more money.

HODGES' ADVICE TO YOUNG ENTREPRENEURS
There are risks and costs to action.
But they are far less than the long-range risks of comfortable inaction.
~ John F. Kennedy

In my experience, I think what holds most people back from realizing their dreams and goals is the inability to jump. Regardless of whether or not we're talking about being an entrepreneur, in order to achieve success in most things, you must be willing to be vulnerable and stretch beyond what's comfortable. So many smart people get stuck in their comfort zone for various reasons. It could be timing or life circumstances or it could be the lack of trust in their own instincts and abilities. For most, however, I think it's the fear of being accountable to themselves…not having someone else to blame for not achieving their goals. This often keeps people from truly committing to their work and/or passions. It keeps them from giving maximum effort, and that gives them an excuse when it doesn't work out. Do your due diligence and calculate the risk/reward. If it passes the test, go for it! You'll never regret those efforts that you were 100 percent committed to, only those that you entered half-assed.

Remember, it's OK to fear failure, but don't be afraid to fail. In other words, the fear of failure can be a powerful motivator, but you can't let fear stop you from taking action. Many wise men and women—much smarter and more successful than me—have been quoted on fear and failure. Confucius, for example, said, "Our greatest glory is not in never falling, but in rising every time we fall." (I think Rocky Balboa may have said it better, actually). Many years later, Michael Jordan added: "I can accept failure, everyone fails at something. But I can't accept not trying."

Exactly. Everyone fails, but not everyone understands how beneficial failing can be. How did Jordan become the greatest basketball player in NBA history after he failed to make the varsity on his initial tryout? He kept his dreams in front of him, he was motivated by the failure and he wasn't afraid of being vulnerable to failing again. He proved that when he retired from basketball in his prime to play baseball and then again when he came back to win multiple NBA championships. Understanding that you will experience failures and that those failures could be the key to making you an ultimate success can inspire you to take action. So, face your fears and take action. And remember that nothing diminishes fears faster than action. Nothing.

Larry and Doug Hodges on the golf course

There are literally thousands of books that outline success and what it takes to attain it. I've read good ones and I've read parts of some that were not so good. There is no magic formula, but here are six things I find important, especially as a young person starting out in life/business:

1. Spend time with your thoughts. I'm not just talking about your dreams, but the actual exercise of thinking those dreams and plans through. If you can't envision it and actually see yourself doing it, it's not likely to happen. Think positive and be a positive influence on others. Attitude is everything.
2. Build great relationships. Relationships are about give and take. Try giving first and always give more than you take. Doesn't it make sense to have a relationship with your doctor before you get sick, your banker before you need money or your professor before you need that extra credit? Find mentors. It's critical to seek counsel and bounce ideas off people whom you admire and respect. Be respectful of their time, and when the opportunity presents itself for you to mentor someone else, do so with enthusiasm.

3. Build a large trust fund. We all have the type of trust fund I'm referencing. Be the type of person who is always true to his word. Be the person who does what he says he's going to do. Be the person who can be counted on to do her part. Be punctual, be accountable for your actions and be someone others can trust. All of these things contribute to your trust fund. In the end, a large trust fund will always pay dividends.
4. Be an effective communicator. Right or wrong, we are often judged by the way we talk, the way we write and our propensity to listen. Most of us will never need to be able to speak to a room of 200, but being able to communicate one-on-one will always be important. The ability to write an effective letter will always be appreciated, and being a good listener can demonstrate to others that you truly care about what they have to say.
5. Find a place or cause to serve. Give of your time, talents and resources, and your successes will be multiplied. There is no greater joy than positively impacting the lives of others. Where and how you choose to serve will likely change throughout your lifetime. The important thing is to find what's calling you, and that you're doing something for someone other than yourself.
6. Just work hard. When all else fails, hard work can carry you, especially when you're young and trying to figure things out. I actually believe that if you work hard doing something you enjoy or are really good at, everything will fall into place. That includes financial success. The other thing I'm certain of is that no matter where you are, you can outwork 90 percent of the people there. You can't always be the smartest guy in the room, but you can always be the hardest worker.

As I've aged, I've found the glue that holds these all together is a mixture of humility and gratitude. There have been times in my life where I began to admire some of my own accomplishments. Achieving successes and being recognized by your peers or members of the community around you can be quite satisfying, but it can also generate an unhealthy dose of self-pride and accomplishment. Through God's grace, I have been blessed beyond belief with an unbelievable family and a tremendous group of friends who support me, but also keep it real.

If you lose your sense of humility and start believing your own accolades, life will smack you upside the head. Actually, life is going to smack you from time to time anyway, which leads me to gratitude. Being grateful for what you have brings joy and contentment. Being able to express your gratitude to others is a gift. In the worst of times, I've been amazed at the abundance of things in my life for which I am grateful. And when life does humble you, it will be your sense of gratitude that keeps you moving forward.

In his book *Good to Great*, author Jim Collins writes that good is the enemy of great. My charge to you is to not settle for good, but shoot for great!

11.

Jay Graham
Co-Founder of WildHorse Resources
Texas A&M Class of 1992

GRAHAM'S PATH TO TEXAS A&M

From left, Jackson, April, Jacob and Jay Graham

My path to Texas A&M was certainly not a direct one, as I was born in 1970 at Marine Corps Air Station Cherry Point in North Carolina, roughly 135 miles southeast of Raleigh and the historic "Tobacco Road" of Central North Carolina. My kids find this hard to believe because nowadays, my father, Joe Graham, is a grandfatherly "teddy bear." At one time, though, he was a grizzly, a certifiable, bad-to-the-bone Marine Corps fighter pilot, who flew F-4 Phantoms, A-4 Skyhawks and Harriers.

Technically, he wasn't part of the United States' Navy Strike Fighter Tactics Instructor program (more commonly known as "TOPGUN"), but he was an elite-level navigator and one of the first 10 Marine Harrier pilots during the Vietnam era. In the early 1970s, he was sent to London to train to fly the vertical liftoff planes. Fortunately, he was never required to pilot any combat missions in Vietnam because the U.S. began withdrawing its troops and military personnel out of the country. My younger brother, John, was born in 1973 at the Beaufort, South Carolina Naval Hospital. Dad left the Marine Corps in 1974, and after a brief stop in Wichita Falls, Texas, our family in 1975 moved back to Southern Oklahoma, where both my mother and father were raised.

In fact, my family tree is rooted extremely deeply in the red dirt of Oklahoma. My father has taken me to a cemetery in the Marlow area of Southern Oklahoma and shown me the tombstones of my ancestors, the oldest of whom was born in the early 1800s in Tennessee and ultimately settled in Southern Oklahoma. My great, great grandfather and my great, great, great grandfather are also buried in that cemetery. In other words, my family arrived in Oklahoma before it was actually a state. Most of Oklahoma was set aside as Indian Territory before the Civil War, and it wasn't opened for general settlement until around 1890. Some of my ancestors were quite literally "Sooners"—settlers who jumped the gun to settle in the territory.

As generations passed, my family lineage also became deeply entrenched in the crimson and cream of the University of Oklahoma Sooners. My father was raised during the glory days of the Bud Wilkinson coaching era at OU, as the Sooners set the national record—a mark that may never be broken—by winning 47 consecutive game from 1953 to 1957. Practically everyone who grew up in Oklahoma during the Wilkinson (1947-63) or Barry Switzer (1973-88) coaching tenures at OU revered the beloved "Boomer Sooners."

My mother, Phyllis, and father were certainly part of the Sooners' fanatical following, which is one of the reasons my dad ended up attending OU through the ROTC program. That's also why my youngest son, Jackson, has the nickname "Boomer."

My paternal grandfather, Jim, was a farmer in Oklahoma, and my dad essentially chose a completely different career direction, earning a degree in accounting. To help him pay his way through college, my father also "roughnecked" in the oilfields of Oklahoma. If you are not familiar with the term, a roughneck is typically a member of the drilling crew who works under the direction of the driller to make or break connections as drillpipe is tripped in or out of the hole. On most drilling rigs, roughnecks are also responsible for maintaining and repairing much of the equipment found on the drill floor and derrick. The roughneck typically ranks above a roustabout and beneath a derrickman. A roughneck can make good money, but the work is extremely demanding, grueling and laborious, and it can be very dangerous. According to a 2013 article in *The Huffington Post*, the rate of fatalities among oilfield workers is 25 out of every 100,000 employees. It was probably perfect training for the Marine Corps, which my father entered right after graduating from Oklahoma.

As previously noted, my father never had to fly any combat missions in Vietnam, and following his time in the military, we moved back to Southern Oklahoma in 1975—the tiny town of Bray, Oklahoma, to be exact—where my father followed my grandfather's footsteps and went into farming. Even with an accounting degree and a background in flying, farming was in the family genes. My father took over the day-to-day farming operations, and my grandfather owned and managed the country store in Bray, which is just to the northeast of Duncan. I grew up on that farm, and I loved the rural living and the small town togetherness. I went to school with roughly 400 other kids in the community, which represented the entire enrollment—from kindergarten through 12th grade—of the school.

Jay Graham's roots are planted firmly in oilfields

My father was eventually the head of the school board, and in that kind of setting, you practically know everyone, and everyone knows you, which tends to keep you out of trouble as a youngster. Of course, there really wasn't much trouble to be found. My childhood memories on that farm involve roaming the ranch with my little brother, driving a tractor from the time I was about nine, herding cattle, shooting quail, playing baseball whenever and wherever I could and fishing at the creek that ran through our property: Wild Horse Creek. Obviously, I never forgot that creek, as it would eventually become the namesake for my company.

Perhaps if farming had continued to meet our family's financial needs, I would have eventually followed my father's path to the University of Oklahoma. Fortunately, fate intervened, and what appeared to be devastating financial event ultimately turned out to be a blessing. In the early 1980s, a severe drought resulted in my father very nearly going broke. It was one of those ground-cracking, stifling droughts like you see in the movies. The land was prepared, the crops were planted and we all prayed for rain. It never came, though. The drought literally drained us financially, so my father took a job with Halliburton in Oklahoma. Initially, he was still farming and working as many hours as possible with Halliburton, one of the world's largest oilfield services companies, which was founded in Duncan, Oklahoma in 1919.

It didn't take long, however, for my father to realize he could make significantly more money utilizing his accounting degree at Halliburton than he could as a farmer. In 1983, he decided to take a job internationally with Halliburton, which maintains operations in more than 80 countries. Our family moved from Bray, Oklahoma, where we knew everybody, to Bahrain, where we knew nobody. Bahrain is an island country situated near the western shores of the Persian Gulf in the Middle East. This was before Dubai became the place to be in the Middle East, so it was a good financial move for my parents. It was, however, a complete culture shock for my brother and me.

I was 12 when we moved from Middle America to the Middle East, and I vividly recall flying from Oklahoma City to Tulsa, from Tulsa to New York, from New York to Geneva, Switzerland and from Geneva to Amman, Jordan. We stepped off the plane in Amman, and soldiers with loaded M16s were lined up through the airport. Amman was intimidating, to say the least. But once we arrived in Bahrain, my brother and I began to fit into our new surroundings. Bahrain was beautiful, and we attended an American school on a U.S. Naval base, which was operated through the Department of Defense. We had American teachers, and the students were from 48 different countries. Many of the elite Arabs and wealthiest residents of Bahrain sent their children to school on the Navy base so they could receive a Western education. Among the people I attended school with was Salman bin Hamad bin Isa Al Khalifa, the current Crown Prince of Bahrain. I became really good friends with a number of Bahrain residents, and I grew to appreciate and respect the many different cultures of people I met.

I also realized fairly quickly I was not the sharpest tool in the naval base school. My small-town Oklahoma schooling had been good, but I was at least a year behind many of my classmates in Bahrain. We had 80 to 100 students per class, and probably somewhere between 1,200 and 1,500 in the entire school. Most of those kids were extremely sharp and had been well-educated. My brother and I both had to bust our butts in the classroom just to keep up. We learned plenty from our teachers, and I learned so much about the world and people from different cultures by sharing classrooms and hallways with kids from around the globe. It's a shame that adults from all cultures often can't interact with the same courtesy and respect that we did as children. I feel fortunate that I was able to experience what I did in Bahrain, but I am also grateful that, after two years in the Middle East, my parents returned to the United States. Bahrain was fine, but it didn't feel like home because it didn't have baseball, and I certainly missed the game while we were overseas.

I loved baseball; I wanted to play it competitively once again; I wanted to start high school in the United States; and my father, after serving his two-year contract with Halliburton in Bahrain, told the company he would like to take his family back to the U.S. Instead of going back to Oklahoma, however, my father was transferred to Houston. The Halliburton office where my dad would work was not too far from Alief Elisk and Alief Hastings High Schools, two massive schools (both Class 5A at the time) that are adjacent to each other and are separated by only the length of a couple of football fields. With our Bray, Oklahoma background, my parents didn't believe either of those schools were a particularly good fit for my brother or me.

Fortunately, my mother had some family members who lived in Tomball, and my parents made the decision to settle in Tomball because, at that point, it possessed a country, small-town charm. Even though moving to Tomball would result in my father commuting about two hours per day (an hour each way), we moved into the community, which featured only one Class 4A high school (Tomball High) at the time. I started school at Tomball for my sophomore year, and I also started playing football on the junior varsity team. I was a pretty decent athlete, especially as a baseball player. I once struck out 24 hitters in a single varsity game, as I pitched 12 innings in what turned out to be a 15-inning, 1-0 loss to Waller.

Baseball was big at Tomball, but football was king. Shortly after our family's arrival in the community, I realized I had moved into a phenomenal football environment under the direction of head coach Lynn Etheridge and quarterback Lance Pavlas. I'd heard that everything was bigger and better in Texas, but Pavlas was practically larger than life. He was a good guy and a great high school quarterback.

As a junior in 1984, Pavlas started flinging touchdowns and leading an offensive attack that was as efficient through the air as it was on the ground. Behind Pavlas' heroics, Tomball rolled to a 14-0 record until falling to Denison, 27-13, in the state championship game. One year later, Tomball started the season ranked No. 1 in the state, and Pavlas was the prized recruiting prospect that practically every college coach coveted. Coaches like Oklahoma's Barry Switzer, Notre Dame's Lou Holtz, Miami's Jimmy Johnson and Texas A&M's Jackie Sherrill regularly walked the halls at Tomball and attended practices. I didn't initially know much about any of the major colleges in the Lone Star State, but Pavlas bled Aggie maroon, and he eventually signed with A&M. Before he landed in College Station, though, he again led our football team to a 14-0 record before falling just short in the state championship game, this time against Sweetwater. In the last two years of his high school career, Pavlas led Tomball to a 28-2 record, passed for 3,410 yards and 46 touchdowns and was back-to-back first team all-state.

I had grown up as an Oklahoma fan, which meant I naturally loathed the University of Texas. Once I landed in Tomball and grew to appreciate Lance Pavlas and his love for A&M, I figured that might be a good fit for me, too. After all, I could still hate Texas and fit right in with the maroon and white crowd. Like it's been said, "the enemy of your enemy is your friend."

During my junior year at Tomball my father took my brother and me to our first Texas A&M game, a 1986 early season contest against Southern Mississippi. Back then, you could roll into College Station and buy your end zone football tickets, along with a burger and fries, at the Dairy Queen. The Aggies won the game, and they also began to win me over. I didn't understand all the yells or the unique traditions, but I could detect the passion and pride of the students and former students. As I learned more about A&M, I grew to appreciate it even more. I have a vivid recollection of watching an A&M-Texas game on Thanksgiving Night in the mid-1980s at my high school girlfriend's house. Her family was filled with Aggies, and the excitement of that game led me to first utter these words publicly: "I'm going to Texas A&M."

My girlfriend's family was excited about that declaration; my own family was not nearly as thrilled. As previously noted, my parents were huge Oklahoma Sooners fans, and Texas was just a stepping stone for them. They spent three years in Houston, and they moved back to Oklahoma with my younger brother the day I graduated from Tomball High. By that time, I had been accepted by A&M and was drinking the "maroon Kool-Aid" in heavy doses.

I arrived in Aggieland in the fall of 1988 with a strong work ethic, a passion for A&M and no real clue as to what I wanted to do with the rest of my life. My first major was in chemical engineering for no other reason than I thought I was good at chemistry. I stayed on that track for just one year. I recall sitting in an 8 a.m. chemical engineering class on the first Monday morning of my sophomore year wondering if the professor was speaking in a foreign language. I literally had no idea what he was saying. After that class, I walked straight to the registrar's office, dropped every one of my chemical engineering classes and switched into general studies because I was going to be a baseball coach, just like my uncle, Lynn Harmeyer, in Oklahoma. I began taking some physical education classes, and I loved the idea of being a high school baseball coach.

My uncle, who taught me the game, had been a high school coach in Oklahoma for three decades. He was extremely successful, and I admired him tremendously. From the time I was seven years old, I sat in the dugout listening and watching him virtually every game. That's why I listened closely when he pulled me aside one day and gave me some straight talk. He told me that after 30 years in the profession, he was earning just $35,000 to $40,000 a year. "That's not much money, especially when you consider how long I have been doing this," he said. "If money is not an issue, then be a baseball coach. But if you want to make money and earn a significant income, choose something else."

If I had not taken those words to heart, I would not be in this book. I'd grown up in Oklahoma with very little money. When we moved to Tomball, I noticed that some of my friends did have parents who drove nicer vehicles and who lived in bigger homes. I also noticed that their lifestyles were less worrisome and stressful than my friends' parents who didn't have much money. I wasn't jealous or envious of my friends who had money, but I didn't want to go through what my father had encountered in the early 1980s because of a severe drought and the devastation it caused to our family farm. To me, my father and grandfather were tremendous entrepreneurs as ranchers because they ran their own business; they were their own bosses; and they had to wake up each day to figure out how to make money. But there were financial limitations in their industry, financial limitations I did not want to encounter.

I wanted to choose a profession where my income potential was virtually unlimited, and as I was reading the *Battalion* one day at the bus stop café in front of the chemistry building, I read an article stating the need for petroleum engineers, who were earning starting salaries of $45,000 or more. That was more than my uncle was making after 30 years of coaching. Besides, I grew up in Oklahoma during a boom in the oil and gas industry, and I could count 25 drilling rigs in view from our ranch. I just figured God was telling me to enter the oil and gas industry, so I walked into the Richardson Building one day and told somebody I wanted to be a petroleum engineer. It would not be so simple today, but that's how I started as a petroleum engineer.

I will be the first to admit I was not a great student. I graduated with a 2.7 GPA overall, and I was just over 3.0 in my petroleum engineering classes. But the education I received at Texas A&M was about much more than merely what I learned in the classroom setting. One of the best things I did in college was to work as a bus driver for three years. By nature, I'm a talkative person, so I met many classmates while driving my bus. People would come up to me in a bar, recognize me as their bus driver and buy me drinks. That was a benefit, but perhaps the best part about driving a bus—aside from the fact that it was one of the highest-paying jobs on campus—was that I was able to register before most of the other students, regardless of my classification. I drove an average of 20 to 25 hours a week, which cut into my study time. Meeting and interacting with so many people, however, was a great benefit. I loved my fellow students, I loved most of my professors, and I loved the camaraderie of Aggieland. And when I walked the stage in 1993, I somehow knew that the connections I made at A&M would ultimately be as meaningful to me as the degree.

GRAHAM'S PATH TO ENTREPRENEURIAL SUCCESS

April and Jay Graham in Scotland at Ardbeg Distillery

Growing up on the ranch, I first began to drive on my own when I was only eight or nine years old. My father placed me on a tractor, and I would plow the fields in square patterns on some days or drive his old pickup through the pasture while feeding the cattle on other days. There was really nothing to it, but it made me feel awfully important. It was kind of like the lyrics from "Drive," the old Alan Jackson song: "*...I'd sit up in the seat and stretch my feet out to the pedals, smiling like a hero who'd just received his medal...a young boy, two hands on the wheel, I can't replace the way it made me feel. Just a dirt road with trash on each side, but I was Mario Andretti when Daddy let me drive.*"

I mention that story because, as I stated previously, one of my most prominent memories of my time at A&M was of driving the bus. After I graduated and landed my first job in the petroleum engineering industry with Halliburton (it didn't hurt that my father provided a nice recommendation), I once again found myself driving. I left college and arrived at Halliburton in Hobbs, New Mexico excited about showing my new employers how much I knew about petroleum engineering. Instead, they handed me the keys to an

18-wheeler, and I drove pump trucks as much as 80 hours per week. It wasn't just me, either. Halliburton wanted its young engineers to know every aspect of the business, so we were all initially truck drivers. I drove so much it nearly drove me crazy.

Ultimately, I "graduated" to driving the frac data van, an extremely expensive vehicle that serves as the centralized command center to control all critical well site equipment while monitoring, recording and supervising the fracturing treatment. Data vans, with all of their computer technology, reduce the number of equipment operators required to complete the treatment while improving job quality through real-time data gathering. Anyway, I was in Hobbs, New Mexico, and one of the big deals for members of the Halliburton field crew was to arrive at the local café at lunchtime as soon as possible. Otherwise, you had to wait for all of the "more seasoned" staffers to order, and you might be waiting a long time. On one particular day, I was determined to be first to the café, so I threw the frac van in reverse and stepped on the gas without even looking behind me. Unbeknownst to me, a pump truck had been moved behind my frac van, and I wrecked the $500,000 vehicle. I suddenly lost my appetite. Instead of going to the café, I found one of my supervisors at the camp and told him about my accident. It had been two years (or more) since the last accident in the Midland division, and the supervisor told me it would not surprise him if I was fired because of the accident.

It's funny how things work out because the division manager was in favor of firing me…until he was made aware that I was Joe Graham's son. My father's sterling reputation with Halliburton saved my butt. The next day my camp manager came to me and tossed me a different set of keys. When I asked him about it, he said I had been promoted to serving as an engineer in a car and that I was to never drive a truck again because I wrecked the frac van. To say I was instantly relieved would be a huge understatement. But then I began to wonder if I should have wrecked something much sooner to be promoted.

Overall, I spent four years with Halliburton, and I learned way more than I earned. After a couple of years working 70 to 80 hours a week in Hobbs, I knew two things: I wanted to return to Texas, and I wanted to run my own business. Of course, I also knew I was nowhere close to being prepared to run my own business. I needed experience; I needed direction; I needed increased opportunities; and I needed a mentor. So, I called the person who has possibly been the most influential man in my life—aside from my father—and asked him if he knew anyone in Houston who might need an engineer with limited experience, but plenty of initiative. When I called that man—the legendary Billy Pete Huddleston—I was a little worried that he might not even recognize my name. Mr. Huddleston is a self-made millionaire and a financial genius, a petroleum entrepreneur who could turn a profit on Wall Street, Main Street or Skid Row. He's brokered deals from Round Rock to Russia, and he has more entertaining stories than some libraries. As a football player at A&M, he survived Bear Bryant's famed Junction; he turned "junk oil properties" into gold; and he built an empire after starting with virtually nothing.

Huddleston, a captain on the 1955 A&M football team that went 7-2-1, went to work for Marathon Oil in Bay City after his graduation and spent six years at the company. With $2,500 in total assets in 1967, Huddleston and his wife moved to Houston and he went into business for himself. From those simple beginnings, Huddleston built a thriving business. In 1971, he started buying small interest oil properties known as "junk." The industry viewed the properties as the equivalent of slum housing, but Huddleston made a fortune on them. In about a decade, he'd made several million dollars. Then Princeton University Endowment Fund partnered with him in the mid-1980s, and his partnerships ran a net cash flow of about $100 million a year. From 1981-98, Huddleston also taught two three-hour courses at A&M. During that time, he taught over 1,000 students, and I was fortunate enough to be one of them.

When I called Mr. Huddleston in 1997, I was worried that he might not remember me. Instead, he told me to come to Houston because he would hire me. I was surprised and elated. I knew that working with Mr. Huddleston would result in tremendous personal and professional growth. Not only was he a great businessman, engineer, entrepreneur and visionary, he was also a man of impeccable integrity, character and ethics. It was the perfect situation for me because I was able to grow under the leadership of a man I admired tremendously. Mr. Huddleston utilized me in a variety of roles and seemed to groom me for bigger things in my future.

I spent four years working for Mr. Huddleston in roles I could not have previously envisioned. I performed expert witnessing for oil and gas cases, and I worked as an operations engineer for the oil and gas companies he owned. I did everything from reserve analysis to operations. Perhaps the most interesting role I performed was after the first Gulf War (Operation Desert Shield). Toward the end of the conflict, the Iraqi military set fire to 700 oil wells as part of a scorched earth policy while retreating from Kuwait after being driven out by Coalition forces. The fires started in January and February 1991 and the last one was extinguished by November 1991. Somewhere around six million barrels of oil were lost each day while the fires burned out of control. We believe over 800 million barrels were lost in total.

Mr. Huddleston was hired by a law firm in Houston that represented the United Nations Compensation Commission. Ultimately, Mr. Huddleston's company was responsible for determining how much oil Kuwait lost and the economic value of that oil. Kuwait did its estimate, and Iraq performed its estimate, as well. Then Huddleston and Co. performed a reserve analysis to determine an unbiased estimate. I made two trips to Kuwait, along with Mr. Huddleston's son, Peter, and one other engineer. It was probably six years after the war, so much of Kuwait had been rebuilt, but some of the big oil tanks that caught on fire and melted were still around. We also went through dusty old well files that had survived the war. In addition, we traveled to Calgary to meet with financial experts and ultimately presented our findings to the United Nations in Geneva, Switzerland. It was a fascinating experience, and it was just one of many roles I performed under Mr. Huddletson's tutelage.

Those four years were invaluable, and I could not possibly overemphasize how much working for Mr. Huddleston developed me and molded me for future success. After four years, however, I also knew I needed to continue broadening my horizons. I moved to a small public company called Tex Oil, which was under the direction of another successful Aggie who had earned a petroleum engineering degree, Jerry Crews. I began working and learning under Jerry and fellow Aggie petroleum engineer Tom Campbell. Within a month of joining Tex Oil, however, the company was sold to a larger public company, Ocean Energy, which was under the direction of John Schiller, another A&M petroleum engineer from the Class of 1981. Mr. Schiller, who was inducted into Texas A&M's Department of Petroleum Engineering's Academy of Distinguished Graduates in 2008 and was named the 2014 Ernst & Young Entrepreneur of the Year, was another tremendous visionary who was great in teaching young engineers. I learned so much from him because he empowered his young engineers to make decisions and cut deals from the start.

By now, any recipe I've compiled for success in petroleum engineering should be clear: Learn as much as you can from the Aggie mentors who are practically everywhere. I worked for Mr. Schiller at Ocean Energy until April 2003, when the company merged with Oklahoma City-based Devon Energy in a stock-swap deal valued at $5.3 billion, which made Devon the largest US independent oil and natural gas company. I could have moved to Oklahoma City to become part of that merger, but I didn't want to leave Houston.

Fortunately, I had the opportunity to stay in Houston and to join other influential leaders at Anadarko Petroleum Corp. like Karl Kurz, Texas A&M Class of 1983, and James T. Hackett, who had been the chairman, president and CEO of Ocean Energy before the merger with Devon. After the merger, Mr. Hackett became CEO of Anadarko in 2003, taking charge of a sputtering company that was considered by many to be takeover bait and turning it into a respected deep-water driller with $45 billion in strategic deals. Mr. Hackett, who earned his undergraduate degree from the University of Illinois and received his M.B.A. from Harvard Business School, was an incredible leader, who was comparable to Mr. Huddleston in terms of his integrity, people skills and value system. Here again, I cannot overstate the importance of learning from great mentors like Mr. Hackett. I didn't work directly under Mr. Hackett, but my admiration for him is the primary reason I went to Anadarko in the first place.

Mr. Hackett was a tremendously devout Christian leader, who believed great companies needed to be value-based first and foremost. Although he never worked at Enron, the energy giant that collapsed into bankruptcy in 2001, Enron's fall shaped Hackett to lead with integrity, character and Christian values. I spent four years at Anadarko, and I grew to admire Mr. Hackett's ability to lead a company with a

Christ-centered perspective and without ever compromising his values. I wasn't surprised when Mr. Hackett enrolled at Harvard Divinity School. His faith has always been first, and inspiration to many of his employees because of his perspective. As he told Bloomberg in "When you make this money, when you provide these jobs, there is a duty you have because blessed by God to shepherd that wealth. And you have to do it well."

I couldn't have asked for better leadership training from the time I started my profession Halliburton until I decided to leave Anadarko in 2007. To this day, I can't really explain my leaving Anadarko when I did. I didn't have another job lined up, and I certainly didn't have all of my ducks in a row in terms of starting a new business. But at 36-years-old and with a five-year-old son and a two-year-old son at home, I knew it was time to begin my entrepreneurial journey. Practically every day after work at Anadarko, I was on the phone with my friend and fellow petroleum engineering classmate at Texas A&M, Anthony Bahr, Class of '91. Anthony received his Master's degree from A&M in '94, and he earned his MBA at Cal State Bakersfield in 2000. He became an Asset Manager at Hilcorp Energy in 2004, and we eventually began talking about doing something on our own.

I realized the future was now in 2007 when I called Anthony and told him I was quitting Anadarko to begin writing a business plan to start our own company. Anthony applauded my decision, but as a testament to how much smarter he is than me, he continued to work at Hilcorp while I decided to move forward. I had not even told my wife, April, about my decision to leave Anadarko when I quit, but I knew she would support my decision. Neither one of us had grown up with any significant money, so we were not afraid to pinch pennies, if necessary. Besides, I have always tried to leave work at work and to never bring the stresses of the job home with me. Family is my top priority, and once I leave the office, I've always tried to focus entirely on my family.

I was at my oldest son's preschool assembly the day I decided to leave Anadarko, and after departing the preschool, I called Mr. Huddleston and told him I was ready to start my own company. He said, "It's about time. Do you have any money?" I told him I didn't, and he committed to loan us multiple millions of dollars to help us start. I was floored, stunned and so naïve that I didn't know what to say. I blurted out, "Is that enough?"

He said, "Heavens no. You are definitely going to need more." I didn't know where to go next, but Mr. Huddleston told me about some private equity companies that I could contact. I didn't even know what a private equity company was, but shortly thereafter, I told April that I was going to quit my job at Anadarko. Just as I suspected, she supported my decision and we vowed to live off her teacher's salary for as long as it took. We had a little money saved up, but not much. Neither one of us was worried, though, because we both had faith that things would work out for the best. Later that day, I called Jim Hackett and Karl Kurz, who was the Chief Operating Officer at Anadarko, and asked if I could come see them. They were trusted friends, and I wanted them to know first. When I told them I was leaving, they asked me where I was going. I told them I was going to start my own company even though I couldn't provide them with any details because I didn't have anything worked out. They must have thought I had lost my mind, but Mr. Hackett was gracious enough to say that if things didn't work out he would gladly take me back. It was a relief to have Plan B already lined up, even though Plan A was a complete mystery. Since that time, Karl has been a trusted confidant and mentor. I've spent many hours talking to him about business and life. Just like Mr. Hackett, he is a Christ-centered businessman who is not afraid to bring his faith into the boardroom.

I walked out of Anadarko in April 2007 with no salary and no real definitive plans in place. I then began working on writing our business plan, which Mr. Huddleston graciously reviewed. I then set up an appointment with a private equity company in Houston to seek funding. They were not impressed and did not volunteer to provide any funding. For the next appointment, however, I wised up. I arranged to use Mr. Huddleston's conference room and I asked him to make an appearance. My meeting was to be held with John A. Weinzierl, a Managing Director and Operating Partner at NGP Energy Capital Management. Mr. Huddleston had been on a Board of Directors at another NGP company, and he entered the room after John Weinzierl arrived, extended his hand and said, "I'm Billy Pete Huddleston, and it's nice to meet you. I known both of these boys since they were in college. Jay worked for me for four years. He was one of the best students I ever had and one of the best engineers I have ever had. I have known his partner, Anthony, as another great student. I am putting my money with these guys, and I think you need to, as well." Mr. Huddleston then walked out of the conference room without saying another word. Of course, he had already said quite enough.

John looked at us and asked how much Mr. Huddleston had committed. We told him, and he then asked us if we had talked to other companies. After we acknowledged that we had spoken with other private equity companies—we didn't mention how bad it gone—he asked us not to speak with any others. He was satisfied with our business plan and Mr. Huddleston's endorsement. He committed to funding us multi millions, and just like that, we were in business. We'd been given a chance, and now it was up to us to make the most of that opportunity.

GRAHAM'S MOST DIFFICULT CHALLENGE

In August 2007, Anthony and I started WildHorse Resources out of my 2,500-square-foot house. It took about six months before we moved into a more traditional office space. By May of 2008, we were ready to execute our first deal and to drill our first well. Unfortunately, our first well was a dud. Literally, we drilled a dry hole, which happens from time to time. When it's your first attempt as a new start-up business, though, it can be a little nerve-racking.

Jay and Jacob Graham in Times Square

Many of the major drilling companies in the United States at that time had left the country to explore international and offshore opportunities. Our plan was to focus on domestic opportunities, including reworking existing older properties where we could renovate, reinvigorate and flip them to make a nice return on investment. Meanwhile, gas prices were all over the map throughout 2008. A gallon of regular unleaded cost $3.05 in early January and then jumped to $3.50 in April and over $4 in May. In July 2008, crude oil prices hit a new record of $147 per barrel, while the U.S. average price for a regular gallon of gasoline climbed to an all-time high of $4.11. The law of gravity, however, is also applicable in the oil and gas industry: that which goes up will also come down.

By mid-October, oil prices fell below $70 a barrel, less than half of its July peak. In November, U.S. gas prices dropped to $1.72 a gallon, and by December OPEC removed 2.2 million barrels from its daily production, as crude oil collapsed to $40 a barrel, the lowest price in almost four years. The danger in doing business in that kind of volatile market is that if you begin buying when the price is really high, you may never be able to recover when the bottom drops out. It was a crazy and unpredictable time, where the challenge for us was to maintain our focus and confidence.

Our next attempt at drilling another vertical well was better, as it produced relatively well. It wasn't spectacular, but it also wasn't a dry hole. That's about all we did in the first two years, and it wasn't until May 2010 where we executed our first formative acquisition, purchasing Petrohawk out of North Louisiana so we could begin moving toward horizontal drilling development. We spent about $15 million on our first horizontal attempt, and it was almost a dry hole. Then we spent another $14 million on the next drilling site, and it was not much better. When we first started the company, the initial equity commitment we had received from NPG was about $35 million. But we had spent almost $300 million in equity—more than eight times the initial commitment—and had essentially struck out and grounded out.

We were discouraged, but we knew we had an asset that was better than those results. It was just a matter of sticking to it and convincing our board to keep funding us money. After our first two wells, though, we were essentially sent to the "principal's office" to meet with our board of directors in the summer of 2011. We were told we were to meet in Houston to discuss the two wells and our plans moving forward to be more productive. The way the meeting was originally pitched to me, I thought it was just going to be a few people. On the day of the meeting, however, I called one of our board members to determine how many presentations I needed. He told me there would be at least 12 people in the room.

A sickening feeling settled into the pit of my stomach as I hung up the phone and raced into Anthony's office. Clearly, this was not a casual meeting about our plans moving forward; this meeting was going to determine whether or not WildHorse Resources would have a future. The pressure instantaneously magnified and multiplied. We were headed to a meeting where our money guys were going to either collapse the company or keep it afloat. If they collapsed it, they would be able to sell the deal and recover most of their money. But Anthony and I would be looking for a job. We were prepared; our presentation was thorough; the meeting went well; and we convinced them to give us some more time.

We made the most of that time on our next well, which we began drilling in November 2011. On January 31, 2012, that well—L.D. Barnett 23 H-1—struck gold, delivering 15 million cubic feet of natural gas and almost 300 barrels of oil a day. Instead of packing the office up and going back to work for Anadarko, I was swapping high-fives with Anthony and our investors. That one well turned it around, as we went from a $300 million company to what is now—at the time of this writing—a $4.5 billion public company. We didn't give up or lose faith. We believed we had a good plan and the right asset, but building a company is never easy. As every entrepreneur in this book can attest, you are going to make mistakes and life is going to throw obstacles in your path. You can either allow those obstacles to stop you in your tracks or you can blaze a new trail.

Looking back, we put it all on the line with that particular well, and I thank the Lord we were provided with that opportunity. Out of the well and out of that play we created Memorial Resource Development, an upstream oil and gas company. On September 16, 2016, we completed a merger of Memorial with Range Resources out of Fort Worth to create a $12 billion natural gas-focused behemoth. We also created Penn-Tex, a publicly traded midstream company. Another acquisition we did through WildHorse seeded about 49 percent of another public company called Memorial Production Partners. In other words, out of one idea and investment, Anthony and I created three different publicly traded companies. We made the most of the biggest opportunity. It wasn't easy, but it was most definitely worth it.

GRAHAM'S ADVICE TO YOUNG ENTREPRENEURS

As previously noted, I was not the world's greatest student at Texas A&M. In fact, I was the definition of average with my 2.7 GPA, but I have managed to do OK for myself. Don't misunderstand me. I am not saying grades are not important. Whenever I speak to students when I return to campus I point out that good grades are a good thing. They are not, however, the only thing that is important. I've seen students who are so focused on their books that they miss out on the golden opportunities that college provides.

Your parents may not necessarily agree, but the best thing you take away from college may not be your diploma. For me, the greatest thing I received from my time at A&M was my contacts. The fact I earned a degree allowed me to get my foot in the door at Halliburton, my first employer after school. The diploma proved I was capable of thinking, learning and performing at a high level. I learned some basic and solid petroleum engineer skills when I was at A&M, but in all honesty, I learned far more in terms of the nuts and bolts of the industry in on-the-job training.

What opened doors for me within the industry—as opposed to merely getting a foot in the door—was my contacts. I would not be featured in this book or be where I am today without the relationship I had with Mr. Huddleston. He was a magnificent mentor, who truly shaped my future. I would strongly encourage any student reading this to develop relationships with your professors, especially the professors within your major. I would also encourage you to take advantage of every guest speaker who volunteers his/her time to return to campus to share knowledge with the students.

Each year, hundreds—maybe thousands—of former A&M students return to campus to volunteer their time and to share their knowledge with the current students in all departments. Don't just attend the lectures they provide; network with the professionals and stay in touch with them.

Jay Graham and his partner, Anthony Bahr

I spend plenty of time on campus already, and I would love to eventually become a visiting professor like Mr. Huddleston. My wife says I must develop some patience before that becomes a reality. But I can assure you I'm going to be patient and as helpful as possible to those students who truly want to learn and who understand the importance of a professional network. One of the things my wife—a Texas Tech graduate—admires the most about the Aggie network is the family embodiment that Aggies have for one another. Whether I am on Wall Street in New York or in a meeting in San Francisco, Aggies are instantly connected by the Aggie Ring. I assure you it is not like that at all other schools. Aggies are also willing to help fellow Aggies succeed far more than ex-students at other universities. Take advantage of that help. Network with your fellow students; get to know people on the bus; introduce yourself to professors; follow up with guest lecturers; collect business cards and cell phone numbers; develop strong friendships while pulling tickets at Kyle Field; and always be looking for ways to connect with other students and former students.

If you examine my career, Aggies of all ages—men like Billy Pete Huddleston, Jerry Crews, Tom Campbell, John Schiller, Karl Kurz, Dick Lonquist, Greg Floyd, Jeff Elkin and, of course, my partner, Anthony Bahr—have shaped and sharpened me as an entrepreneur and a man. Aggies are willing to help you, too, if you are sincerely interested in helping yourself…as opposed to just earning a diploma.

I would also advise that you commit to giving back in whatever way you can as soon as you can. I cannot tell you how blessed I have been because of the commitment Anthony and I have made to give back. Because of my own struggles in the classroom setting, I decided to endow 10 roughneck scholarships for petroleum engineering students who have a GPA below 3.0. Many great engineers have come through A&M for decades upon decades who may have struggled on tests or who worked their way through school, which affected their GPA. The scholarships we endowed have helped those types of students gain entrance and graduate from A&M. I've been blessed by the relationships I've developed with those students.

Anthony and I also contributed $6 million each with my donation going to the petroleum engineering department and his $6 million going to the business school to create an entrepreneurial program, the Graham Petroleum Ventures Program, where engineers can cross-train and take finance classes or finance majors who have an oil and gas interest can familiarize themselves with petroleum engineering. It's a two-year program that helps aspiring entrepreneurs to build a company, staff it, finance it and so forth. When Anthony and I did our first major deal, we didn't know how to finance it. We are helping to equip today's students with practical skills that will prepare them to expect what was unexpected to us. The great thing about giving back is that Anthony and I have received tremendous satisfaction in developing relationships with A&M's administrators, professors, staff members and the students. I regularly call on those contacts for professional advice, to discuss current events or to inquire about prospective employees. The law of reciprocity is powerful, because we have received many times what we have donated in time and money. If you can't yet afford to give back in terms of your financial commitment, it's never too early to give back your time and knowledge. You will be amazed at how giving back—whether it's to A&M, your church or some other charitable organization—will inevitably bless you.

Finally, have faith in yourself. If you are a student at A&M or a recent former student, you have been gifted with an incredible ticket that can help you get your foot in the door. Once you have that foot in the door, make the most of it. Do things the right way; be on time; exceed the expectations of your bosses; and make the most of the Aggie network. How you treat people in college—good or bad—is going to either come back and help you or hurt you in the future. I promise the relationships you nurture and develop now will only benefit you and your loved ones down the road. Conversely, if you're dishonest and disrespectful now, burning bridges and looking out for only you, it will come back to bite you. Whether you are in the classroom or inside Kyle Field for Midnight Yell, you are building your résumé all the time.

That is something I stress to my own kids every day, especially in this society of social media. One of the first things we do on a background check when we are looking to hire someone is to research the person's social media accounts. Be careful what you post on social media. Remember, what you post—good or bad—becomes part of your résumé and reputation. You are always building a brighter or bleaker future… the choices you make every day will determine your direction and your destiny. God bless you!

Casey Oldham
Chairman/CEO of Oldham Goodwin, LLC
Texas A&M Class of 2002

OLDHAM'S PATH TO TEXAS A&M

Casey and Sarah Oldham

At the end of *Cast Away*, Tom Hanks' character finds himself at the intersection of U.S. Route 83 South and Interstate 40. In reality, these crossroads place you at the Dairy Queen in Shamrock, in the Texas Panhandle, where my story begins. Shamrock is best known as a welcoming stop for travelers along old Route 66 between Oklahoma City and Amarillo, highlighted by the historic U-Drop Inn, considered one of the most impressive examples of Route 66 architecture in Texas. Continuing with the movie theme, the renovated U-Drop Inn was featured in the 2006 Disney animated film *Cars* as the inspiration for the fictional Ramone's body shop.

Shamrock is a rural, isolated community (population 2,029 people) and just as it proved inspirational to Hollywood in creating major movies like *Cast Away* and *Cars*, it inspired me to dream big and move forward. Shamrock is where I first experimented with the idea of becoming an entrepreneur. Quite frankly, my dream has always been to be an entrepreneur. While other kids were dreaming of becoming professional athletes, pilots, doctors and so forth, my vision was to run my own business. I didn't know what type of business I would be running, but I knew I wanted to be in business for myself no matter what the business.

Fortunately, my parents provided me with a foundation for success, raising me to understand that hard work, perseverance and determination are important character traits to be successful in life and business. I arrived in Aggieland in 1998 with an unformed plan, but a strong desire to work for myself and to earn a degree. I never imagined my work would lead me to be included in a book celebrating entrepreneurism; I am honored to tell my story alongside this illustrious group of individuals. While we each have our own unique path, hopefully these stories are relatable to you or encourage you to discover your path to success. If your dreams take you far from your beginnings, perhaps my story will show that your success lies solely in your hands.

I didn't know my paternal grandfather, but the stories of his life helped to seed my interest in working for myself. He was a cattleman in Shamrock, trading cattle back when Route 66 was still a hopping highway. Unfortunately, he died suddenly from a heart attack, so I never knew him. Tragically, my father, Dusty, who was only a teenager at the time, was the one who found him. To help support the family after my grandfather's death, my dad went to work on a cotton farm with his oldest brother, J.H. Oldham. An extremely successful Shamrock businessman and landowner, Fred Nicholson, leased the cotton farm to my uncle and took a special interest in our family. Mr. Nicholson was a Texas A&M alumnus and played on the Aggie golf team. One day, as my father was on a tractor working the farm, Mr. Nicholson pulled up and asked him if he ever thought about going to college. My father shook his head and explained that he had but the family could not afford it, as it was just he and my grandmother.

"I'll make you a deal," Mr. Nicholson said, "I will see you through school at Texas A&M. My only stipulation is you have to join the Corps of Cadets and keep your grades up. As long as you do that and take care of business, I have you covered."

Truly, that was a remarkable act of kindness. Through Mr. Nicholson's generosity, many young men were given the opportunity to attend Texas A&M. This is a testament to the character of Texas A&M alumni. Mr. Nicholson's offer changed my father's life…and ultimately shaped mine, as well. To this day, part of the reason that my wife and I give back to the Texas A&M and the golf program through an endowed scholarship is because of what Mr. Nicholson—an Aggie golfer—did for my family. Naturally, my father accepted that offer, made the eight-hour trip from Shamrock to College Station and graduated from Texas A&M in 1973. During his time in Aggieland, my father joined the Corps of Cadets, Spider D, and even more significantly, met my mother, Joyce Noski.

Mom was raised in Anderson, a small community 30 miles southeast of College Station. Mom's parents were Polish, with my grandmother attending school through eighth grade and my grandfather attending through sixth grade, not uncommon for their generation. They were hard-working people who worked to live and weren't concerned with the things they did not have. In fact, my mother did not have running water until she was a teenager and never even tasted a slice of pizza—a delicacy at that time for her family—until she met my father at a dance hall and they began dating. My parents were married right after my dad graduated from A&M. As a result of her upbringing, Mom has always encouraged and supported my sister and me to pursue our dreams.

Casey Oldham consoles his father after receiving dire financial news

My father earned his degree in animal science from Texas A&M as he initially planned to go to veterinary school. But life took him in a different direction. I was born in Denver where my father worked as a managing broker at a commodities firm. Like most young kids, I did not know exactly what my father did for a living, but I idolized him as a father and a businessman. I knew I wanted to be just like my dad when I grew up. I loved watching him work; he was always working hard and making deals. My father traded commodities like gold and silver, which eventually led him to a bankruptcy. Although moderately conservative in social and political matters, he was a risk-taker in his business dealings. He seemed to love uncertainty, thrive on unpredictability and excel while living on the edge in business. Unfortunately, the gambling aspect of trading can also come back to bite you. In essence, he placed all of his chips on the table and bet heavily on metals, but a crash ensued and my father paid the price. I have a vivid memory of my father taking the devastating call that changed our lives.

While my father worked to recover financially, he led our family on a whirlwind tour that took us from California and on to Florida before bringing us back to Texas. Looking back, a truly impactful moment of my childhood occurred when I was seven. We had packed up everything in a single-cab truck (the only possession my dad had left) and were headed to California where my father apparently had a job opportunity. We stopped at some fleabag motel, and I remember my dad sitting on the edge of the bed with his face buried in his hands. I had never before seen him cry, but the tears were flowing. I hugged him and tried to make him feel better, even though I did not understand what was wrong. Many years later, I realized he had gone bankrupt only a few days before.

As he worked to come back from this financial blow, my father took a job in a beef-packing distribution house, overhauling locations that were not productive and loading boxes at night for extra money. Once he had an operation running smoothly, it was on to the next destination. After a brief stop in Florida, we moved in with my grandmother in Shamrock, and my father's connections led him back to the commodities business as a wholesale meat trader. He made a couple of significantly prosperous moves, putting him in a position to start his own business, C.D. Meats, which was named after my sister, Darby, and me. That business was later incorporated into Shamrock Meats, which is still in existence today. My father never gave up, and his efforts paid off. He ended his full time career as president of a local bank in which he owned an interest. My father also served as president of the school board and became a highly respected pillar in the community. He was not defeated or defined by his bankruptcy. He worked diligently to reinvent himself and rebuild his wealth. Watching through the eyes of youth, I learned so much about business from my father, without realizing at the time the full value and importance of the lessons I was learning. His experience shaped both my desire to be in business for myself and my entrepreneurial philosophy. But the most valuable lesson he taught me was this: never let the fear of failure deter you from your goals. That's a cliché, but one that he and I strive to practice to this day.

Fears often sabotage all hope for success, and many people are terrified (rightfully so) by the fear of failing, poverty and loss of money. Those fears typically cause people to avoid risk of any kind and to reject opportunity when it is presented to them. Many people are so afraid of failure that they become almost paralyzed when it comes to taking any chances. But if you don't tackle and control your fears, you will never take the risks necessary to be successful or make the best decisions. By watching my father, I gained great courage and realized that a key to success is to focus on things we desire, not dwell on the things we fear. My father instilled that courageous attitude in me, and I've never been fearful in my entrepreneurial efforts.

Dad is a man's man, who enjoys a diverse set of people. Likewise, people enjoy being around him. Even in the midst of staging a business comeback in Shamrock, he always made time for his family. With me, he shared his love of golf. My father taught me how to play, and it became an important part of my life. Golf is a sport that teaches you much about yourself and your ability. You can play golf competitively against anyone, but, ultimately, it comes down to competing against yourself, controlling your emotions, developing good habits and not trying to do too much, lessons that are applicable in life and entrepreneurship. I practiced all the time, and what I lacked in athleticism, I made up for in work ethic. While playing for the Shamrock High School golf team, I was on track to win the individual state title, but on the first hole of a sudden-death playoff, I choked, missing an easy putt against a talented player from Normangee. While I won the first round against him, he ended up winning the playoff. However it wasn't the last time I would encounter him or his impressive set of golf clubs. Even though I didn't win that individual title, I did have the privilege of leading our team to the state Class A team title twice during my Shamrock High School career.

In addition to his love of golf, my dad shared his passion and adoration for all things maroon and white. Throughout my childhood and adolescence, I accompanied my father on numerous trips to College Station for football games, class reunions and other events. As a result, there was never a question as to where I wanted to go to college, only if I would be accepted into A&M. Even as many of my friends longed to go to Texas Tech, I never even applied to a school other than Texas A&M. Fortunately, I was accepted, and I enrolled at A&M in the fall of 1998, just in time to be a part of the cheering crowds as the Aggies won their only Big 12 football championship.

In a conversation that echoed my dad's with Mr. Nicholson decades before, my father made a deal with me. He said he would pay for everything during my time at Texas A&M—room, board, tuition, books, and all—as long as I went through the school of agriculture. His reasoning for this request was he wanted me to meet kids from similar, rural backgrounds. He stressed the importance of developing a lifelong network of friends in college, and he believed it would be easier to accomplish this with people from a similar background. He also made it mandatory for me to take at least one animal science class, which I was adamantly opposed to doing.

At the time, I didn't really understand his requirements, but in hindsight, I acknowledge my father led me in the right direction. I didn't know a soul when I arrived at A&M. Not one. While I am sure there are friendly people in every degree program at A&M, I quickly and easily developed a rapport with the group of students in agriculture. I eventually focused my education on agriculture economics, which I knew little about at the time. Nevertheless, it was a good fit for me, and I was eventually inducted into the Tyrus R. Timm Honor Registry of Former Students in Agricultural Economics. The Honor Registry is named after 1934 graduate Tyrus R. Timm, who led the department for 20 years during its rise to prominence in teaching, research and extension.

Within the agriculture economics department, I found a great group of friends, and even benefitted—much to my surprise—from the animal science class I took with Dr. Howard Hesby. During his 35 years at Texas A&M, Dr. Hesby helped more than 15,000 students, and I am honored to be one of those students. Dr. Hesby, who died in 2005, was one of the most charismatic and impactful teachers I have known. He was engaged with his students, truly wanting to know and understand them. He was also quite famous on campus for taking classes on field trips. That class and the people I met through it, have a special place in my collegiate memories.

Casey Oldham has been a longtime winner on the golf course

Another special person who was a tremendous help to me at A&M was Pam Vernon, who in 2014 was presented with one of the Dean's Outstanding Achievement Awards in the areas of advising and student relations. She served as a Senior Academic Advisor in the agricultural economics department for 25 years. Pam connected with me and so many other students and truly understood that a college education encompasses much more than merely what students learn in the classroom setting. Pam realized I was a go-getter and an entrepreneur. She respected and understood that I had many roles and responsibilities in the community that were helping me move toward my dreams of becoming an entrepreneur. She analyzed my time constraints and guided me in choosing classes and schedules that would permit me to excel in the classroom, as well as allowing me to develop my real-life business skills.

Joining a fraternity was also beneficial for my college experience and in starting me on a path toward eventually building my business in College Station. I initially considered joining the Corps of Cadets as my father had done. While I admire the discipline instilled by the Corps, I decided that it was not the best choice for me. In my sophomore year I pledged Phi Delta Theta, which ultimately opened doors for me that I never envisioned.

My long-term career plan was not clear, unless planning to graduate and becoming an entrepreneur counts. When I first arrived at A&M my goal was to earn a business degree, return to Shamrock and work with my father in the banking industry. In 1999, following my freshman year in college, I went back to Shamrock and worked with him at the bank. I planned to work there following my sophomore year, as well, but my father sold his interest in the bank. There weren't any other similar summer employment opportunities in Shamrock so I began looking for a job in College Station. It turned out that I was able to create a job and help my fraternity at the same time. Phi Delta Theta was in desperate need of a new fraternity house. The existing house was off the beaten path, and we needed something that would be appealing to potential pledges. Nobody had successfully taken the lead in finding a new house, so I stepped forward to take up the charge.

I contacted former Phi Delta Theta members to raise the funds needed for the purchase of a new home, and I found a realtor who helped us locate an ideal place on West 26th Street in Bryan. We also needed legal help to clear a few hurdles. I was referred to J. Fred Bayliss, who specializes in real estate law. I scheduled an appointment with Fred, explained what we were attempting to do and convinced him to represent us. I did not know exactly what to do, but apparently I was doing something right. Fred was impressed with my resourcefulness and asked me to come to work for him on the spot. The timing was perfect, and I gladly accepted the role offered even though I knew little about it.

In retrospect, this was a pivotal moment for my career. This was my gateway into the real estate industry. I learned so much from working with Fred. He was a mentor and facilitated my introduction to the business community in College Station. While I impressed Fred right away with my resourcefulness, I am quite certain that I underwhelmed him soon after with my lack of computer skills. Growing up in Shamrock, I was not on the cutting edge of technology. In fact, I didn't know what email was and did not have it until I was at A&M. My new role in the office was to perform clerical and paralegal work, and I was struggling with just powering up the computer to create documents. I wanted to be an asset to the office, but I was dreadfully slow and everybody knew it.

One day I was flipping through the pages of *The Battalion* as I was eating in Sbisa Dining Hall and I noticed an ad for a job that sounded just like mine. I continued reading and recognized Fred Bayliss' office number. I quickly called the office manager to find out if I was being fired. While Fred liked me and truly didn't want to fire me, he did need to find someone who was much better suited to do the clerical and paralegal work he had originally hired me on the spot to perform (I like to remind him this was where two fools met). Given my terrible performance, it didn't take long to fill the position with a more qualified employee. Fortunately, I was able to convince him to create a new job where I could be an asset to the firm in a different way by resolving some of the more unique and challenging problems for a variety of his clients.

In this capacity, I proved my worth to the firm and accomplished some meaningful things. For example, one of Fred's clients owned a mobile home park in which several of the homes had been severely damaged by a fire. A contractor who was originally hired for an outrageous amount of money had failed to tear down the homes in a timely manner as promised. Instead of going with another contractor, I challenged Fred to let me handle it even though I didn't have a clue regarding how to complete it. I quickly acquired a permit, rented equipment and hired some operators to help coordinate the tear-down for significantly less money and on time. In another meaningful role for me, Fred's client was having issues with a civil contractor while developing a residential subdivision. Fresh off the success of my last "bail-out job," I rented equipment, hired a crew and we took it over, which was a big undertaking considering the fact I was a still a college student and this was only my second coordination job. We did great work again and soon others were hiring me to do what they could not or would not get done. These types of jobs were usually complicated, dirty and hard—the kind of work that few people wanted to handle. Eventually, the opportunity to do what others did not want to do or couldn't led me to start a freelance business as an independent contractor. I developed a reputation for tackling roles that others were not willing to do, which became a principle for building my future businesses.

Fred was supportive in allowing me to take on these additional freelance projects while continuing to work for him. One of the more interesting assignments that followed involved assisting with an eviction. I went to the house to start the eviction process, and as I surveyed what valuables had been left behind, my attention was pulled to a set of golf clubs in the corner of the room. As fate would have it, these were the same clubs that my opponent used when he beat me in the high school state championship. To make a long story short, we evicted the tenants, and I asked for the clubs to be included as part of my compensation. Flash forward to a Wednesday night at the Bryan Municipal Golf Course a few months later. I ran into the golfer from Normangee who beat me in the state title playoff. He recognized the clubs I was using and asked if he could buy them back from me. I told him they were not for sale, but after I finished that round, I ultimately gave the clubs back to him. It makes for a good story, but mostly I use this as a reminder to myself that we live in a small world in which we should, whenever possible, avoid burning bridges. Life is an oval track: What comes around, goes around.

My college years were extremely busy socially and professionally. I continued working in a variety of capacities, carrying a full load of classes at A&M and enjoying a social life through the fraternity whenever I could fit it in. I was making good money as I entered the summer after my junior year, allowing me to have a lot of fun in my free time. I was planning on attending law school after graduation and applied at South Texas College of Law in Houston. Those plans soon changed when I met the woman of my dreams, Sarah Kathrine Barger, in a country and western dance class at A&M. Sarah was an electrical engineer major from Needville, and I soon discovered that I could not live without her. She is beautiful, grounded, brilliant and everything I was looking for in a woman and a wife. We dated for about a year and were engaged to be married during my senior year at A&M. Engagement made me realize that it was time to take a serious and organized approach to our financial future. At that point, I didn't know exactly what I wanted to do with the rest of my life, but I knew I wanted to spend it with Sarah. She helped to give me the focus and desire to begin working on a meaningful plan for the future. Then and now, she has always allowed me to be me.

OLDHAM'S PATH TO ENTREPRENEURIAL SUCCESS

Casey and Sarah Oldham on his A&M graduation day

Growing up, I often thought my parents were ridiculously over-protective; they would not let me stay out late at night, especially on the weekends. On the other hand, my parents displayed an amazing amount of trust in my abilities when it came to financial matters. My father permitted me to borrow significant amounts of money with him co-signing on my name when I was in high school so that I could buy calves to start a light cattle operation. I have always possessed this entrepreneurial drive and interest in all business, even as a child, constantly looking for ways to make deals and make money. For instance, I sold cell phones in junior high, the big bag phones and the early flip phones available in the late 1990s, profiting from the sale of each phone and earning residual income, as well. I also traded cars in high school; I promoted concerts in college; and at one point at A&M, I believed I had found a start in real estate.

While I was in college, I bought my first residential investment, a small home that required me to put just three percent down. I lived in one room and rented the others to generate cash flow. This was working so well that I began to buy more homes and rented them out to fellow students, producing even more cash flow. This income was in addition to my other entrepreneurial efforts. To some of my classmates from bigger cities, College Station was a sleepy, bedroom community. Coming from Shamrock, I viewed the Bryan-College Station community as a land of opportunity. In the late 1990s and early 2000s, Texas A&M, the community and the real estate industry were all experiencing tremendous growth. Great things were happening and I was ready to dig in and be a part of it. As I built a small portfolio of residential properties, I was beginning to apply one of the major lessons my uncle, J.H. Oldham, taught me early in life on the cotton farm. As we would drive around the farm, he talked about the importance of ownership of assets without debt and of buying things like land that would appreciate in value and that would pay for themselves. Looking back, the time I spent with my uncle cemented the fact that real estate was in my blood.

As graduation neared, I decided to continue with the work I had started in college. It seemed like a natural progression to build on what I was already doing. I was involved in the local community, had developed a solid reputation through my freelance projects and was solidly invested in the residential real estate market. At the very least, I decided to practice real estate until Sarah graduated and then attend law school. I earned my real estate license and landed a job with a local real estate firm one year before my graduation from A&M in December 2002.

It didn't take long, however, before I realized that residential real estate sales was not a good career fit for me. For one thing, I simply lacked the patience and desire to be an effective residential realtor. It requires a different skill set than I possess. I knew realtors who were doing well locally, and I believed I could be successful—if only temporarily—in the field, as well. At the time, there were approximately 600 realtors in our community, and most of them had far more patience than me. Initially, I focused on for-sale-by-owner homes, scanning the newspaper daily and contacting sellers in an effort to convince them to list their home with me. It didn't take long to learn that for-sale-by-owner clients were often difficult; I ended up working much harder, for much less profit than many of my peers. I was making a tough career as difficult as it could be. Of course—as noted earlier—I have always been willing to do things that other people are not willing to do. For example, even to this day, I still make cold calls to procure new business when so many people hate to make cold calls or feel it is beneath them.

I remember an incident with one young couple as if it was yesterday. We worked diligently together to rebuild their credit and to create a budget. We looked at six or seven houses that were within their price range and fit the description of what they said they were looking for, but they found an issue with each one we toured. At about the seventh house, I realized that if I sold this couple a house, I would earn about $6 an hour. During this showing (what would ultimately be my last), the client said she liked the house, but the curtains just weren't the right color. Reaching the end of my patience, I said, "Ma'am, here's the deal, if you will please buy this house and I will buy new curtains in whatever color you want." Not surprisingly, I didn't make a sale to that couple (any good realtor would never have shown them seven houses in the first place). I have great respect for realtors who possess the necessary skills and patience to thrive in residential real estate, but it is not my niche. If memory serves correctly, my monthly income while I was in college was higher than what I made my first six months in residential real estate. I really liked sales in real estate, but I just needed to find something I believed in and stirred my passion. Residential real estate, however, just wasn't for me.

I have always believed that God works in truly mysterious ways, and He blesses those who are willing to work hard. He opened a door for me. My first commercial real estate transaction came together quickly and smoothly, a stark contrast to my first six months in residential real estate. This alone convinced me it was time to take my career in a new direction. It was a "sign" I needed. The first commercial lease I negotiated was for a client planning to open a maternity store in the Bryan-College Station area. I showed the client and the prospective investors one commercial space (not seven). They immediately liked it, and I received the lease comments from the landlord. We quickly reached an agreement and I was paid a commission the next week. At that moment, I made a conscious decision to practice commercial real estate full time until Sarah graduated and I could begin law school. At that moment, I also knew that I was going to make this work, no matter the cost, because so many friends and associates had encouraged me to get a job instead of trying to do something on my own. But I wanted to do something on my own, and I felt like if I didn't make this work, I would reluctantly need to go work for someone else because I needed to earn a living. After all, I was getting married. I had responsibilities. Once I found my confidence and passion, I really started to hustle. I got focused and began making contacts and decisions that gave my commercial real estate career a kick-start.

My first substantial client was a large Bryan-College Station property owner who lived in California, who had a larger-than-life persona with an equally large portfolio of commercial investment holdings in the community. He was at times difficult to work with, taking what I politely call "challenging" positions on deals. Fortunately, I was able to maintain my professionalism and integrity in fairly difficult situations. From this, I gained a great deal of experience and earned a good reputation within the industry for how I handled these challenging positions. Another key influence was a gentleman named Robert Todd, who was one of the first brokers in the community to specialize only in commercial retail (something my firm continues to do well today). Robert was accomplishing things in the community that no one else had tried locally, and he was a source of inspiration for me. He opened my eyes to the potential success of commercial specialization in this community. Ultimately, that led me to refine the idea of a multifaceted and specialized commercial real estate firm in BCS that would later be known as Oldham Goodwin.

At every opportunity, I learned as much as I could from the people around me. Just as I learned by watching my father while I was growing up, I continued to observe and examine both the mistakes and successes of the people in my life. I realized that if I could learn from the mistakes of others and avoid repeating them, I could stay ahead of the game…or at least stay in the game. My inquisitive nature drives me to understand the people I meet, to question what drives them, what led them to the place they are in their lives; I want to hear their stories of inspiration, disappointment, success and failure that makes each person unique. This drives me, personally and professionally. From the cab driver to the *Fortune* 500 CEO, I am not shy about asking people about themselves and what drives them.

The deal that led me to have the courage to found the Oldham Group was the transaction of a large apartment complex that not only placed me on firm financial ground, but also helped me to cement the opportunity to specialize in investment real estate (now called capital markets). I realized the Bryan-College Station area could attract institutional-grade investors. This was a major turning point in my career. I realized that I no longer needed to take on just any client. This realization, along with some financial stability, positioned me to establish the business specializing in multiple facets of the commercial real estate business.

The Oldham Group launch in 2004 was well-timed and received by the market. Commercial real estate was thriving, not only in our community but nationwide. My connections had become more widespread and I began negotiating major commercial investment sales of all types across the state and throughout the country. To facilitate this type of work for the clientele we were attracting, we needed real substance, past success, a track record and an understanding of investment real estate from A to Z, including property management. Investment real estate really inspired me, and it took all my talents to be successful at it. Pursuing a law degree was no longer important; this business venture was challenging, fulfilling and fully engaging.

As I was transacting these commercial deals for clients, another critical element for success became apparent. After closing, these properties are typically handed off to property management firms and the success of the investment hinges on the ability of the management company to properly handle all aspects of operating the property profitably. Property management is a tough business; it is a difficult business in which to make a profit; it revolves around matching the right people and processes to the requirements of the property. It was difficult, yet I saw a great opportunity to expand the business by taking on this challenge.

A short time after forming the Oldham Group, I added the commercial real estate management division, initially focusing on small multi-family and commercial projects. In the start-up days of this division, operating in a rented building on 29th Street, I was fortunate to have the support of Brian Stephen, a business associate from my early days working with Fred and a good friend to this day. He shared his property management know-how and introduced me to Rick Lemons, a hard-working entrepreneur who had just sold his restaurant and was looking for a new and challenging career. To entice Rick into the business, I gave him a small percentage of ownership of the company. Rick was a great partner and helped guide the successful development of property management division. We made more right decisions than wrong, and we soon found ourselves with 22 employees in the little office on 29th Street. It was cramped, crowded, chaotic...and up until then, the most exciting time of my life. The real estate market was booming; we invested time and effort into developing a presence in California, putting on seminars and bringing clients to Texas for investment opportunities. At that point in my career, I possessed complete confidence in my leadership, the business and my business model. I knew I had found my niche and I was onto something big.

Sarah only enhanced my determination to succeed and my confidence with her constant support. We married before I started Oldham Group and she has been understanding of the demands of both the real estate business and the intense focus and time involved in starting and managing business endeavors. Without her understanding, either our marriage or the business would have suffered. It is emotionally and physically exhausting to start and run a business. She encourages me to pursue my passion, in spite of the constant demands on my time and attention. It is helpful that she is successful in her own right, building a successful career as an electrical engineer. While it is impossible to ignore the sacrifice and dedication that is required to establish and run a successful business, there is also reward. Sarah and I have the opportunity to travel and enjoy the luxuries that result from our hard work and dedication to our careers. It is a blessing to share this journey with a partner who understands the demands and celebrates the successes, equally.

Sarah and I have not always had a blissful marriage. Like most other couples, we've endured struggles, fights and the highs and lows of married life. But we are truly a team, and we value and respect each other. There is no doubt in my mind that I would not be where I am today or who I am without Sarah as my life partner.

I never envisioned adding a full partner to my business; it was my intention to run the operation on my own and in my own way. In my experience, there have not been many successful business partnerships. It's a risk to take on a partner. Having my partner in life, Sarah, was enough for me. Therefore, it was a great surprise to encounter Hunter Goodwin. While I was not looking for a full business partner, I was fortunate to find not only a strong business partner, but also a great friend. Hunter has helped to transform my company from good to great. The day Hunter showed up at my office with a million questions was a game-changer. After the initial meeting in my office, where I answered his rapid-fire questions, he showed up at my front door one evening with a new list of questions. We were sitting at my kitchen table and I remember thinking, "Man this guy is relentless; I need to step up my game and do my homework."

Hunter was an All-Southwest Conference offensive lineman at Texas A&M in the mid-1990s, and from 1996-2003, he was a tight end with the Minnesota Vikings and Miami Dolphins. Former NFL running back and longtime ESPN commentator Merril Hoge once referred to Goodwin as "the best blocking tight end in the league." He was still playing in the NFL when we first met, and Hunter and his wife, Amber, lived on the same street as Sarah and me. Hunter was investing in local real estate while he was still in the NFL. Our initial business relationship began when Hunter and some of his real estate partners were considering becoming involved in a duplex development project. Hunter and his associates were referred to me by a well-known builder, Joe Courtney, to help them find land and develop a duplex project in College Station. I met with them and convinced them to break up the track and to invest first in a retail development project. Quite frankly, that made Hunter uncomfortable because he had never been a part of a retail project. But that's when Hunter and I began to learn so much about each other as we began to work extensively on that project.

Hunter is an impressive, intriguing, insightful and unendingly inquisitive man. His questions, right from the start of our business relationship, were thought-provoking, and his instincts were accurate. I certainly appreciated his involvement, and what he realized from our business dealings, was that I made as much money from the transaction as he did, although he was carrying all of the risk. We talked about that deal, what he wanted to do and an investment he had in a hotel venture that was not going the way he

Casey and Sarah Oldham with Hunter and Amber Goodwin

expected. He saw an opportunity to take over the hotel's operation to recoup his investment and potentially make it profitable. He asked me if I wanted to take on the management agreement with him. It was not something I had a strong interest in doing, but I told Hunter I would pay him to run the hotel and see how things worked out. That was in 2004. By 2006, we were full partners in Oldham-Goodwin.

Hunter was open to suggestions, but he really wanted to wrap his arms around the marketplace, the trends, the pros and cons of commercial real estate, the potential returns on investment and so much more. It was immediately apparent to me that he is extremely sharp and possesses tremendous business acumen. When we began talking about working together, I discovered he had done his homework on me and the projects I had undertaken and completed. He asked dozens of questions that shed light on his genuine and sincere desire to begin preparing for life and a career after football. Throughout his football career, he had been involved with the players' union and had developed strong connections with general managers, agents, owners, team sponsors and others in the business. He took full advantage of the doors that were opened as a result of his NFL career, which is rare among professional athletes.

Hunter has enhanced our business through his contacts, passion and energy. He also expanded our organization as the catalyst for our entry into the hospitality business. Since we first formed a full partnership, we have transformed who we are and what we do. At times, we fight like brothers because we are so similar in nature, but we share a belief system and a friendship that allows for respectful debating to be a valuable part of our relationship, not a disruption. We both firmly believe in hard work, doing the right thing, putting others first and staying true to our word. We play to each other's strengths in the boardroom, and that is a strong suit for us. I don't know where our organization would be without Hunter's input and direction. But I do know that our combined strengths, along with a talented, hardworking group of employees, has positioned the Oldham-Goodwin Group for a powerful and prominent future. Most significantly, Hunter is one of my best friends. Our wives are great friends, as well, which brings us together for relaxing times and traveling together. That gives our business partnership an added dimension.

I would be remiss if I didn't mention another relationship that has benefitted me, the friendship I've been fortunate to develop with Donald A. Adam, one of the most successful and influential men I've ever known. We don't do much business together as ours is more of a true friendship, but Mr. Adam has served as a mentor to me in so many ways. We've traveled together; our families have spent quality time together; and he has shared wise advice with me. He is a man of great detail and a gentleman in every sense of the word, and he has probably forgotten more business and entrepreneurial knowledge than I will ever know. Whenever you are able to spend time with a person you admire tremendously—like I respect Mr. Adam—value that time and learn as much as you possibly can. I have learned to cherish friendships like the ones I have with Hunter Goodwin and Donald Adam.

OLDHAM'S MOST DIFFICULT CHALLENGE

Former United States Treasurer Ivy Baker Priest once described perspective this way, "The world is round, and the place which may seem like the end may also be only the beginning." Author Robert Brault stated it just as eloquently when he wrote, "So often in life a new chapter awaits. You ride off into the sunset and discover it's the sunrise." I wish I could articulate a one- or two-line quote to sum up my perspective just as expressively and powerfully. But that is not going to happen, so I will say it this way, "Be careful how you view the world and yourself because your perspective becomes your reality." It is extremely important to check yourself on this, just as it is imperative to keep in mind that situations or circumstances are rarely as good or as bad as they may seem while you are in the midst of the experience. In reflection, there are three main challenges I have encountered that prove to be common in starting and building a business:

1. Proving your relevance and having others take you seriously as you are first starting out.
2. Being a steady producer, and at the same time, building a new business.
3. Staying focused and consistently working the business plan; there is a new shiny thing every day that can distract you.

Simply staying focused on your mission is a key to success. The more successful you are perceived to be, the more often people will approach you with a "golden opportunity" or a "can't-miss" investment. It can be tempting to diversify and become involved in a million different things, but those things can often take you off course. It is sometimes beneficial to branch out into new endeavors, as was proven to me by the addition of Hunter Goodwin and our entry into the hospitality business. But opportunities must be well-chosen, as well as strategic and truly integrated, especially as you are laying the foundation of your business. Be extremely selective; in most cases you do not want to stray too far from your core business.

Every businessperson will be tested constantly and relentlessly. I can practically guarantee it, and it will wear you down if you let it. In the midst of those challenges, maintain perspective and remember the biggest obstacles teach us how to hurdle, and the toughest burdens broaden our shoulders. Or, as American essayist Ralph Waldo Emerson so eloquently said, "We acquire the strength we have overcome."

I will be frank and candid. Because of the risk and sacrifice involved, I don't think every individual is suited to be an entrepreneur. Risk does not always result in reward, and that is and can be a tough pill to swallow. Sometimes you are going to make bad investments (hopefully not too many) and lose money. But a bad day or a bad investment should not be confused with a bad life. Even in the darkest times, an entrepreneur is just one relationship or one deal from turning things around. Utilize the lessons learned from failure or the trials you've faced to ensure success in the future. If entrepreneurism is your chosen career destination, make sure you possess the right temperament and the proper perspective. Don't get too high or too low and always try to learn from every deal and every encounter. As Henry Ford once said, "Failure is only the opportunity to begin again more intelligently."

OLDHAM'S ADVICE TO YOUNG ENTREPRENEURS

People want to know: How do I become a successful entrepreneur and get rich quick? The cliché is that it doesn't happen overnight. And it's true.

Most people who know me say I have always had a good knack for business or that I just "get it" when it comes to opportunity. But the reality is that I show up to work and to seek opportunities. Every day. It really is that simple…and that hard. But, it works. At the age of 35, I built a successful business that employs more than 600 people. Once I am engaged, I strive to put more than 100 percent into whatever I am doing that day, whether it is working at a real estate deal, building my business or being present for family and friends on a day off. There are some basic principles that have certainly helped me to achieve my goals. But first, know you want to be in this for the long haul. You must truly want it and understand that there is no substitute for hard work. Sacrifice is a must, and without that willingness, you will fail. Be ready to completely immerse yourself in your business. To say it was only tough in the early days is misleading; running a business is 100 times more work than you anticipate. When you are not at the office, you are thinking about the office.

There are plenty of ruthless, manipulative and unscrupulous entrepreneurs who have made it big by doing whatever is necessary, whether it is immoral, illegal or irresponsible. I encourage you to stay true to your beliefs and take the right path, not the path of least resistance. Treat people the right way in every situation. Remember that everyone has a back story that fuels his actions and reactions. You can only control your own. I am committed to what are considered "old-fashioned" values, the ones my parents instilled in me as I was growing up. I encourage you, from the day you start your career until the day you retire, to lead your business with honesty and integrity. As I have matured as a businessman, I have also grown in my Christian walk. I do not pray for riches or expect to be financially blessed simply for doing the right thing. It is my belief that God blesses us when we follow his will; treating others as you would like to be treated and being a person of integrity are two of the things we are instructed to do in this life. Your marriage, partnerships and pursuits are to be conducted in a way that glorifies God. I do not live this out every day and fall short of it often, but others should see God through you as an entrepreneur.

Integrity and treating people well should not be confused with allowing others to push you around or take advantage of your good nature. It is important to know how and when to stand up for yourself. As the leader of an organization of any size, you must strike a balance between being an authority figure and being calloused. Some people think you must be ruthless to command respect; I don't believe that. It is possible to demand excellence without being a dictator, to handle confrontation without becoming hostile. You can deliver constructive criticism to an employee or cut ties with a partner or client with respect and professionalism, allowing you and the other party to retain their dignity. In business, I am known to be hard-edged, straightforward and blunt, but not a bully or cruel. While Hunter has a more intimidating presence, I am the go-to "no" guy of our team. I have an aptitude for identifying the difference between someone who is being genuine and someone who is attempting to manipulate a situation, and I have become good at handling situations in an unemotional, matter-of-fact manner. I don't mind being headstrong and tough, but I avoid being malicious or spiteful. Maintaining your composure, even when your blood is boiling with anger, will earn you a great deal of respect and is vital to developing and maintaining long-term relationships. You must control your emotions or be prepared to be controlled by them in business. It is fine to walk away from the table in negotiations, but try to do so with a handshake and a smile whenever possible.

Finally, it is imperative to surround yourself with good people. Not just people who are agreeable, either. I have seen many businesses and sports teams fail or fail to reach their potential because the leaders surround themselves with "yes" people. I hire people who are smarter than me (which is easy to do); I want to associate with people who have great ideas and opinions that may be different than mine. I am drawn to people who are not afraid to disagree or to challenge my thinking — in a respectful manner —as it creates a stronger business. I seek out people who have vision and push me to be a better leader. We are fortunate to have an outstanding team at Oldham Goodwin, one that supports and grows the business with passion and integrity. We continue to search for sharp, motivated and enthusiastic individuals who want to make a difference by doing things the right way.

Live with a delayed gratification mentality in all aspects of your life to minimize risk. If you are working in a bad situation, don't just endure it; learn from it. Study people around you and learn what you want to do and what you want to avoid. Learn from good and bad examples, both will contribute to your success. I encourage you to be observant; it has served me well. Don't just take a paycheck as you are working toward your entrepreneurial start; take lessons from every place God leads you. Starting a business involves inherent risk. Be conservative in your finances to balance the risk. By planning carefully and paying attention to the details, you will be taking a calculated risk with a higher chance for success.

So, you have an idea, your business plan is sound and you are ready to work harder than everyone around you? What's next? Go to work! Believe in yourself, even when no one else does . . . and just go do it. There is no time like the present.

CPSIA information can be obtained
at www.ICGtesting.com
Printed in the USA
LVOW06s2033160817
545293LV00005B/8/P

reached out to me about buying Pumpco. For years and years and years, we had invested practically everything we made back into the company. We were growing, and we were doing well, but I didn't personally have a line of credit large enough to take the business to another level and have complete peace of mind. In some ways, I had stepped onto the treadmill, running fast but going nowhere. But in 2007, MasTec CEO Jose Mas contacted me about his desire to diversify his company. We began talking rather seriously, and once I learned that MasTec did not own another pipeline construction business, I was quite interested, especially when I learned that they wanted me to continue overseeing the operations of Pumpco. Basically, MasTec offered us enough to give us the flexibility and financial stability to take things to an entirely new level. MasTec is now a $3 billion company, and its financial support allowed Pumpco to go from a successful, family-owned business to a thriving, financially secure major pipeline construction company.

Since the buyout became official in 2008, we have expanded our horizons in numerous ways. We have started other companies; we've delegated more; we've stressed less; and our family vacations have evolved from road trips to Austin and Waco to fishing trips in Alaska and vacations in world-renowned destinations. Pumpco now has more than 1,500 employees, and in 2012, our payroll exceeded $80 million. After more than 30 years in business, it is no longer necessary to invest every bit of profit back into the business. We now have complete financial security and freedom, which has allowed us to invest back into the things that mean the most to us: our church, our charities, our family passions, Texas A&M, Aggie athletics, dream vacations, fishing boats and so much more. But please allow me to reiterate a point: We didn't travel to Italy, France or Australia when we first made a profit; we didn't buy dream homes when we were investing in backhoes; and we didn't overextend our finances when we were extending the hours we worked and the demands we accepted.

ROBERTS' ADVICE TO YOUNG ENTREPRENEURS

In all sincerity, I am somewhat uncomfortable in giving advice. But I am more at ease highlighting a couple of the key points that have been essential to my success as an entrepreneur. First and foremost, I believe it's critical to follow your heart. It's probably not impossible to be successful in an industry that you don't enjoy, but life is too short to be miserable in your profession. Besides, if you enjoy what you do, you are at least twice as likely to be successful at it financially and to be satisfied and/or fulfilled. As the Chinese philosopher Confucius once said, "Choose a job you love, and you will never have to work a day in your life."

I'm thoroughly convinced that I did the right thing by leaving the accounting field less than two years after I started in it. It didn't fit me, even though I tried desperately to convince myself that it was a good career and that I could be happy as a CPA. But I finally realized I could not be happy by living out my father's dreams. Even though I knew he would not be pleased with my decision to initially leave my white-collar career to start my own oilfield repair service—to use my hands to make a living—it was something I felt like I had to do. Telling him was tough, but it was easier than staying in a career field that bored me. Eventually, even my father realized that I had done the right thing. I've always believed that if you follow your dreams and work hard, success will eventually follow you. That has certainly been applicable in my life and my career.

Another critical component to what has made me successful is my commitment to treat people the right way. Not just my friends. Not just my customers or prospective customers. I have always strived to treat everyone around me the way I would like to be treated. That's the biblical "Golden Rule," and it should also be a top priority for any entrepreneur or business owner. Quite frankly, I believe treating people with respect, dignity, kindness and compassion should be a top priority for every person on the planet, regardless of whether you are building a business or not. But it is especially important to treat every employee as a key employee, which will create loyalty, unity and solidarity.

Today, we do so much to reward and encourage our employees. We host tailgates at sporting events—particularly Texas A&M football games—where we have numerous televisions set up around our RV, and we have hosted as many as 175 people, who were all employees, family and friends. At the 2013 Texas A&M-Alabama game in College Station, we literally had so many people at our tailgate that we passed out wristbands to make sure we could manage the crowd. Throughout the years, I cooked and prepared food for everyone before and after games. I could have had it catered, and I certainly could have hired people to serve everyone. But that would have defeated the purpose of hosting the tailgate. I wanted to show my appreciation toward my employees, customers, colleagues and friends by serving them.

We have created a tremendous team-oriented atmosphere, and I truly believe most of our employees are quite pleased to be working for an organization that values them and their efforts. We work hard, and I expect great things from our employees, but I try to be a leader who coaches, inspires and motivates instead of merely acting as a dictator. When you encourage someone to perform at a peak level it is far more effective than demanding someone to do more. It's a subtle distinction that makes a world of difference. And through the years I've been able to retain great people because they enjoy working for us. I've even been able to hire longtime friends and some family members, making our atmosphere even more enjoyable. My brother Jimmy, for example, came to work for me after a career in teaching and banking, and he now oversees all of our safety policies and procedures, and I am proud of our safety record.

In addition to investing in people, Robyn and I have always invested back into the company by purchasing equipment, upgrading technology and providing our staff with all the resources to be successful. For roughly three decades, I didn't really take a salary. We paid our people, paid the bills and paid for more "yellow iron" before we took any income for ourselves. Even the most expensive purchases—like an airplane and helicopters—have been made to propel our business ventures. We're doing work in Wyoming, North Dakota, New Mexico and various other locations across the country, which makes a private plane far more of a necessity than a luxury. But as an added benefit, we have been able to use the plane and the helicopters to help people in a variety of other ways.

Our plane contributed indirectly to one of Texas A&M's national championships, as I occasionally accompanied former A&M women's basketball assistant coach Vic Schaefer to Kansas City to recruit Danielle Adams, the star of the Aggies' run to the 2011 women's basketball national championship. Vic really didn't like to fly. So, we would go together, and he would talk to the player and the family, while my pilot and I would hang out at the airport. We would then fly back, stopping in Dallas for dinner at a place like Pappas Bros. Steakhouse and then we'd drop him off back in College Station.

Of greater importance, we've also been able to use the plane and helicopters to help friends and family in times of need. In the summer of 2010, Vic Schaefer's son, Logan, had a severe wakeboarding accident at a camp that required emergency surgery in Tyler. At the time of the accident, Vic was with his daughter, Blair, at a basketball tournament in Cincinnati, while his wife, Holly, was at home in College Station. We were able to immediately fly Holly from College Station to Tyler, and after Vic caught a commercial flight from Cincinnati to Dallas, we had the helicopter waiting for him at the airport to fly him to Tyler. Fortunately, everything worked out for the best. Logan recovered from the subdural hematoma he had suffered, and we felt blessed to make sure that his family was together as quickly as possible. We couldn't have done that without our longtime commitment to investing in tools for the company. It would be my strong recommendation to any prospective entrepreneur to do the same thing, practicing delayed gratification for any personal luxuries and unnecessary expenses, while investing everything you can back into your business.

Finally, I believe it is imperative to establish yourself within any industry as a businessperson of integrity, honesty and morality. I see businessmen and women who cut corners and fail to deliver on their promises all the time. Some people really believe that the key to making a profit is to over-charge and under-deliver. But if you focus on doing things the right way, treating people the way you would want to be treated and exceeding expectations, you will eventually distinguish yourself and your business within any industry. Focus on building a strong reputation and everything else will take care of itself. As Albert Einstein once said, "Try not to become a man of success, but rather, try to become a man of value." Success will follow men and women of integrity, honesty and value.

Christ-centered perspective and without ever compromising his values. I wasn't surprised in May 2013 when Mr. Hackett enrolled at Harvard Divinity School. His faith has always been first, and he has been an inspiration to many of his employees because of his perspective. As he told Bloomberg in a 2015 article, "When you make this money, when you provide these jobs, there is a duty you have because you've been blessed by God to shepherd that wealth. And you have to do it well."

I couldn't have asked for better leadership training from the time I started my professional career with Halliburton until I decided to leave Anadarko in 2007. To this day, I can't really explain my reasoning for leaving Anadarko when I did. I didn't have another job lined up, and I certainly didn't have all of my ducks in a row in terms of starting a new business. But at 36-years-old and with a five-year-old son and a two-year-old son at home, I knew it was time to begin my entrepreneurial journey. Practically every day after work at Anadarko, I was on the phone with my friend and fellow petroleum engineering classmate at Texas A&M, Anthony Bahr, Class of '91. Anthony received his Master's degree from A&M in '94, and he earned his MBA at Cal State Bakersfield in 2000. He became an Asset Manager at Hilcorp Energy in 2004, and we eventually began talking about doing something on our own.

I realized the future was now in 2007 when I called Anthony and told him I was quitting Anadarko to begin writing a business plan to start our own company. Anthony applauded my decision, but as a testament to how much smarter he is than me, he continued to work at Hilcorp while I decided to move forward. I had not even told my wife, April, about my decision to leave Anadarko when I quit, but I knew she would support my decision. Neither one of us had grown up with any significant money, so we were not afraid to pinch pennies, if necessary. Besides, I have always tried to leave work at work and to never bring the stresses of the job home with me. Family is my top priority, and once I leave the office, I've always tried to focus entirely on my family.

I was at my oldest son's preschool assembly the day I decided to leave Anadarko, and after departing the preschool, I called Mr. Huddleston and told him I was ready to start my own company. He said, "It's about time. Do you have any money?" I told him I didn't, and he committed to loan us multiple millions of dollars to help us start. I was floored, stunned and so naïve that I didn't know what to say. I blurted out, "Is that enough?"

He said, "Heavens no. You are definitely going to need more." I didn't know where to go next, but Mr. Huddleston told me about some private equity companies that I could contact. I didn't even know what a private equity company was, but shortly thereafter, I told April that I was going to quit my job at Anadarko. Just as I suspected, she supported my decision and we vowed to live off her teacher's salary for as long as it took. We had a little money saved up, but not much. Neither one of us was worried, though, because we both had faith that things would work out for the best. Later that day, I called Jim Hackett and Karl Kurz, who was the Chief Operating Officer at Anadarko, and asked if I could come see them. They were trusted friends, and I wanted them to know first. When I told them I was leaving, they asked me where I was going. I told them I was going to start my own company even though I couldn't provide them with any details because I didn't have anything worked out. They must have thought I had lost my mind, but Mr. Hackett was gracious enough to say that if things didn't work out he would gladly take me back. It was a relief to have Plan B already lined up, even though Plan A was a complete mystery. Since that time, Karl has been a trusted confidant and mentor. I've spent many hours talking to him about business and life. Just like Mr. Hackett, he is a Christ-centered businessman who is not afraid to bring his faith into the boardroom.

I walked out of Anadarko in April 2007 with no salary and no real definitive plans in place. I then began working on writing our business plan, which Mr. Huddleston graciously reviewed. I then set up an appointment with a private equity company in Houston to seek funding. They were not impressed and did not volunteer to provide any funding. For the next appointment, however, I wised up. I arranged to use Mr. Huddleston's conference room and I asked him to make an appearance. My meeting was to be held with John A. Weinzierl, a Managing Director and Operating Partner at NGP Energy Capital Management. Mr. Huddleston had been on a Board of Directors at another NGP company, and he entered the room after John Weinzierl arrived, extended his hand and said, "I'm Billy Pete Huddleston, and it's nice to meet you. I have known both of these boys since they were in college. Jay worked for me for four years. He was one of the best students I ever had and one of the best engineers I have ever had. I have known his partner, Anthony, as another great student. I am putting my money with these guys, and I think you need to, as well." Mr. Huddleston then walked out of the conference room without saying another word. Of course, he had already said quite enough.

John looked at us and asked how much Mr. Huddleston had committed. We told him, and he then asked us if we had talked to other companies. After we acknowledged that we had spoken with other private equity companies—we didn't mention how bad it gone—he asked us not to speak with any others. He was satisfied with our business plan and Mr. Huddleston's endorsement. He committed to funding us multi millions, and just like that, we were in business. We'd been given a chance, and now it was up to us to make the most of that opportunity.

GRAHAM'S MOST DIFFICULT CHALLENGE

In August 2007, Anthony and I started WildHorse Resources out of my 2,500-square-foot house. It took about six months before we moved into a more traditional office space. By May of 2008, we were ready to execute our first deal and to drill our first well. Unfortunately, our first well was a dud. Literally, we drilled a dry hole, which happens from time to time. When it's your first attempt as a new start-up business, though, it can be a little nerve-racking.

Jay and Jacob Graham in Times Square

Many of the major drilling companies in the United States at that time had left the country to explore international and offshore opportunities. Our plan was to focus on domestic opportunities, including reworking existing older properties where we could renovate, reinvigorate and flip them to make a nice return on investment. Meanwhile, gas prices were all over the map throughout 2008. A gallon of regular unleaded cost $3.05 in early January and then jumped to $3.50 in April and over $4 in May. In July 2008, crude oil prices hit a new record of $147 per barrel, while the U.S. average price for a regular gallon of gasoline climbed to an all-time high of $4.11. The law of gravity, however, is also applicable in the oil and gas industry: that which goes up will also come down.

By mid-October, oil prices fell below $70 a barrel, less than half of its July peak. In November, U.S. gas prices dropped to $1.72 a gallon, and by December OPEC removed 2.2 million barrels from its daily production, as crude oil collapsed to $40 a barrel, the lowest price in almost four years. The danger in doing business in that kind of volatile market is that if you begin buying when the price is really high, you may never be able to recover when the bottom drops out. It was a crazy and unpredictable time, where the challenge for us was to maintain our focus and confidence.

Our next attempt at drilling another vertical well was better, as it produced relatively well. It wasn't spectacular, but it also wasn't a dry hole. That's about all we did in the first two years, and it wasn't until May 2010 where we executed our first formative acquisition, purchasing Petrohawk out of North Louisiana